Praise for *Tough Luck*

"A terrific read that should draw interest from all general nonfiction readers."   —*Library Journal* (starred review)

"Vigorous storytelling at the intersection of crime and sports history."
                    —*Kirkus Reviews*

"A fascinating must-read for anyone who loves good history, the NFL, and is interested in the price of fame. It is compelling as the journey of a great athlete from an unusual background . . . Highly recommended."   —Leigh Steinberg

"Thoughtful, moving . . . Simply put, this book is about the greatest reverse play in the history of football."
                    —Steve Wulf, former executive editor of *ESPN the Magazine*

"Rosen artfully blends fascinating tales of the rise of the National Football League with the bloody demise of the mob."
                    —Bill Geist, author of *Lake of the Ozarks*

"A great read."
 —Nicholas Pileggi, screenwriter for *Goodfellas, Casino,* and *City Hall*

"A terrific job of reporting and writing."
                    —Ira Berkow, author of *Hank Greenberg:
                    The Story of My Life* and *Giants Among Men*

"An incredible book. Exceptional in many ways. More than a good sports book, it is a great history of the times and the gangs of New York."   —Upton Bell, author of *Present at the Creation: My Life
                    in the NFL and the Rise of America's Game* and former
                    general manager of the New England Patriots

"Fascinating . . . Rosen's history is wonderful reading for a wide audience." —*Illinois Times*

"A magnificent book."
—Marv Levy, Pro Football Hall of Fame Coach

"A warm, fluent writer whose book flows with subjects he loves: Chicago, football, the intricacies of family politics, mysteries hidden in plain sight." —Lincoln Caplan, lecturer in English at Yale University and former staff writer at the *New Yorker*

TOUGH LUCK

Also by R. D. Rosen

NONFICTION

Such Good Girls: The Journey of the Holocaust's Hidden Child Survivors

*A Buffalo in the House: The True Story of a Man,
an Animal, and the American West*

Psychobabble: Fast Talk and Quick Cure in the Era of Feeling

*Me and My Friends, We No Longer Profess Any Graces:
A Premature Memoir*

MYSTERY NOVELS

Strike Three You're Dead

Fadeaway

Saturday Night Dead

World of Hurt

Dead Ball

HUMOR

*Not Available in Any Store:
The Complete Catalog of the Most Amazing Products Never Made*

With Harry Pritchett and Rob Battles:

Bad Cat

Bad Dog

Bad Baby

Bad President

*Throw the Damn Ball:
Classic Poetry by Dogs*

TOUGH LUCK

SID LUCKMAN, MURDER, INC., AND THE RISE OF THE MODERN NFL

R.D. ROSEN

Grove Press

New York

Published simultaneously in Canada
Printed in the United States of America

This book was set in 12.5-pt. Centaur MT by Alpha Design & Composition
of Pittsfield, NH.

First Grove Atlantic hardcover edition: September 2019
First Grove Atlantic paperback edition: September 2020

Library of Congress Cataloging-in-Publication data is available for this title.

ISBN 978-0-8021-5736-2
eISBN 978-0-8021-4711-0

Grove Press
an imprint of Grove Atlantic
154 West 14th Street
New York, NY 10011

Distributed by Publishers Group West

groveatlantic.com

20 21 22 23   10 9 8 7 6 5 4 3 2 1

In memory of Robert Baskin Rosen,
brother in every sense

Sometimes you find the panel, but it doesn't open; sometimes it opens, and your gaze meets nothing but a mouse skeleton. But at least you've looked. That's the real distinction between people: not between those who have secrets and those who don't, but between those who want to know everything and those who don't. This search is a sign of love, I maintain.

—Julian Barnes, *Flaubert's Parrot*

Contents

Introduction: The Quarterback Next Door   I

1   Hog-Tied and Trussed   11

2   The Erasmus Terror   18

3   One Heartless Tangle   28

4   A Worrisome Gent   43

5   Specialized Persuasions   50

6   A Good Future in Trucking   61

7   Up the River   83

8   Captive City   89

9   A Fast Passing Game   99

10   Runaround   113

11   Rookie   121

12   They All Laughed   129

13   Whiners, Crybabies, and Quitters   139

14   Barrage   150

15   Temptations   159

16   High-Priced Help   168

17   Another Botched Job   173

18   Almost to a T   180

19   With a Thud   190

20   Casualties   197

21   A Surprising Comment   206

22   Last Dance   213

23   Bingo Keep It   223

24   A Congestion of Quarterbacks   232

25   Gifts   242

26   Secrets   255

27   Who Do You Think You Are, Sid Luckman?   262

     Postgame Commentary and Acknowledgments   275

     Selected Notes   283

     Bibliography   291

     Index   295

Introduction:
The Quarterback Next Door

In 1959, when I was 10 years old, I was fascinated by the new occupants of a big redbrick colonial house around the corner from my family's quirky custom split-level. Word had spread quickly throughout Highland Park, our suburb on the North Shore of Chicago, that the new occupants were former Chicago Bears quarterback Sid Luckman and his family.

This was of particular interest to me, since I had recently become a rabid Chicago Bears fan. An embarrassing amount of my mental and emotional life was consumed by the team and its fortunes. My most noticeable talent in those days was my drawing ability, and my school notebooks were filled with pictures of football players and the hash-marked turf at Wrigley Field, where the Bears played their home games until 1971. On autumn Sunday mornings, while I fidgeted in confirmation class at Congregation Solel—our activist Reform rabbi had temporarily stopped believing in the bar mitzvah—I emerged from my football reveries only long enough to write an occasional essay about the nonexistence of God. Judaism was my faith, but the Chicago Bears were my religion.

And Sid Luckman was professional football's Moses, having led the Bears, the first modern pro football dynasty, to the promised land. Although I was too young to have seen Luckman play, his legendary status was reinforced every time I heard fans of my father's generation exclaim—usually when one of Luckman's lesser successors overthrew an open receiver—"Where's Sid Luckman when we need him?" The great quarterback presided over my obsession with the Bears, even though I was too young to appreciate, or even know about, his specific deeds. Only later would I learn that he had once led the most feared team in the National Football League—the "Monsters of the Midway"—to five national championship appearances and four titles in seven years during the 1940s; that in his first year as starting quarterback, the Bears had manhandled the Washington Redskins 73–0, still and probably forever the most lopsided victory in NFL history; that Sid Luckman was the first man to throw seven touchdown passes in a game and the first to throw for more than 400 yards; and that he held the record for the highest percentage of passes in a single season that went for touchdowns. Despite the rapid evolution of the passing game, most of Luckman's several team records wouldn't be broken for 65 years.

More important, however, was this: the intricate T-formation offense he spearheaded had ushered in the modern era of pro football, elevating a sport that had been the grimy sideshow to the more popular rah-rah college game. This historical achievement was memorialized in the Bears' fight song, "Bear Down, Chicago Bears": "We'll never forget the way you thrilled the nation / With your T formation." If the song was catchier than most, that was because it was written by the man who had already penned "Bibbidi-Bobbidi-Boo" and "A Dream Is a Wish Your Heart Makes" for Disney's movie *Cinderella*.

I knew the words by heart because I was lucky enough to go to several Chicago Bears games in the late 1950s and 1960s, when the song was blared scratchily over the loudspeaker. Of all the memorable experiences of my childhood, nothing captured my imagination quite like Bears games at Wrigley Field. In those media-deprived days, before home games were even televised, attending a Bears game was a rare glimpse of a special kingdom full of pageantry and armed battle. As my father and I walked up North Sheffield Avenue, the air crackled with the pregame chatter of Jack Brickhouse and his sidekick, newspaper columnist/color man Irv Kupcinet, pouring out of hundreds of Sony transistor radios—a new phenomenon. And now we were through the clicking turnstiles and mounting Wrigley's ramps until the scene was revealed in all its glory: the brilliant green turf; the meticulously limed lines; the fans in their seats already unscrewing their thermoses of coffee and nipping from their flasks to stay warm; the ivy on Wrigley's outfield walls turning brown, yellow, and orange, or gone altogether, leaving a spindly network of vines stuck to the brick. Most exciting of all were the Bears players themselves, warming up, military in their navy-blue jerseys and helmets and immaculate white pants; immense in their shoulder pads; practicing passes, pinwheeling placekicks, and high revolving punts; running phantom plays under the cold sun. And everything was in saturated color, not the faded hues of our first Zenith color television.

I knew Luckman only from a few photos—old publicity shots in which he was poised to pass, right arm cocked while the left pointed downfield to an imaginary receiver, or of his big, square handsome head stuffed into a flimsy leather football helmet. In the town that Carl Sandburg had labeled "City of the Big Shoulders," no shoulder was bigger or more revered than Sid Luckman's right one.

That Luckman now lived a mere 100 yards from my house—and across the street from where I was developing into a sticky-fingered receiver in neighborhood touch football games—didn't quite make sense to me. Powerful figures lived in our midst, but they were doctors, lawyers, and small titans of business whose achievements were obscure and uninteresting to a 10-year-old boy. Sid Luckman, however, was part of history—a treasured relic of an era before face masks, before the integration of American sports, before television came along to broadcast pro football's appeal. And that name! Was there a better one in all of sports, joining two of the most vital elements of athletic success at mid-century, luck and manliness? It was so perfect that he hadn't needed a nickname, unlike other early pillars of Bears history such as Harold "Red" Grange, aka the Galloping Ghost; Bronislau "Bronko" Nagurski; or George "One-Play" McAfee—or future pillars like "the Kansas Comet," Gale Sayers.

The only aspect of Luckman's arrival in my neighborhood that made any sense to me was that he was Jewish. Highland Park was a lush, lakeside, liberal suburb that had opened its doors to Jews years before, while neighboring towns like Kenilworth and Lake Forest discouraged upwardly mobile refugees from the crowded Jewish ghettos of Chicago. Even so, I was too young to fully appreciate the irony and pathos embodied by a Jewish quarterback who had led the meanest team in professional football during the very years the Nazis were murdering two-thirds of the Jews in Europe. Like boxer Barney Ross and baseball greats Hyman "Hank" Greenberg before him and Sandy Koufax after, Sid Luckman symbolized the strength, endurance, and greatness of the Jewish people.

I was even too young to have heard him give a talk to the Highland Park High School student body. In any other profession, Luckman would have been hitting his stride, but by 1959 he had been retired from football a decade already, done with playing at 33, his best years behind him a few years before that. He was still young and looked like a movie star, perhaps like Gregory Peck, born the same year, 1916. If the students expected to hear about some of Luckman's triumphs, they were disappointed. Decades later, my older brother told me that Luckman had regaled the teenagers with the story of his first NFL game at quarterback, in 1939, during which he said he had done almost nothing right. All kids like a story about the fallibility of adults, especially one who rose to the very top of his profession.

More than half a century later, my interest in Sid Luckman was reignited by the discovery that I could watch him in action during the 1940s on YouTube and see at last what everyone had been talking about when I was child. I was seized with the desire to know more about this figure who had remained just beyond my reach for so long.

And not only beyond *my* reach. For some reason, Sid Luckman had never been the subject of the documentary or biography he deserved. Where was his valedictory autobiography? More than most famous athletes, he had revolutionized the game he played, pioneered the modern role of quarterback, and set several enduring records. There have been countless refinements since the 1940s, and better athletes, but Luckman was the prototype of the modern quarterback. Yet he remained something of a marginal figure in the panorama of the 20th century's greatest sports figures. Among that tiny subgroup of Jewish hall-of-fame athletes, Hank Greenberg, Sandy Koufax, the NBA's Dolph Schayes, and swimmer Mark Spitz have been treated to biographies, even award-winning documentaries—but not Sid Luckman.

The reason, it turned out, was buried deep in the Internet, in an item that was simply too unbelievable to be true. It seemed impossible that virtually no one knew of it, that there was ever a time when something that had once been so public could have remained so unknown. What I stumbled on was a tragedy of Shakespearean dimensions that had been remembered by almost nobody.

Had it not been for a chance conversation in a suburban Washington, DC, coffee shop shortly after Sid Luckman's death, in 1998, at the age of 81, the story might well have died with him.

A Washington, DC, sports columnist named Dan Daly, who was researching a book of anecdotes about the NFL's early days, was sitting with one of his loyal readers, an old-timer who was a valuable source of information about professional football's past. The conversation turned to Luckman's recent death, and the old-timer clucked, "It's an embarrassment what happened with his father."

"What happened?" Daly asked.

"You know, he went to prison for murder."

Daly was stunned that a story like that could be kept under wraps for so long. When he looked into it, he discovered that the murder wasn't the half of it.

In 2012, Daly published a book called *The National Forgotten League: Entertaining Stories and Observations from Pro Football's First Fifty Years*, in which he included several pages about Sid Luckman's father among almost 400 pages of quirky facts and anecdotes. No one seemed to notice.

I traced Daly's footsteps into newspaper archives and then drilled deeper, troubled at every turn. I finally picked up the phone and with some trepidation dialed the number of Sid Luckman's only son, now a 75-year-old retired businessman. I introduced myself as a former Highland Park neighbor, and told Bob Luckman I wanted to write about his father, one of my childhood heroes. He was intrigued and immediately offered a few stories about the father he admired so much.

"Bob," I eventually said, "can I ask you about your grandfather?"

After a brief pause, he said, "I'm surprised you know about him."

"To tell you truth, I am too," I said. "I found it on the Internet. What do *you* know about Meyer Luckman?"

The answer turned out to be, not much. Bob was almost 50 before he knew anything at all. When the rough spots between his father and him had long been sanded smooth, Bob had suggested to his father, then in his 70s, that he write an autobiography. There had once been an autobiography, *Luckman at Quarterback*—ghostwritten back in the 1940s—but it was long out of print, and so much had happened since then.

"I can't, Bob," his father said, explaining that there was something in the family past he didn't want to come out, and if he wrote a book, someone was sure to bring it up.

Sid shared only the barest outline of the story, recounting that his father, the grandfather that Bob had been told had died young, had in fact been convicted—falsely, Sid claimed—of killing someone and had gone to prison. But Bob could tell by his father's demeanor that it was probably not a good idea to press for more details.

"Something happened in a warehouse is all I know," Bob said. "I don't even think my sisters know."

That Sid's own children had been kept in the dark showed that the secret had grown an impenetrable shell.

"Bob," I told him, "I'm in the awkward position of knowing a lot more about your grandfather than you do." It was an invitation for him to ask me what I knew, but strangely, he didn't say anything.

It became obvious as I continued my research that if I had any intention of writing about Sid Luckman, I would have to come clean with Bob. I could not separate Sid's story from Meyer's. A few weeks later, I made arrangements to fly to Chicago and meet Bob for breakfast at a Jewish deli in our hometown, Highland Park.

Bob is a large, robust presence, just under six feet tall like his father, with a Florida tan, light blue eyes, and a head of silvery hair. I begin by stressing my admiration for his father, lamenting that I never met him, and that I've been a hopeless Bears fan for most of my life. Bob responds with several stories about Sid, including an example of his legendary generosity. He mentions that his father's nose was broken seven times, five in the pros. Given that he didn't wear a face mask, I wonder why it wasn't broken 700 times. I ask Bob about his own playing days—the football scholarship to Syracuse, the ankle injury, the failed comeback in his junior year there.

Once again, the specter of Meyer Luckman looms too large to be ignored. "You know that I can't write about your dad without bringing in his childhood and the terrible stuff that happened."

"With all the athletes and celebrities I know, I can't believe no one ever mentioned my grandfather to me."

"Your father made sure almost no one knew."

"Look, I don't care for myself, but Sid"—he referred to his father only as "Sid"—"never wanted it to come out."

It occurred to me that this was the moment I had been dreading, running afoul not of Bob Luckman but of his father's imposing ghost. I had given some thought about what to say.

"It was a very long time ago," I told him. "It's an important piece of history. Your father was an important part of history. And it's already out there." Anyone can pick up Daly's book and run with the story.

"Well, I know there's nothing I can do to stop you."

"I think of it as maybe your father's greatest victory," I said, spinning it as best I could, "to overcome his family's tragedy and become who he became."

Did I believe that? Well, yes. It could never have been far from Sid Luckman's mind for long, what his father had done, what Sid had left behind. Not being derailed by it, sticking to football, taking any job he could to afford college when the family finances collapsed, psychologically surmounting the shame—by comparison, memorizing the Bears' playbook and suffering seven broken noses had to have been nothing.

I had the sudden urge to tell him more. It would serve no one to be cagey. "Do you know who the victim was?" I asked.

He shook his head.

When I told him, he took a moment, before saying, "I don't like going against what I know Sid's wishes would be. Some people came to me ten years ago to do a documentary on Sid, and I said no, because I knew he wouldn't have wanted it to come out."

"I'm sorry. I didn't go looking for it. And I need your help because I can't tell the good parts of the story without you."

In the parking lot, I gave Bob Luckman a DVD I had tracked down that contains rare film footage of his father playing for Columbia University—a token of my determination to do his father justice. The DVD includes two games from 1937 and 1938, played before Bob was born, when Sid was just a young man dealing with the reality of a father who was in prison for a crime that his grandson would soon enough know more about than he would like to.

As I drove off, I was torn between excitement about the project and anxiety about taking a good man's secret into my own hands. Some secrets, once revealed, do real damage, but so do many unrevealed secrets, as I had learned writing a book about Holocaust survivors and their offspring. Unacknowledged trauma gets passed down in the genes, a poisonous and unavoidable heirloom.

We live in a world in which privacy has become almost obsolete, so it may be hard to imagine that the story of Meyer Luckman has been a secret for 80 years—especially since the secret was hardly one to begin with. In fact, Meyer Luckman's crime had made headlines in New York City on and off for two years. He had been linked in headlines to one of the most notorious criminals of the 1930s. How had a story as uniquely and perversely American as this one—one family's journey from mob murder to Monsters of the Midway in a few short years—slipped through the cracks? A homicidal father whose son became a seminal figure in the one sport that mimics the nation's history of territorial gang violence? You couldn't invent it if you tried.

But it happened, even if it was suppressed, misplaced, forgotten—and finally silenced by time.

1

Hog-Tied and Trussed

At approximately 8:30 on Sunday night, March 3, 1935, the Brooklyn police received an anonymous call that "a man was screaming" at the Luckman Brothers Trucking Company garage at 225 Moore Street, a nondescript, windowless, redbrick warehouse in a dimly lit neighborhood of Bushwick, where many buildings were abandoned. Patrolman John P. McAuliffe, around the corner in his radio car, was the first to arrive at the scene. Finding all the doors locked, he climbed through the office door transom, after being given a boost by Patrolman Eugene Stahl, and opened the door for the eight or so other officers who had by now arrived.

In the pitch black, one of the cops found the switch to a single electric bulb hanging over the middle of the garage, revealing a fleet of more than two dozen delivery trucks. In the pale light, several men followed a trail of blood; there was so much of it that a *New York Times* reporter would think, when he slipped in it half an hour later, that it was motor oil. The blood led to a Ford coupe with New Jersey license plates. In the rumble seat, wrapped in a bloodstained, "crudely home-stitched canvas bag," lying on an oilcloth to protect the upholstery, the cops discovered the battered corpse of 35-year-old Samuel Drukman, one of the firm's employees. His body was still warm.

He had been hog-tied and trussed like a chicken. His own necktie had been cinched around his throat and then tied tightly to a rope attached to his wrists, which were tied behind his back. A second rope around Drukman's throat was tied to his ankles, which had been forced behind his back so they almost touched his wrists. It was a professional job, using a method that caused the victim to strangle himself with every attempt to move or free himself. Sam Drukman may not have been in much of a position to move, since his skull had also been bashed in with a sawed-off leaded pool cue that the policemen found nearby. It was bloodstained and broken in two, possibly from the force with which it had been used on Drukman. When McAuliffe picked it up, he would testify, lead pellets fell out. The blood spatters on the adjacent trucks suggested the victim had fought hard against his assailants before being immobilized.

The policemen heard sounds—rustling, whispering—coming from the rear of the huge garage. The police approached, guns drawn, and found three men hiding behind a truck. Two of them ran toward the center of the garage and were seized, while the third, a portly older man, escaped through a door onto the street. McAuliffe gave chase, slipped, lost ground, and then fired a warning shot over the man's head—"in order to facilitate matters," he would later explain—at which point the fugitive stopped, and McAuliffe took the man, one Meyer Luckman, his hands and clothes bloodied, into custody. One of the other men, Meyer's nephew Harry Luckman, was covered in blood. The third man, also bloodied, was a middle-aged ex-con and bootlegger named Fred J. Hull, who would be described in one newspaper as "a professional killer." They were an odd-looking bunch. Hull carried his 200 pounds on a five-foot-10-inch frame, but Harry Luckman was built like a bowling ball—also 200 pounds, but only five–foot–two. Meyer Luckman, 58, would later be described in court as "corpulent and unkempt."

Meyer Luckman had $3,000 in cash on him, which he claimed was a loan. He said that he had gone out for cigarettes and on his return had found six men (never identified), who had beaten up his nephew and Hull and killed Drukman in the process. But when a police surgeon examined the three arrested men (a fourth, a neighborhood drunk also found in the garage, was eventually released) later that evening, he found no wounds. Meyer Luckman would subsequently change his story and admit he *had* been in the garage, but only to see about renting some trucks to "a fellow," when the same six alleged men came in and murdered Drukman. Which hardly explained why the bloodstained Ford coupe, the "kill car" in which the corpse had been awaiting a ride to be disposed of, was registered to Meyer Luckman's cousin Morris Luckman, of Hopatcong, New Jersey. The men had been caught red-handed—literally. Brooklyn's assistant city toxicologist would testify that the Luckmans' clothing was "saturated" with blood.

As the *New York Times* would describe it, the Luckman Brothers Trucking Company was owned by first-generation Russian American brothers Meyer and Ike Luckman, neither of whom, it was reported, could read or write English—although that was a slur. They "enjoyed a lucrative monopoly in the trucking" of flour and other foods to New York City bakeries—although the newspaper seemed unaware of how this domination had been achieved. The victim, Samuel Drukman, a company employee responsible for collecting the payments from Luckman Brothers' drivers, had allegedly been siphoning off money to pay his substantial gambling debts. Meyer Luckman had been convinced of Drukman's embezzlement—also known as "peculations" in the press—for some time. In the Jewish and Italian mob-controlled Brooklyn of the 1930s, stealing from your own was a capital offense, and eliminating the miscreant was often the outcome. Ordinarily, a job like this would be outsourced to a professional, but Luckman may have wanted his victim to know who his killers were, to teach him a special lesson.

This was entirely possible, since if anything was unusual about this crime in murder-ridden Brooklyn, it was that Sam Drukman was Meyer Luckman's wife's younger brother. And 18-year-old Sid Luckman's favorite uncle.

In April, a grand jury was convened to hear the evidence. Most of the witnesses were policemen. The suspects' bloodstained clothing, the toxicology reports, and the $3,000 in cash that had been found on Meyer Luckman when he was arrested were shown to the jury members. It appeared to be an open-and-shut case.

Surprisingly, although these sorts of things happened in Brooklyn, on May 10 the grand jury declined to return any indictments. The evidence—including the bloody garments and the coupe—was returned to its owners. The men were free to go.

The Drukman case would have been pigeonholed with numerous other unsolved murders, had it not been for a letter that a 25-year veteran of the police force, Charles Corbett, one of the first men on the case, wrote to the police commissioner that summer, saying that he had been offered $100,000 to quash the case. In one version, Corbett reported he was offered the money by an assistant district attorney named Kleinman to "go easy" on the Luckmans. Corbett said that he had been approached by Leo Byk, a Brooklyn slot-machine czar with a criminal record who happened to be a good friend of Kleinman's boss, none other than Brooklyn district attorney William F. X. Geoghan.

Detective Corbett was called in by the police commissioner to defend his accusations, but the matter was soon dropped amid talk within the police department that Corbett was a man of dubious mental stability. Many police reporters, however, considered him an honest cop, albeit one who made a habit of proudly discussing all the bribes he had turned down. Time would reveal him to be a person with only a habit of exaggerating the truth.

Once again, Sam Drukman was in danger of becoming another quickly forgotten casualty of the dark workings of mobbed-up Brooklyn. But 1935 was an election year, and Brooklyn DA William Geoghan's challenger, former New York City comptroller Joseph McGoldrick—who wasn't thought to have much of a chance against the incumbent—decided to enliven a dull election campaign during a speech he delivered at the Methodist Episcopal Zion Church on October 7, 1935. He accused Geoghan of mishandling the Drukman case and making "murder safe in Brooklyn."

For now, the entire Luckman family of 2501 Cortelyou Road in the Flatbush neighborhood of Brooklyn breathed a sigh of relief. For Meyer Luckman's wife, Ethel, the relief was complicated by grief over the murder of her younger brother. But her own children demanded her attention. Leo, her oldest, had just gotten married, but Blanche, Sidney, and David were still at home. Until her husband's arrest, life in America had been good for the two immigrants from Lithuania. Ethel had been a political activist in Russia, part of the underground that had helped Jews escape the country, and she herself had fled to America in 1905. That her husband might be in trouble and unable to support the family was terrifying; that he might have had anything to do with her brother Sam's murder was unimaginable. Until now, one of her greatest anxieties, besides the welfare of her poor parents, had been the safety of Sid, a star football tailback for Brooklyn's Erasmus Hall High. Had it had been up to her, Sid would never have gone anywhere near a football field. She refused to see him play so brutal a sport.

As a boy Sid had bonded over the sport with his father. Meyer took an unusually intense interest in his son's progress. As Sid's high school coach found out, Meyer was not a man to be ignored; during many of Sid's games he insisted on sitting on the bench, where he could bark both encouragement and criticism. He had what Sid would one day describe as "an addiction to the game," and spoke of football "in terms of how it benefited a youngster, kept him from being spoiled, gave him self-reliance and drive."

In truth, Sid needed some supervision. He was, by his own later assessment, "a perpetually gloomy runt," and rebellious too—certainly if an episode at Hebrew school a few years earlier was any indication. The bearded rabbi with whom Sid at 13 had prepared for his bar mitzvah had a habit of falling asleep during their lessons, his grizzled head slowly descending to the table between them, where he began to snore gently, his face in the Torah. One day Sid took the wad of gum he had been surreptitiously chewing and used it to attach the rabbi's beard to the table. Then he got up and walked out.

Meyer Luckman's love of the game was a tribute to his adopted country. "What affected Dad most about my rise in football," Sid Luckman wrote at the end of his playing career in an autobiography for which he shared the credit with writer Norman Reissman, "was the democratic attitude he saw throughout the game, and especially the unbiased ways of my coaches. Irish coaches and Italian and Bohemians, who brought a Jewish boy out of Flatbush and worked their heads off to make a high-priced football man out of him."

When Sid and his older brother, Leo, were young, Meyer frequently drove them to the Polo Grounds in upper Manhattan to watch the New York Giants and their outstanding young tailback, Benny Friedman, another son of Russian Jewish immigrants, who had grown up in Cleveland's Jewish ghetto and graduated from the University of Michigan. In the fall of 1929, when Sid turned 13, Friedman threw an unprecedented 20 touchdown passes and led the Giants to a 13–1–1 record. George Halas, the founder of the still young National

Football League and owner and coach of the mighty Chicago Bears, called Friedman "the first pro quarterback to recognize the potentialities of the pass," in an era when the forward pass was still a novelty. Before Friedman, teams didn't risk passing until they had crossed the 50-yard line. Fascinated by Friedman, and a fledgling passer himself, Sid besieged his father with questions about how Friedman managed to throw the ball so well.

Leo suggested their father introduce Sid to Benny Friedman himself. In those days, it was easier to accomplish such things, and after one Giants game, Meyer approached Friedman outside the locker room.

"I have a future pro for you, Benny," he told the player, his hand on his stocky son's shoulder.

Friedman returned to the locker room and came back with a football and showed Sid exactly how he gripped it along the laces, no small matter since the ball in those days was fatter. Sid was mesmerized. Little did any of them—Sid, Leo, Meyer, Benny Friedman— know how influential a role Friedman would play in Luckman's career down the road. A few years later, he would coach Luckman on a Manhattan all-star team, and a few years after that he would have a key, if somewhat devious, role in determining the course of Luckman's entire life.

Meyer Luckman had already changed his son's life with a single act. He had presented Sid on his 11th birthday with a six-dollar football that had some big-league player's name on it. His father told him that owning a football in his hurly-burly Brooklyn neighborhood was like owning real estate; it conferred tremendous status in a community in which few boys could afford one. "Dad could barely afford it himself," Luckman would recall. "He used to take odd jobs during the week for small trucking concerns."

In a sense, owning a football was the most pivotal event in Sid Luckman's life. "They *had* to let me play quarterback," he often said.

2

The Erasmus Terror

By 1934, Sid Luckman had matured into a football star at Erasmus Hall High School, a public high school a five-minute walk from the Luckman home. It was a school to be reckoned with—over the years, a virtual factory for famous people. Future luminaries of all kinds, nurtured by the striving immigrant communities of Brooklyn, had already passed, and would pass, through its doors.*

Unlike most of them, Sid Luckman was already making headlines during his high school days, although not during his freshman

---

* Today, the school can claim among its graduates NBA player and coach Billy Cunningham, Yankees pitcher Waite Hoyt, Olympic silver medalist Cheryl Toussaint, team owners Al Davis (Oakland Raiders) and Jerry Reinsdorf (Chicago Bulls, Chicago White Sox), and New York Knicks founder Ned Irish. Several graduates succeeded in Hollywood, that dreamworld conceived by first-generation eastern European Jews, foremost among them Clara Bow, Mae West, Barbara Stanwyck (real name: Ruby Stevens), and Norma Talmadge. Moe Howard (Moses Horwitz) of the Three Stooges dropped out. Eli Wallach and Michael Rapaport would come later. In the other arts, the school can claim writers Frank "Mickey" Spillane, Betty Comden (Basya Cohen), and Roger Kahn: singers Beverly Sills (Belle Silverman), Barbra Streisand, Neil Diamond, and Marky Ramone (Marc Bell); record executive Clive Davis, Joseph Barbera of Hanna-Barbera Productions and Tom and Jerry fame, Nobel Prize–winning scientists Eric Kandel and Barbara McClintock, and chess master Bobby Fischer. In Luckman's class of 1935 alone, there were future stars Susan Hayward (Edythe Marrener) and Jeff Chandler (Ira Grossel).

year, when he had sat out the football season after breaking his hand
while slugging a kid who had called him a name during a touch football game in the park. He soon made up for it; for three autumns, the
city's sports pages were full of Sid's exploits for Erasmus Hall's varsity.
In November 1932, just a week after he turned 16, Luckman scored
four touchdowns, two on long runs, as the Erasmus Hall Dutchmen
crushed Boys High 37–0 in front of 15,000 at Ebbets Field—a larger
crowd than saw the football game there that same month between
the NFL's New York Giants and the Brooklyn Dodgers. "Powerful
Offensive Led by Luckman Enables Erasmus Hall to Triumph Again,"
read the *New York Times* headline, next to a photo of Luckman scoring
one of his touchdowns. "Resembling a wild bull tormented by a
matador waving a red flag before him," read one account, written in
the purplish sports-reporting prose of the day, "Luckman, an elusive
individual, thrived in heavy going to put on a thrilling display of ball
carrying. . . . [He] put on one of the greatest exhibitions seen on a
scholastic gridiron in many a moon. . . . Sid's punts average 50 yards,
his passing was a revelation, but it was his toting of the oval that made
him the most conspicuous." He was soon "Sid Luckman, sensational
three-way luminary, the outstanding schoolboy ball carrier in the city."
At the end of his first varsity season, he was named all-city.

The *Brooklyn Daily Eagle* called him "the Erasmus Terror" and
"a corking back, who can run and heave passes with undying accuracy. . . . He played like a well-seasoned veteran." "Hopes of Erasmus
Put on Luckman," ran another *Daily Eagle* tribute to the "precocious
sixteen-year-old lad who casually throws a football fifty yards and
who punts consistently about that distance." The praise rolled off the
presses: "For the remainder of the game, it was all Luckman. . . . Erasmus Hall added the name of Sid Luckman to its legendary scholastic
heroes. . . . As a triple threat, he was in a class by himself." The competition for best high school tailback between Luckman and James

Madison's Marty Glickman, future Olympian sprinter and New York broadcaster, was followed as closely as most professional sports rivalries.

When he had shown up as a high school freshman in 1931, Luckman was so reminiscent of Benny Friedman that the *New York World-Telegram* was already calling him "an embryo Benny Friedman," but passing played a small, wobbly role in the single-wing offenses of the day. In pro football film from the 1920s and 1930s, quarterbacks and tailbacks often look as if they are shot-putting the rotund ball. Erasmus Hall football coach Paul Sullivan, a graduate of Michigan State and New York University, urged Luckman to find his own passing style, as Luckman recalled in his 1949 autobiography: "Keep the fingers closer together across the laces and throw in a long and free movement, not short and stiff like Friedman. You'll feel a lot better using your own method." When Luckman grew frustrated that he couldn't throw farther, the slim, balding Sullivan told him to concentrate on his footwork—the footwork that would catch George Halas's eye in a few years. "Practice stance and pivot," Sullivan told him. "Keep at it and maybe you'll heave it eighty yards before you're able to vote."

Luckman had learned to mix it up in the streets of Flatbush, "a hotbed of grid-lunatics," as he put it, "where victory grew into a *religion*." But toughness was something else. At Erasmus, Sullivan weeded out boys who weren't equipped with "nerve, stubbornness, and spirit." "Gentlemen," Luckman recalled Sullivan addressing them, "I don't want it on my conscience that a squirt was banged up prematurely under Paul Sullivan. When he lacks the stuff for self-protection, he's a menace to himself." The game, he stressed, was not a mob sport. Sullivan drilled the boys on technique: how to carry the ball, how to stay low to expose less to your opponent, how to pivot to avoid tacklers, how to take a man down by hitting him low and rolling. He taught his boys how to walk and talk like football players. "If you should get laid out by your own boneheadedness," Sullivan said, "why,

Sullivan would take the blame. It would be a sad blow to Sullivan. So if I don't teach you another blamed thing at Erasmus, I'm going to teach you to survive this sport."

Luckman's precocious passing skill, however, made him feel entitled to some special treatment. "It was my natural forte," Luckman recalled, but admitted, "I may have been guilty of feeling that I should have it easier than the rest, and escape the drudgery. After all, good young passers are few and far between." The deference his comrades may have shown him on the streets of Flatbush simply because he owned the football wasn't forthcoming on a real team with dozens of footballs. Coach Sullivan was onto him: "Luckman, before you get any ideas, let's see if you can't bounce along with the others. Football isn't all passing. There's also blocking, running, punting, and tackling." When Sullivan sensed the other boys' growing jealousy and their resentment of Luckman's cocky attitude at tailback (the passing back in the single wing), he called him to his home on the eve of a game to tell him that the others were sore that Luckman was calling so many plays for himself to run and pass the ball.

"I didn't think I was being hoggish, Coach."

"It's my fault, anyway, Sid," Sullivan was quick to say. "When we played the Madison bunch, I advised you to try a passing game whenever we reached a tight spot. But listen, jealousy can't help a team. So tomorrow, you forget your own signal. Don't call it at all until I learn that everything's OK. I'd rather take a beating than have this attitude continue among the rest of the gang." Against Alexander Hamilton High the next day, when Erasmus fell behind by two touchdowns in the second half, Luckman continued to obediently call plays that involved him blocking for his teammates.

After a few running plays went nowhere, the team's right guard turned to Luckman in the huddle and called him a damned fool. "What're you trying to do—lose this game for us? Call passes now, and nothing but passes." Hamilton couldn't stop the onslaught, and Erasmus Hall came from behind to win 30–24. "But the main victory," Luckman would write much later about the episode, "was over dissension, the kind of victory that lasts throughout a season." By the time he wrote those words, the lesson learned under Paul Sullivan had helped to carry Luckman and the Bears to four championships under George Halas.

As a junior in 1933, Luckman was already fielding interest from college coaches at, among others, Princeton, Penn, the Naval Academy, and the University of Michigan, his idol Benny Friedman's alma mater. He also had his eye on New York University, where former NYU all-American and New York Giant pro football star Ken Strong, who had been one of his summer camp counselors, was an assistant coach. Columbia University, nearby in Manhattan, wasn't on his radar screen. Luckman had read about Columbia's revered coach Lou Little, who had led the Lions to successive 7–1–1 seasons in 1931 and 1932, but the university didn't award athletic scholarships and seemed out of academic reach. Then the freshman football coach at Columbia invited Sid and his older brother, Leo, to the varsity's game against Navy in October.

Sid and Leo traveled to the northern tip of Manhattan to watch Lou Little's varsity team beat Navy 14–7 at Baker Field on its way to an 8–1 record. Navy had already made a strong bid for Sid, and Edgar "Rip" Miller, Navy's athletic director, took him to Columbia's locker room afterward to meet Little. Miller must have felt no harm would come of this, since Columbia didn't have much to offer Luckman, but Sid was impressed by Little. Born Luigi Piccolo in Leominster, Massachusetts, Little had played some pro football and was an impressive man. The previous January, on a rain-soaked field in Pasadena's Rose Bowl, Little's 7–1–1 Columbia team had beaten the heavily favored Stanford Indians 7–0, behind quarterback Cliff Montgomery. Stanford had been scored on only four times all season, and Columbia's victory in the mud is considered one of the greatest college upsets of the 20th century. Adding to the coach's allure, especially for a rough-edged kid from Flatbush like Sid, was his impeccable wardrobe, which included, or so Little claimed, a different pair of shoes for every day of the year. Although he looked like a well-dressed professor in his rimless glasses, he was a frequent visitor to New York City's nocturnal hot spots.

"Right away," Luckman said later, "I could see there was something about the man; he had a certain charisma, a certain air about him. I felt from the start that if I could spend four years with a man like that it would enhance my life." For Little, the feeling was mutual. "The first time I saw him," the coach would recall, "he had class written all over him." It also didn't hurt Columbia's chances of landing Luckman that the school had produced the durable, humble Lou Gehrig, about to start his 12th season for the Yankees. In the end, though, a deciding factor may well have been Little's eyewear. "When I think about it, I guess," Luckman admitted, "it was not really the university I chose, although I love it with all my heart; it was the person, Lou Little, that I really chose. He reminded me very much of Franklin Delano Roosevelt with the pinch glasses."

In the locker room after the Navy game, the dapper Little regaled Sid and his brother Leo with all the reasons Sid should come to his school. No doubt aware that Leo was concerned that his kid brother be prepared for a successful career after football, Little didn't bring up football in the conversation until he had extolled Columbia's academic virtues and performed the usual song and dance about turning boys into men, not just football players who had nothing to fall back on after graduation if an athletic career didn't pan out. "I'm out to make men first, and then football players," Luckman remembered Little saying. To hammer home his point, he offered the cautionary tale of another promising player who had breezed into Columbia, quit early, and failed at the pro game because he lacked experience and humility. "To make a long story short, Sid," Little said, resettling his rimless glasses on his nose, "do you know where that halfback wound up? I can take you to him at one of the big freight yards downtown. Got wind of his whereabouts from an old grad."

The strategy worked. "Between the two of them, Mr. Little and my brother," Sid recalled, "I was left with doubts about the value of my prep name."

Sid's smaller, older, more practical brother Leo, just out of Syracuse, where he had been Phi Beta Kappa and a first-team all-American soccer player, had been opposed to Sid's ambition. "Remember this," he counseled Sid. "Football is primarily a game for glory and hurrahs. And it can turn into false glory unless you are the one in ten thousand who can climb up to pro ball and stay there. How many college stars are pounding the New York streets looking for half-decent jobs?"

"Maybe I wasn't a hotshot after all," Luckman remembered thinking. "Maybe the Brooklyn sports pages had exaggerated my Erasmus Hall feats."

"Coach Little," Leo said, "if you're talking about a swell-head, no need to worry about Sid. His dad whaled all the big-headedness outta him a while ago."

"I'm sure of it," Little said. No doubt he had discussed Luckman's family situation with Paul Sullivan at Erasmus. Sullivan could have assured Little that Meyer Luckman cared deeply about Sid's football career, and had even contrived to sit on the bench with Sullivan during Sid's games.

Now, in the early spring of Sid's senior year, disaster had struck. His father, so devoted to his football fortunes, was accused of an act that, on the face of it, was too absurd to be believed, but the damage was done within the walls of Erasmus Hall. Walking down the halls, the best high school football player in the biggest city in America could hear classmates whispering, "Get away! Get away fast! That's the murderer's son!"

If Meyer talked about the arrest at all in front of the family, he would have laughed it off. And he was apparently right; there *had* been nothing to worry about. By May, the grand jury had voted not to indict Sid's father, his cousin Harry, or Fred Hull. The cloud that had settled over the family lifted. Sid would be going to Columbia, but with an asterisk. His grades weren't good enough for Columbia College, so he would be admitted to the New College for the Education of Teachers, an undergraduate school that was within Teachers College at Columbia, where he could major in physical education. Meanwhile, in the spring of 1935, Sid was again the starting shortstop for the Erasmus baseball team.

And he was in love. He was as shy around girls as he was aggressive on the football field, but Estelle Morgolin had approached him. In the fall of 1934, before the business with his father, friends had been trying to recruit him to run for class office, but he was willing only to stump for the team's student manager, Edwin Klein. At a school assembly, he took the stage wearing a large school monogram on his chest and intoned, "Has anyone in this school ever risen to such fame? Ladies and gents, I assure you that by putting Mr. Edwin Klein in office you'll make Erasmus Hall the pride of Brooklyn!"

An attractive brunette classmate in the audience came up to him afterward, shaking her head, saying there was something wrong with this picture. "Why don't you run for office yourself?" she said. "I think Edwin has the wrong qualifications for office. He should have been all-city last season and football captain, like you." Sid might have been used to the flattery of coeds, but never had attraction been so cleverly framed as political advice.

Estelle was the beautiful, sensible, football-loving only child of Max Morgolin, who had come from Russia at the age of 12, and his wife, Elsie. Although Sid couldn't be convinced to throw his hat in the political ring, he knew a good romantic running mate when he saw one. He took Estelle to the senior prom, and soon they were a couple.

In his 1949 ghostwritten autobiography, when Luckman looked back from his perch as one of the two best quarterbacks in pro football, he saw his family through a lens that had already been tinted and re-tinted—a family in which his mother, Ethel, became the central figure. As always, she had been worried for his safety.

"Organized football is hardly like street football," Sid assured her. "We are protected, Ma, believe me. And I'm a little bigger myself."

"And she'd nod her head carefully as though to ponder whether I actually had grown up," Luckman recalled. "I wondered myself—for if ever a group of offspring remained young and sentimental, ours did. The Luckman Clan might not have been unusual in that respect, but so far as family ties were concerned, it was hard to beat. Ironies and depressions, and a dependency on one another, produced a closely knit team. . . . Having learned a tough lesson out of poverty, we became a pack of young dreamers—the boys thirsty for something big, feeling they had been pushed around."

In fact, Ethel was married to a violent man who had demonstrated his terrible temper long before his arrest on March 3, 1935. However much Meyer may have loved his immediate family, he often ruled them through fear. Several stories trickled down through the generations, none more terrible than the one that Meyer's daughter, Blanche, eventually told her daughter, Ronnie Suslow. Back in 1915, there had been another child—an infant daughter—born after Blanche and before Sid. The housekeeper had left the infant unattended for a moment on the ironing board and she had fallen off and died. Ethel knew that if she told her husband the housekeeper was responsible, he would kill her—literally. So she told him that two-year-old Blanche had left the infant on the ironing board. The housekeeper's life was saved, but Blanche spent the next 70-odd years thinking she had accidentally killed her baby sister. No one had bothered to tell her the truth until the subject came up on the way to a funeral in the 1980s, when Blanche said, "You know I did it," at which her brother Leo exclaimed, "You thought you did it? You've thought all these years that you killed her? You didn't do it!"

Blanche's life had been influenced even more profoundly by her father. When Blanche wanted to marry a man in the 1930s, Meyer forbade it because he insisted she marry into the Fleischer family, owners of the Flagler Hotel, the first and grandest of the Catskills resorts. "He wanted her to marry my father because he was a big shot at the Flagler," Blanche's daughter recalled. "And he figured Fleischer had the money and that's where she should go." And so it came to pass.

Sid, too, had faced his father's fury as a youngster. Meyer had bought Sid a bicycle on one condition—that Sid never ride the bike in the street. When Meyer found him doing just that, Meyer took the bike and chopped it up with an ax.

Of course, none of these incidents appeared in Sid's sanitized 1949 autobiography, or anywhere else. The only allusion to Meyer's anger in that book was exceedingly oblique. Sid wrote that his mother tried to apply the brakes to the Luckman males' "big ideas." Ethel was "overly anxious about keeping the family on an even keel—afraid it might be hurt by its own ambitions," he wrote. "She often lectured us on the danger of wanting too much out of this world. Money? Never crave more than your share. I'm sure she'd have been fully satisfied to have a family of honest but small-paid tradesmen. And when Dad's business went on the rocks, this philosophy helped keep us on a sound level."

3

One Heartless Tangle

On November 14, 1935, six months after the grand jury had returned no indictments against him and his two alleged accomplices, a disheveled Meyer Luckman was returning to the family home at 2501 Cortelyou Road in Flatbush—why he was coming home at 7:30 in the morning is anyone's guess—when Homicide Detectives James Sloan and Frank Sarcona of the Brooklyn police confronted him.

The men faced one another uneasily on the sidewalk in front of the Luckmans' neat little two-story redbrick house on the corner of Cortelyou Road and Lott Street, with the enclosed porch in front and the garage in back. Sloan said he had a warrant for Luckman's arrest.

When Luckman protested that the grand jury hadn't found anything in May, Sloan told him there was a new one. Since when, Luckman wanted to know. Since district attorney Geoghan changed his mind. The arrest of "the rotund little garageman" would make front-page headlines in Brooklyn for the next three days.

In a photograph of his booking at police headquarters, the heavyset Luckman, in his overcoat, stands between nattily dressed detectives, his hair matted, gazing downward. One eyelid is drooping.

He looks like a man who had been out all night. A captain read Luckman the short affidavit, charging him with homicide in the Luckman Brothers Trucking Company garage on the night of March 3, 1935. "Jaunty for all his 230 pounds," reported the *Brooklyn Daily Eagle* in that afternoon's edition, "he was by turns cool, aggressive and defiant as Acting Capt. Daniel Mooney hurled a rapid fire of questions at him in the glare of light on the lineup platform." When Mooney read the murder charge, Luckman interrupted.

"That's not right."

"Were you present when Drukman was killed?" Mooney asked.

"Yes."

"Did you see him killed?"

"No."

"Did you know him?"

"Yes."

"Relation?"

"Yes."

"Ever have any trouble with him?"

"No trouble."

"How was he killed?"

"Six fellows they were with him. They killed him."

"Where was Drukman when you first went into the garage?"

Luckman didn't answer.

"Who were the six men?"

"I don't know, but they killed him. They even hit me with something in their hands."

"Why were you there that night?"

"I'm there. That's my garage."

"Every night? Are you?"

"I had an appointment that night for a fellow to hire a truck. I been through this fifty times before."

Later that day, in Brooklyn Homicide Court, Luckman was smiling again, this time into the lenses of numerous cameras, as his attorney, Joseph Solovei, tried to get the complaint dismissed. But the magistrate granted the assistant DA's request to adjourn the matter until November 19 and sent Meyer Luckman to Raymond Street Jail without bail. In another photo, Luckman stood in a doorway as he left for jail, his fedora back on his head, glaring menacingly at the camera. Still later, he was snapped standing in his cell in Raymond Street Jail, still wearing his fedora but now looking somewhat chastened.

As Meyer Luckman sat in his cell, he couldn't have known that three members of the police department were already facing departmental trial as a result of persistent rumors of having accepted bribes in connection with the Drukman case's first grand jury. He couldn't have known that more than two dozen witnesses had already been called before a new grand jury. He couldn't have known that the police had issued an eight-state alarm to find Harry Luckman and Fred Hull. He couldn't have known that his cousin Morris, in whose coupe Drukman's body had been found, had also been charged with first-degree murder.

District attorney William Geoghan had been voted back into office that month by a large margin, insisting that the Drukman case was closed. His opponent, Joseph McGoldrick, had unsuccessfully petitioned New York governor Herbert Lehman to investigate, a move that Geoghan histrionically called "just a cheap political trick and I am amazed that my opponent would stoop to such low and unethical tactics." It was bluster; Geoghan had been wounded by his opponent's accusations that he had completely bungled the case. Under growing pressure, Geoghan did a quick about-face after the election and got permission, on the basis of "new evidence," to reopen the case.

Among other matters, the grand jury established that the Luckman Brothers' $35-a-week bookkeeper, Harry Kantor, who was thought to be the only possible eyewitness to Drukman's murder and therefore the source of the anonymous tip to the police that night, had been in New York for nearly three weeks afterward without appearing before the original grand jury. He then had been permitted to leave New York with his wife, Dora, and their daughter, thereafter moving from city to city, "apparently well supplied with cash," the *Times* reported, eventually suffering a mental breakdown in Chicago. A month earlier, in October, Kantor had died in that city, of injuries sustained when he mysteriously fell out of a window of the sanatorium where he had gone to recover.

Kantor's death had capped an autumn of increasing intrigue surrounding the Drukman case. McGoldrick was right; the manipulation of the first grand jury defied belief. It turned out that the very motive for the murder—Sam Drukman's alleged embezzlement of company funds—had been withheld from the first grand jury. It turned out that a member of the jury was distantly related to the Luckmans. Detective Charles Corbett's accusations of a $100,000 bribe and jury tampering could no longer be ignored. Police commissioner Lewis Valentine had obtained the minutes of the original grand jury and opened his own investigation into the police officers who had handled the case, formally charging three detectives with returning evidence to the suspects. On November 24, with Meyer Luckman in custody, Governor Lehman stepped into the fray after initially refusing to address the controversy. He summoned DA Geoghan and police commissioner Valentine separately to "discuss the case and all the alleged crimes associated with it."

In Brooklyn (which at the time would have been the third-largest city in the United States were it not technically a borough), the indictments were handed down in late November. The *Daily Eagle*'s banner front-page headline read: INDICT 2 LUCKMANS IN DRUCKMAN CASE.

(Morris would soon prove he had been unaware of the killing and be released before trial.)

The whole thing smelled of the corruption and rackets that had ruled the city since long before Prohibition. After studying the records of the new grand jury, the governor decided to open an extraordinary term of the state supreme court and, once the criminal trial was over, have a special grand jury investigate the alleged bribery scandal surrounding the initial grand jury.

On December 23, Harry Luckman, 36, of Brooklyn; and Fred Hull, 52, of the Bronx, presented the prosecution with a Christmas gift—themselves. They surrendered at district attorney Geoghan's office, where they were arrested. Harry Luckman identified himself as a "foreman truckman," Hull as a "driver." They were well dressed and, according to the *New York Times*, "seemed unperturbed." In an Associated Press photograph from that day, plainclothes policemen escort them down the sidewalk from Brooklyn police headquarters. In his overcoat and striking white fedora with a black hatband, the ruggedly handsome, six-foot-tall Hull, eyes cast downward, purses his lips in deep thought—or perhaps he's whistling. Next to him, the human bowling ball, double-chinned Harry Luckman, smirks in his overcoat and dark fedora, his face as pale and doughy as a kreplach. They would say nothing about where they had been for the past month and a half, during which the police had sought them along with Meyer Luckman. They joined Meyer Luckman in jail, all of them held on charges of first-degree-murder.

Two weeks later, on January 7, 1936, police wielding a grand jury subpoena paid a visit to the Brooklyn headquarters of the Luckman Brothers Trucking Company and, after a thorough search, took away so many company records that the patrol wagon was filled almost to capacity. When they also found an unloaded automatic pistol and 39 bullets in an office cabinet, they took away two more members of the Luckman family: Meyer's 27-year-old son-in-law, Harold Fleischer, who was married to Meyer's daughter, Blanche, and lived with the Luckmans at 2501 Cortelyou Road; and Meyer's 24-year-old son Leo. The young men were later released without being charged.

Two days later, yet another Luckman was in the news. The wife of Meyer's brother and business partner Ike, 46-year-old Anna Luckman, collapsed while testifying to the grand jury about a visit she had made to the Luckman Brothers Trucking Company's recently deceased bookkeeper Harry Kantor.

The second grand jury indicted all three men on January 18, 1936, and the trial began in February, in Kings County (Brooklyn) Supreme Court, with a sequestered jury and packed courtroom, with more spectators pressing to get in, and front-page headlines. On February 18, the *Daily Eagle* front page blared the headline NIECE TELLS OF THREATS BY LUCKMAN. "Meyer Luckman's niece—frail, reddish-haired Dora Kantor, speaking in a trembling voice and on the verge of collapse—charged in Supreme Court today that her uncle had threatened to kill her and her husband, Harry." Dressed in black for the recent death of her husband, she testified that Meyer "came to my home and demanded the $900 that had been taken from him. He said that if my husband didn't pay he would kill him. He turned to me and said, 'I'll kill you too.' My husband got very scared and I said why not to go to Sam Drukman and Louis Gross [another employee], they took the money. Meyer said, 'We'll take care of them later.'" After her direct examination, by special prosecutor Hiram Todd, "she staggered off the witness stand in a state of near collapse. A matron took her to an adjoining room, where she was permitted to lie down, wrapped in a blanket."

The trial featured eyewitness testimony that Meyer Luckman had also tried to choke Kantor a year before, shouting that Kantor and

Drukman had been stealing money from him. On another occasion, Meyer and his brother Ike had confronted Kantor at his home, told him he was fired, and then offered him a raise if he would tell them the truth about Drukman's theft of company funds. "It was common gossip downtown" that someone was stealing from Luckman, a business associate testified. "Everyone knew it."

Testimony by a betting commissioner and "a bookmaker's runner" established the scope of Drukman's gambling losses: the $60-a-week employee once lost as much as $425 in one day.

The case was littered with Luckmans. It was a confusing family constellation, not made any clearer by the fact that both Meyer and his brother Ike had sons named Leo and Sidney. Ike himself had disappeared and would remain a fugitive until 1940, when he turned himself in to plead not guilty to conspiring to fix his brother's and his son's cases. A week before the murder, the Luckman Brothers Trucking Company's regular day watchman was let go and replaced by Meyer's other brother, Abraham. On the day of the murder, Abe's wife testified, he had come home early and not gone back.

The owner of the West 126th Street bar where defendant Fred Hull worked testified that Hull had asked to take off the afternoon and evening of the day of the murder. The first grand jury's decision not to return indictments in the spring was looking more and more outrageous.

Now, as if to atone for its corrupt and craven conduct the previous spring, the prosecution, over the defense's strenuous objections, carried into the courtroom a shockingly realistic dummy that made the spectators rise from their seats to get a better look and gasp audibly. The dummy was trussed like the victim—and dressed in Samuel Drukman's actual bloodstained clothes, down to suspenders, socks, and necktie. An enlarged crime-scene photo would have done the job almost as well, but Judge Erskine Rogers allowed the theatrics. The other murder weapon, the broken, leaded pool cue, was laid next to the effigy.

Gruesome as it was, the effigy was not the trial's emotional climax. It was not even the most emotional event to take place that day. That occurred when special prosecutor Hiram Todd announced that the victim's father, Abraham Drukman, would testify. Todd added that the man's health was so fragile that his physician, who had accompanied him to court, felt that testifying before a crowd of spectators would be detrimental to him. Judge Rogers ordered the spectators to leave the courtroom, and the grumbling hardly had a chance to begin before the attorneys for Meyer and Harry Luckman insisted on their right to a public trial. This time they got their way; the spectators could remain. But out of consideration for the witness, court attendants removed the dummy dressed in Abraham Drukman's son's bloody clothes.

"A door from a corridor flung open," reported the *Times*. "Supporting hands at his elbows, Abraham Drukman tottered in, a man aged far beyond his 60-odd years. He was a slight figure, stooped and furrowed, his face draining with tears that flooded his spectacles. His hands trembled violently and his knees seemed to buckle as he was helped up the step to the witness chair. He appeared scarcely able to raise his hand for the oath."

Drukman then burst into sobs.

"He happened to look up," the paper went on, "and saw, perhaps for the first time, the figures of the three solidly built defendants. The old man gulped, leaned forward, rose from his chair. His arm flung out toward them, he cried in Yiddish: 'They murdered him! They murdered him! Meyer killed him!'" Judge Rogers did not have it in him to reproach the man for his outburst as Drukman collapsed on his interpreter's arm, but he directed the jury to disregard the outburst and asked the two Yiddish-speaking jurors not to translate it for their fellow jurors.

During the tearful next half hour, Drukman kept referring to his son's murder as his son's "misfortune." When asked to identify one of prosecutor Todd's assistants, who had just helped him into the courtroom, he drew a blank, saying, "Who knows? My head is in a whirl. I don't know what's going on here at all. I am not looking into people's faces lately. I don't see people because of the aggravation since my son's misfortune." He was competent enough, however, to testify that, at six o'clock. on the evening of his son's murder the previous March, he had tried to keep his son at home, where he lived with his parents, but Sam insisted he had to keep an appointment with Harry Luckman, with whom he was planning, over his father's objections, to go into the trucking business. We'll never know why Sam Drukman, while being pressured by his boss to confess to stealing company funds, didn't wonder more about why, suddenly, Meyer's nephew wanted to go into business with him.

The *Brooklyn Daily Eagle* reported that day's testimony on the front page, under the headline "Drukman Case Proves Tangle of Family Ties: Conflicting Affections Are Bared as Murder Trial of 3 Goes On":

> The Sam Drukman murder trial today promised to develop into one of the most heartless tangles of conflicting blood and marriage ties in the history of Brooklyn courts. . . . A taste of the conflict between family branches came late in yesterday's session when Mrs. Ethel Luckman, seated on a spectators' bench, saw her aged father point an infirm finger at her husband, the defendant, Meyer Luckman, and accuse him of the murder of her brother, Sam Drukman. Mrs. Luckman blanched and started forward as aged Abraham Drukman tottered to his feet and shouted hysterically in Yiddish, "That's the murderer, Meyer Luckman."

The "conflicting affections" in the *Daily Eagle*'s headline referred to the paradoxical generosity of Meyer Luckman toward his in-laws, the Drukmans. As the murder victim's brother admitted on the stand on cross-examination, Meyer Luckman had bought the Drukman parents a house and paid for two operations. In addition, to bolster his client's case, Meyer Luckman's lawyer told the court that Meyer's "tall, husky" son Sid had been one of the deceased's favorite relatives.

Few people in the courtroom could have been more incredulous at the Luckman clan's entanglements than Sid himself; he was the witness's grandson, the victim's nephew, and the defendant's son. The *Brooklyn Daily Eagle* described Mrs. Luckman, "sitting with her son, Sid Luckman, Columbia University football star, in the front row directly behind the three defendants." For the first time, Sid had made the papers for something other than what he had done on the football field. "The two Luckman defendants," reported the *New York Herald Tribune*, "are squat, saturnine men with receding brows, but Sidney looks like someone from another tribe, a handsome, open-faced fellow. He is so tall that he quite hid his mother, sitting beside him."

The defense, which had continued to argue fruitlessly that Drukman had been murdered by mobsters over his horse-racing debts, rested without calling a single witness. This was a bad sign in a trial that already looked terrible for the defendants. McGoldrick was more right than he knew to have challenged the first grand jury's refusal to indict; if bribes could protect these men, murder wasn't just safe in Brooklyn—it was actually abetted by law enforcement. On February 19, during their own lawyers' summations, the three defendants wept openly, crocodile tears we have to assume, presumably over the miscarriage of justice that had placed them in such jeopardy.

Their mood was different the next day. Had the prosecution provided an eyewitness to their crime, the men would have been eligible for first-degree murder convictions and the electric chair. As it was, the weary sequestered jury found all three guilty of second-degree murder, and when Judge Rogers sentenced them all immediately to 20 years to life "of hard labor" in Sing Sing, the state prison in the upstate town of Ossining, the *Times* reported, "The three rotund defendants listened to their fate with the same blank expressions with which they had heard the parade of State's witnesses. Mrs. Meyer Luckman and her four children, including Sid, Columbia University football player, sat in a row inside the railing and retained their composure while the verdict was announced and sentence pronounced." All three men appealed their convictions immediately.

While everyone in the family felt the shock, Meyer Luckman's conviction had a drastic and immediate effect on Leo, the oldest son, and his new wife, Leona. Instead of pursuing his academic future, Leo would have to step in and run the Luckman brothers' trucking business. It was hardly what either of the two bright, college-educated New Yorkers had envisioned for themselves. More than 80 years later, Leo and Leona's son, Peter, who eventually took over the company from his father, would still be shaking his head over it: "How many Jewish girls do you know who would have married someone thinking she would have a good life, and three months later her father-in-law commits a murder, and she sticks with his son for sixty-four years? You could say it was a different time, but still."

No sooner was the murder trial over than the extraordinary grand jury probe into the conspiracy to fix the earlier grand jury was in full swing and looking into allegations of a bribe slush fund totaling as much as $175,000—equivalent to $3 million today. Two weeks after being convicted, Meyer Luckman was accompanied to the courthouse to testify, while hundreds of curious onlookers, held back by police, strained to get a good look at him. He was by now a celebrity convict, and the crowd was almost a parody of the throngs that his middle son's exploits had attracted on Saturday afternoons.

When Meyer Luckman emerged after his testimony, handcuffed to a sheriff, he was smiling (reporters frequently singled out the elder Luckman's arrogant smile), apparently unperturbed by his imminent confinement at Sing Sing, which began on March 4, 1936, a year and a day after Samuel Drukman's murder.

The effects of the crime rippled outward. The jury-tampering investigation would itself become the target of at least one jury-tampering attempt. Special prosecutor Hiram Todd's team would call 500 witnesses and ruin reputations, careers, and lives. Sid Luckman's bank account statements were subpoenaed along with those of 38 others. By late March, Todd had determined that the bribe slush fund totaled nowhere near the six figures that policeman Corbett had bandied about. It was in the neighborhood of $25,000 to $35,000 and had been raised mostly among "the huge Luckman family," with a lesser amount "contributed by friends and business associates."

On March 22, the *Brooklyn Daily Eagle* reported that Meyer Luckman, "now serving a 20-year term in Sing Sing, had no sooner been arrested than emergency calls went out to all branches of the family to rush contributions in to the fund." Ike's 27-year-old son Leo (not to be confused with Sid's brother Leo), who was promoted to the murdered Drukman's job, admitted withdrawing $3,000 from his bank account after the murder and giving $2,000 of it to his uncle Meyer. In addition, a Yiddish-speaking policeman named Sedlak had overheard Meyer and Harry Luckman talking in their cells on the night of the murder, already discussing a sum of money that had changed hands to help them. As early as the morning after the night of the murder, Meyer Luckman had struck a deal with Detective Charles Hemendinger; and Ike Luckman's wife, Anna—who was also Ike's niece—had removed money from Ike's safe-deposit box.

She gathered $11,000 in all from various accounts and individuals, money she believed was going to pay for lawyers, she told investigators. Anna's confessions were hard won; on being asked by the prosecutor whether she remembered March 4, 1935, the day after the murder, she began to shriek hysterically, and later began to shriek again and sob uncontrollably when asked about her husband, who had disappeared the previous Christmas, claiming to be sick and needing to get away.

Detective Hemendinger, 56 years old, had an even more violent response to his interrogation; rather than return for further questioning about suspicious deposits to his bank account, Hemendinger committed suicide, in April. Meanwhile, Meyer's other brother, Abraham, the garage's newly hired watchman who had been told to go home on the day of Drukman's murder, used a different avoidance tactic. On the day he had been subpoenaed to testify at the conspiracy trial—he had already been questioned by the grand jury, so he knew what to expect—one of Abraham Luckman's neighbors notified the police of the smell of gas coming from his apartment. Abraham was found by the police in "a dazed condition in the gas-filled kitchen of his three-room apartment at 45 Cook Street in Brooklyn," standing in front of his gas stove, from which gas was pouring out of two jets. He refused treatment by an ambulance surgeon from Saint Catherine's Hospital and went out to the street to "get some air," at which point he simply disappeared.

By the fall of 1936—the start of Sid Luckman's sophomore year at Columbia—18 coconspirators had been named and eight indicted, including Meyer Luckman's own lawyer and two members of the original grand jury. Five went to trial. The other 10 conspirators had earned immunity; one of them, Mrs. Lillie Lipiansky, was described in the *Brooklyn Daily Eagle* as a "member of the vast Luckman family, who was supposed to have furnished funds for Harry Kantor to stay out of town." Harry Luckman's brother Louis would be convicted on the third try of perjury and sentenced to 18 months to three years of hard labor at Sing Sing. Even with a scorecard, it was difficult to keep the Luckmans straight—to say nothing of non-Luckmans. Bribes had been offered to detectives, prospective witnesses, members of the district attorney's staff, and jury members. The probe ended up convicting only three defendants on misdemeanor charges in a trial that featured another attempt to tamper with a juror.

Two other defendants—Meyer's brother Ike, considered the mastermind behind the bribery conspiracy; and Max Silverman, a mob lieutenant, "labor adjuster," and friend of Meyer Luckman—were fugitives from justice, and for good reason. The two men, more than any others under investigation, could connect Meyer Luckman's crime to the city's bakery racket, run by Brooklyn's Jewish mob bosses, Louis "Lepke" Buchalter and Jacob "Gurrah" Shapiro.

It was as if the sloppily handled murder of Sam Drukman had been an unimportant loose thread that, having been pulled, now threatened to unravel the entire, carefully woven fabric of Lepke Buchalter's and Gurrah Shapiro's multimillion-dollar rackets. "The slaying of Sam Drukman, more or less a routine affair as murders go, attracted barely a ripple of attention when it was committed on March 3, 1935," the *Brooklyn Daily Eagle* wrote in the fall of 1936. "In fact the public was for the most part unaware that the crime had been committed which was to develop into one of the most notorious scandals in the history of Brooklyn. . . . Thus was launched a chain of events which subsequently became so involved and complicated that no one can remember all the details and side issues."

The *New York Times* weighed in, writing that "the killing of this obscure bookkeeper in a Brooklyn garage may result in the obtaining of valuable evidence against rackets. . . . Most of the 'big shots' in the game are not known to the public . . . they live well and pass as prosperous businessmen." As the *Times* would later report, in uncharacteristically hard-boiled prose, "They lived in swanky apartments facing Central Park, drove around in big, black, fast automobiles, spent their Winters in the South or California, their Summers at the beach and apparently most of their profits in fast living and betting on race horses."

Manhattan special prosecutor Thomas Dewey, the Bronx DA, and Hiram Todd, the Brooklyn prosecutor now in charge of the Drukman case, joined hands to fight the rackets with everything at their disposal. "With all the forces now concentrated on one problem with a thousand facets," wrote the *Times*, "there is reason to hope that eventually the elusive racketeer may be forced to give up his hold on business men and working men who turned over many millions of dollars yearly for 'protection'—the need of which is created by the same gangsters that collect the money."

And the once obscure Meyer Luckman would be revealed to have played a bigger role in Brooklyn's underworld than his family could ever have imagined.

4

A Worrisome Gent

Six months after his father went off to Sing Sing in March 1936, Sid began his sophomore year at Columbia's New College for the Education of Teachers, but the *Brooklyn Daily Eagle* had jumped the gun in calling him a "Columbia football star" during his father's trial. Between his need to get up to academic speed and the part-time fraternity house job he needed to pay his tuition after his father's conviction, Sid had had to give up football for the fall of 1935. When he complained to Coach Little that he wanted to quit school altogether, Little wasn't pleased. Sid needed to stay in school, he said, and he himself needed the young man to return the Columbia football team to glory in the fall. "Coach put his arm around me and said, 'The only time you're ever going to leave this university is when you have your degree,'" Luckman recalled, "'and I promise you'll have your degree,' and with that I got two or three jobs—I was a babysitter on Friday and Saturday night. It was the only time I had the chance to study."

The Columbia football team's habitual role in recent decades as the Ivy League's weak link makes it hard to credit how important the team was in New York's sports landscape in the 1930s—in part because the fledgling National Football League offered little competition and in larger part because Coach Lou Little had spoiled locals with excellent teams several seasons in a row. In Luckman's own words, "Fans went nuts over the team." The unlikelihood of another Rose Bowl championship didn't dampen expectations about Luckman himself. Great passers were rare—the forward pass was still something of an innovation, not unlike air travel itself—and word that Little had landed the best thing ever to happen to an airborne football traveled fast. One day after practice early in the 1936 season, Little asked Luckman to put on a passing demonstration for the press. The city's football reporters crowded around Baker Field to admire 60 or 70 of Luckman's spirals, and their ensuing reports only intensified the pressure on a young man who had recently endured a family calamity that almost defied description.

Among reporters and football fans in the months following Meyer Luckman's conviction, it had to have been common knowledge that the team's messiah was his son. But although it was an era in which newspapers thrived on crime, gore, and scandal, reporters were squeamish about piercing the privacy of law-abiding citizens. For sports reporters, who could not do their job without the cooperation of athletes and the largesse, food, and alcohol of the teams they covered, discretion was assumed when it came to ballplayers. Sid Luckman was a single degree of separation away from a sensational crime, and yet, not once, from the late 1930s on, did any reporter, in the sports or any other department, refer to Sid Luckman as the son of a convicted murderer.

The year without football didn't seem to have hurt Sid. In his college debut on October 3, 1936, against a weak University of Maine team, Luckman ran for a 38-yard touchdown and passed for two others in a 34–0 cakewalk in front of 15,000 at Baker Field. This team would not be confused with Little's recent ones, however. Luckman was still untested, the team was full of sophomores, and no Columbia lineman weighed more than 200 pounds. Next up was formidable Army in a game at cavernous Yankee Stadium in front of 50,000 fans. The NFL Giants drew fewer than half that number for its home games at the nearby Polo Grounds. A nervous Luckman threw an early interception but settled down to throw a touchdown and run for another. The team played respectably in the 27–16 defeat, and Luckman, as usual, monopolized most of the coverage.

"The criticism that was raised over the fact that Sid Luckman had been singled out and showered with such flattering praise before he had played a game of varsity football was pretty well answered last Saturday by the man himself," the *New York Times'* Allison Danzig wrote. "It is not often that a sophomore comes through so handsomely in his first real test as did the new pride and joy of Baker Field against the powerful Cadets. . . . The youngster from Erasmus Hall has the stuff to take his place among the unforgettables of Columbia football." The "sensational three-way luminary" of Erasmus Hall was on his way to becoming what the paper called "one of the best passers Columbia has had in recent years." The *Brooklyn Daily Eagle* wrote that the "sophomore triple-threat sensation has given the Morningsiders verve, fire, and a real punch. He may be the making of the team."

But it wasn't only his athletic skill that was beginning to impress people. "The thing that the coaches liked particularly about the young man," Danzig noted after the loss to Army, "was his readiness to lend a helping hand to his mates. Between the halves, there was a discussion between the coaches and the backs as to what plays the latter thought would go best." Luckman, no doubt remembering his talk with Erasmus Hall coach Paul Sullivan three years earlier, immediately recommended a play calling for him to block for other ball carriers.

"It wouldn't appear from this," Danzig wrote, "that the lad is stuffing his pockets full of clippings about Sid Luckman."

After shutting out Virginia Military Institute 38–0, Columbia traveled to Ann Arbor to be blanked 13–0 by Michigan; it was the first time Luckman had ventured west of the Hudson River. The next week, Cornell's all-American end Jerome "Brud" Holland broke two of Sid's ribs in Columbia's 20–13 loss at home, and Luckman could only watch as his team won two of the last three, including a 7–0 victory over visiting Stanford (the same score by which Little's 1933 Columbia team had beaten Stanford in the Rose Bowl), and finished the season with a 5–3 record. By the spring of 1937, Sid was healthy again and ready to play shortstop for the baseball team— "a fair shortstop (not a sensational one)," he called himself—while finding time to hone his passing arm during spring football practice by throwing at an archery target for photographers when he wasn't working with live receivers.

With a nucleus of seniors now gone, Luckman and the other starters played both offense and defense, and the team struggled through the 1937 season, winning only two games, one of them an opening day romp over an uncompetitive Williams College. The following week, Luckman contributed an 85-yard kickoff return for a touchdown in a 21–18 loss to Army, but the team scored only 18 points over the last six games, finishing with a 2–5–2 record. Columbia would have avoided one of those losses, 7–6 to Brown, if Luckman, also the team's punter and placekicker, hadn't fudged the point after touchdown.

Coach Little had a gift for keeping his overmatched players inspired week after week by rarely criticizing their shortcomings and mistakes. For Luckman, however, he had some specific advice. "You're a flat-footed passer, Luckman," he said. "Keep up on your toes, and hop around a bit. Play it smart." Luckman was taking a beating, both running and passing out of the tailback position in the single-wing formation. Bruised legs and ribs, and broken noses in that era before the face mask, were his weekly punishment, and avoiding worse was his primary motive for learning to be lighter on his feet and gain a precious extra second to find open receivers.

Conscious of Sid's family tragedy and very much needing a new offensive leader to replace the departed quarterback and 1934 Rose Bowl hero Cliff Montgomery, and childless himself, Lou Little had multiple reasons to mentor the young man. In Meyer Luckman's absence, he was becoming an important presence for the Luckman family. He had already helped to allay Ethel's anxiety about Sid. "Believe me," he wrote to her, "Sid will amount to something yet. It is only too bad you didn't send me a couple of Sids for next year. I sure need them." One night after dinner, when Sid was visiting from Columbia, his mother said to him, "This Mr. Little—he is a terribly nice man. I'm satisfied that he's taking such good care of you. The Lord knows someone has to take care of you." Ethel began a tradition of sending the coach a box of oranges every Christmas. She could now displace her safety concerns onto Sid's scrawny, 136-pound little brother, Dave, who had joined the Erasmus Hall team.

Sid discovered that Lou Little and he were more alike than he thought—he called Little a "worrisome gent" beneath all that well-tailored toughness. They were both bundles of nervous energy wrapped in hard work and discipline, immigrants' children with boundless ambition.

As Sid fell under the influence of the first of his two famous father figures, Meyer's role in his life evaporated. In *Luckman at Quarterback*, Meyer disappears for 135 pages. Moreover, in the entire book Luckman can't bring himself to use his father's first name, lest it stir sleeping memories for reviewers, readers, and sportswriters. The closest he can come to the truth is to dedicate the book to: "The late Dad Luckman, who played the toughest game of all."

*   *   *

In Luckman's senior year, the Columbia Lions won their first two games, against Yale and Army, but only one more the rest of the season. They weren't as bad as their record might indicate; they lost two games by a single point and another by five. However, far more important, Columbia had pulled off the upset of the year in the East by beating powerful Army 20–18 the second week of the season, and had done it at Michie Stadium, at the US Military Academy at West Point. In front of 25,000 spectators, Army appeared likely to dispose of Columbia quickly. At the end of the first quarter, "A Cadet eleven that looked supremely invincible," Arthur J. Daley wrote in the *New York Times* the following day, was up 12–0. "Columbia's chances of winning would not have been worth a plugged nickel." At the half, it was 18–6, Columbia's score coming on a Luckman pass to John Siegal. Columbia scored late in the third, with Luckman kicking the extra point—by no means a sure thing—to make it 18–13, whereupon, the *Times* declared, "the hysteria of the spectators reached new heights." Army missed a short field goal at the other end in the fourth quarter, and then, with time running down, Luckman moved the team from its own 20-yard line down to Army's three on the strength of three long passes, the last of them to Siegal. With five minutes to go, fullback Gerry Seidel carried the ball in, Luckman kicked a second straight point-after, and Columbia made the two-point lead hold up.

In succeeding pass-happy eras of football, Luckman's numbers that sunny October 8 would not merit much fulsome praise, but few young passers of the day could complete "forwards," as passes were often called, under intense pressure. What the *Times* referred to as Luckman's "passing wizardry" consisted of only nine completions in 19 attempts, for 115 yards and no interceptions, but he manifested a rare form of leadership against a physically bigger Army team that was out of Columbia's league and would finish the year with an 8–2 record.

The country took notice of Luckman's rare achievement—a long fourth-quarter, come-from-behind touchdown drive achieved largely through the air. Two weeks after the game, Sid Luckman's muddy, matinee idol's face, beaming from beneath a Spalding leather helmet, filled the cover of Henry Luce's revamped *Life* magazine, now selling more than a million copies a week. The terse cover line, on the October 24, 1938, issue, said it all: "Best Passer." Inside, the two-page spread of photos and text hailed the "22-year-old Jewish boy" (he would not be 22 for another month) who was now "the most talked about football player in the U.S." Despite his rapidly expanding fame, the article went on, Luckman "considers himself only a fair player. On the field he never swears, never ventures to call Coach Little by his first name." The article contained a small photo of Luckman's right hand gripping a football to pass, as if the photographer was sharing an arcane secret—which, in 1938, the proper way to throw a football largely was.

Life's packaging of Sid's evolving legend gave him a modest background, calling him "the husky but shy son of a Brooklyn truck driver." Period. With that one disingenuous touch, *Life* magazine chiseled Sid's official thumbnail biography in media stone.

At the very moment that Luckman's Columbia Lions were beating Army on October 8, his father—the father who would never see his son play a single college or professional football game—was across the Hudson River and 15 miles south of Michie Stadium, serving the 31st month of a 20-years-to-life sentence at Sing Sing.

5

Specialized
Persuasions

By the mid-1930s, much of Brooklyn was under the thumb of Louis "Lepke" Buchalter, a mild-mannered but ruthless mastermind of the protection rackets. Born in New York in 1897, Lepke was the Alger Hiss of the underworld, the valedictorian of the class of Jewish gangsters who had expanded their territory from the claustrophobic Lower East Side to the wide-open spaces of Brooklyn. No one seemed able to stop him, when he had so many legitimate businesspeople, cops, and prosecutors in his pocket. Unlike Jacob "Gurrah" Shapiro, his coarse, volatile, apelike partner in organized crime, Lepke looked like a prosperous, law-abiding citizen. He wore tailored suits, pocket handkerchiefs, and a discreet yellow-gold pinkie ring; liked to take the baths in Carlsbad, Germany; and lived with his British-born wife, a widowed nightclub hostess named Betty Wasserman, and her teenage son, Harold, on the Upper West Side. He had an office on Fifth Avenue. Unlike most mobsters of the era, Lepke avoided nightlife, didn't play the horses, didn't carry a weapon. His most conspicuous habits were passing pocket change from one hand to the other and looking at his jewel-studded gold pocket watch every five minutes or so, toying with the chain.

You might not have suspected him of ordering the murders of dozens of men when you looked at him, but he enjoyed a fine sociopathic indifference to human life—even to his own, in the end. In one famous photo of Lepke in custody, he has the boyish, twinkly, big-nosed looks of a young Jimmy Durante or Ed Wynn, but he is otherwise as nondescript as a slightly pudgy junior executive. When Brooklyn's assistant district attorney Burton Turkus finally got a good look at Lepke in 1939, he was taken aback by Lepke's eyes. In fact, he became obsessed with them. A mobster's work usually hardened his gaze, and in FBI files Lepke's eyes had been described as "alert, shifting," but in Turkus and Sid Feder's classic book *Murder, Inc.: The Story of the Syndicate*, Turkus called them "soft collie-dog eyes" and "bucolic brown eyes," and at different points in the narrative referred to Lepke as a "soft-eyed rackets overlord," a "cow-eyed plunderer," and "a soft-eyed extortionist," and his countenance as "curiously bland." It was as if Turkus had fallen in love, not with Lepke, but with the mystery of how somehow so benign-looking could have so little regard for human life. Even the psychiatrists who examined him found him "affable" and "diffident."

Even the name he was known by, Lepke—a further contraction of *Lepkeleh*, his mother's diminutive name for the youngest of her too many children—sounded less like the name of a mobster than like a tasty Jewish appetizer. And the list of his aliases compiled by the FBI sounds less like a bunch of pseudonyms for America's most wanted criminal than a tongue-twisting comedy routine: Lepke, Lopke, Lepky, Sefky, Lipke, Lefky, Louis Kuvar, Louis Kuver, Louis Buckhouse, Louis Buckholtz, Louis Cohen, Louis Buckholter, Schnozzle, Murphy (the code name that telephone callers had to use), and Judge, the name by which his syndicate colleagues and underlings addressed him. The honorific says much about the Lepke's quietly punitive temperament.

That the uneducated, diminutive Lepke would become a mob boss seemed no more likely than that a Jewish kid from Flatbush would lead the NFL into the future. Lepke Buchalter had been raised in the Lower East Side neighborhood of Manhattan, a breeding ground in the early 20th century for the very best and the very worst of immigrant Jews, who often enough turned out to be siblings in the same family. The difference between model citizenship and a life of crime might be nothing more than a quirk of fate—or birth order. Lepke's Russian-born father, Barnett Buchalter, owner of a small hardware store, and his London-born Russian mother, Rose, a door-to-door herring peddler, had raised 13 children, from previous marriages as well as their own. Lepke's father died in 1909, when Lepke was 12, and his exhausted mother, tired of both children and herring, went to live with her son from her first marriage, a rabbi in Colorado, and passed Lepke on to one of the boy's older sisters.

Effectively orphaned, and possessed of only a grammar school education, Lepke fell into petty crime with ease. The neighborhood abounded with promising crooks; in 1918, the cops hauled in three young toughs named Maier Suchowljansky, Salvatore Lucania, and Benjamin Siegel, who were fighting over a woman. The cops might not have let them go as easily as they did if they knew the three were going to grow up to be Meyer Lansky, Lucky Luciano, and Bugsy Siegel. Lepke's older siblings and half siblings had been exposed to the Lower East Side's worst elements, but survived to become a dentist, a pharmacist, the aforementioned rabbi, a schoolteacher, and the social director of a Berkshire summer camp. However, just like his siblings, and in accordance with the prevailing Jewish immigrant ethos, Lepke too strove for excellence, gravitating toward the local power brokers, such as Little Augie Orgen, whom he and Gurrah

Shapiro eventually removed from their own path to success in 1927, by murdering him.

Lepke figured out how rackets worked when he was still in short pants, robbing Lower East Side pushcart peddlers and then exacting protection money from them for the privilege of not being robbed again. When he was 19, after two arrests for burglary, he and an accomplice stole two suitcases of jewelry samples in Bridgeport and were sent to a Connecticut reformatory, where his file stated: "Inmate is a clean cut intelligent Hebrew, who led a normal life in spite of little supervision until Aug. 1916. . . . He got in with a bad crowd doing petty jobs. His delinquency was probably result of mental conflict coupled with companions. Outlook excellent."

Lepke jumped parole and then served a year and a half in Sing Sing for grand larceny. He was discharged in 1919, but returned five months later to serve two and a half more years for attempted burglary. After he was paroled, "fully reformed," in 1922, he got serious about crime; and by playing alliances brilliantly, using Italian muscle, not getting too greedy, and keeping his head down, he built his empire. Between 1922 and 1933 he was arrested 11 times for offenses ranging from assault to homicide, but the charges were always dismissed. He was no less an escape artist than Harry Houdini.

Lepke and Gurrah Shapiro, his personal id, waged war in the 1920s on the numerous manufacturers of fur garment linings, punishing all who refused to join their protective agencies and pay tribute, while they played the other side as well, skimming union dues. The unions themselves were at the mercy of competing factions, mainly Communists and Socialists. Lepke and Shapiro knew the goons who could keep "labor peace," but by 1926 the New York City garment district was a war zone. Later, during the Great Depression's shrinking economy, the leading companies banded together to protect their interests against the vagaries of the free market. Smaller, nonunion "runaway" businesses needed to be put out of business. From this chaos, Lepke and Gurrah emerged as the dominant force in "labor relations," which would be to the 1930s what Prohibition had been in the 1920s: fertile ground for making lots of money. Mobsters threatened their prey with a fatal disease that only they could transmit and for which only they had the vaccine.

The rackets were not so far removed from what had always gone on in the shadows of democracy. "What the public learned now," historian Albert Fried wrote in *The Rise and Fall of the Jewish Gangster in America*, "was that racketeering was hardly indistinguishable from ostensibly legitimate practices in certain industries. . . . For [the racketeers] were perceived as operating within the system, surreptitiously giving the orders to no one knew how many unions and companies and politicians." Rackets could be looked at as less genteel cousins of the administrators of the New Deal's 1933 National Industrial Recovery Act, which "sanctioned the establishment of industry-wide cartels or protective associations" to stabilize industries. The rackets worked because they solved problems efficiently—if you averted your gaze from the collateral damage.

The mob made communities run smoothly; it looked after the poor, provided turkeys at Thanksgiving, and kept the streets safe from criminals and interlopers it didn't know. The price that law-abiding citizens paid to stay in business was often preferable to the economic and social chaos that afflicted many industries and, since the beginning of the Great Depression, society as a whole. In any case, the price was often unavoidable if you wanted to feed your family.

Moreover, Prohibition had given being a scofflaw a good name; crime was built into people's lives; it was nothing to be ashamed of. For immigrant groups like the Jews, Italians, and Irish, subject to unspoken professional quotas and outright discrimination, organized crime was in some respects simply the rational revenge taken on a predatory capitalist society that marginalized and excluded them.

Of course, the rackets employed their own brand of coercion. One industry after another fell victim to what Turkus and Feder called the application of Lepke's "specialized persuasions," which included lead pipes, stink bombs, acid-throwing, and the occasional defenestration. The rackets' bread and butter, though, was to strike and shut down uncooperative businesses, and eventually the baking industry came into Lepke's view. Almost everyone ate bread. Lepke and the syndicate could hardly resist taking over the trucking of flour to wholesale bakeries and then the trucking of baked goods to retailers. Just as he had earlier targeted the garment industry's Achilles' heel, the tiny cutters' union, which the industry needed in order to operate at all, Lepke understood and attacked the baking industry's weak point—trucking. "Early in his manipulations in trade and economics," Turkus and Feder wrote, "Lepke discovered what amounted to the atomic secret of labor-industry racketeering: Stop transportation and you stop an industry; control the truckers and you control the work." First, Teamsters Local 138 fell into line, rendering unto the rackets a piece of every loaf and pie its drivers moved. Thanks to his organizational abilities and the ready supply of Jewish and Italian killers to dispose of his enemies, Lepke gradually brought more and more of the industry under his control.

And so followers of the Drukman murder saga in 1936—it had now been making headlines on and off for nine months—learned of something called the Flour Truckmen's Association. It was an organization of wholesale truckers of flour to the city's huge baking industry, which had evolved from a thousand mom-and-pop shops to a handful of large commercial bakeries on the city's outskirts. As they had done with the leatherworking, garment, and fur industries, and would do with the film industry, Lepke and Shapiro grew (and stayed) rich by "protecting" the baking industry from the violence and sabotage only they themselves could, and would if they had to, provide. They would police those who couldn't be trusted to police themselves. Lepke's thuggish deputy in this enterprise was Max Silverman. The Flour Truckmen's Association was now collecting weekly dues of $10 from its members, plus a quarter for every barrel of flour transported to bakeries in its members' vehicles.

The association was very effective at recruiting members. One large concern, the United Flour Trucking Company, refused at first to play ball with Lepke but submitted finally after its efforts to call the authorities' attention to the racket were ignored. The police were not motivated to interfere with a system from which they too benefited. Despite his compliance, the owner found one of his trucks in the river. Max Silverman, the association's head, told him pleasantly, "You're marked lousy with the boys, and we had to do something to show you that we mean business."

As a director of the Flour Truckmen's Association, Meyer Luckman worked for Lepke. He was a link in the chain that enforced the industry's compliance with Lepke and Shapiro's racket. Moreover, Meyer Luckman had seen firsthand the racketeers' violent retribution in action, the swift punishment that could be meted out for lapses of cooperation: He had been present at one of Brooklyn's most famous mob executions, that of William Snyder. Earlier in the 1930s, William Snyder, the nominal president of Teamsters Local 138, had begun to resist the mob's control of his union; in response to the Flour Truckmen's Association's demands for a pay cut, the union had called a strike, which Snyder supported. On the evening of September 13, 1934, Snyder was called to an arbitration meeting by the Flour Truckmen's Association conference in the banquet room at Garfein's Restaurant on Avenue A on New York's Lower East Side.

Snyder came, and at around 10 p.m., Wolfie Goldis, the racketeering vice president of the union, got up, went outside, and opened one of the restaurant's casement windows. He signaled to his brother Morris, who entered the private dining room and, without saying a word, shot Snyder in the back. Snyder sprang out of his seat and turned to face his assailant, at which point Morris Goldis shot twice more, hitting Snyder once in the body. It hadn't gone quite as planned; Snyder was still alive. As a courtesy, Max Silverman drove him to the hospital, where Snyder expired two days later, not having named his assailant.

Not one of the 13 other men at the table, including Meyer Luckman, could identify the killer for the police. As for two waiters at the restaurant who positively identified Morris Goldis as the triggerman for the police, they thought better of testifying, after all. Goldis went free and was soon placed on the local's payroll by its new president, his brother Wolfie.

Meyer Luckman couldn't have failed to marvel at the swift resolution of the association's predicament—and the ease with which witnesses kept their mouths shut or were silenced. Six months later, Luckman faced a problem of his own that had resisted peaceful resolution: he had hired his wife's younger brother to manage the office, no doubt with the understanding that Sam Drukman would do something about his gambling habit. Picking winners was not one of his gifts, and he was stealing company funds to keep his creditors, who happened to be mobsters, off his back.

Stealing from one's own was a capital offense, equivalent to talking to the cops, turning state's evidence, and defying the syndicate. The fact that racketeers considered themselves honorable businessmen—"My rackets are run along strict American lines," Al Capone famously said—made embezzlement an unforgivable violation of the code of honor among thugs. Meyer Luckman, who had started out hauling bags of flour in a horse-drawn cart, was beside himself. Fear didn't seem to play a big enough role in Sam Drukman's life. But Meyer respected fear. Fear—feeling it and instilling it—made the world go around. Respecting fear was the difference between him and William Snyder, between him and any number of corpses.

The situation was perhaps even more dire. If Drukman's theft of company money wasn't enough to cover his debts, and he still owed mob bookies more, Lepke's henchmen would have told Meyer that he needed to make good on Drukman's remaining debts immediately. A man, they would have said, is responsible for his own family. Take care of it, Meyer might have been told. Perhaps Meyer feared for the safety of his own family if he didn't act.

One thing was certain, of course: the matter needed to be taken care of quietly. Lepke controlled a stable of a couple of hundred $125-a-week "schlammers" and "torpedoes" who would have been happy to take on the job. These were men who whacked bigger fish all the time. In fact, in October 1935, the month before Luckman was arrested for the second time, Lepke had had to arrange the contract for one of his own highest-profile associates—34-year-old Dutch Schultz, né Arthur Flegenheimer, of the Bronx, who had made the mistake of defying the syndicate. Manhattan special prosecutor Thomas Dewey had just filed charges against Schultz and threatened to put an end to his shakedowns of Manhattan's finer restaurants. At the same time, Mayor Fiorello La Guardia was clamping down on Schultz's slot-machine business. Afraid of losing his grip, Schultz vowed to put a hit on Dewey. The syndicate—everyone except Gurrah Shapiro—rejected his plan, convinced that rubbing out Dewey would accomplish nothing but invite the wrath of God, or at the very least the muscle of the National Guard, to shut its operation down. Schultz was told that he needed to take the punch for the good of the mob.

When Schultz wouldn't back down, Lepke didn't hesitate. He hired one of his best men, Charlie "The Bug" Workman, who shot Schultz in the men's room at Newark's Palace Chop House on October 23, 1935, although it took Schultz two delirious days in the hospital to die.

Yet Meyer Luckman took the Sam Drukman problem into his own hands—and he botched it. Instead of being relieved of his life with a single shot or two in the back of the head, Drukman had died a slow, noisy death that was discovered immediately by the police. Meyer's original arrest with his nephew and Fred Hull back in March 1935, for a murder only tangentially related to the inner workings of the rackets, raised the possibility that, if they were indicted, they might exchange information about the operation of the baking industry racket for a lesser charge or even their release. Lepke didn't need the headache, but the threat was negligible once enough money had been spread around to make sure the grand jury gave the three men a get-out-of-jail card, even if it was hardly free.

Had Luckman gotten out again on bail after being rearrested in November, his life might have been in danger. But he remained in custody, locked up in Sing Sing for the foreseeable future. The two imprisoned Luckmans, Meyer and Harry, had second thoughts about appealing their convictions and exposing themselves to the possibility of being retried and convicted again, this time for first-degree murder, and given the death penalty. They withdrew their appeals in December 1936.

The third defendant, Fred Hull, was more optimistic about his chances and was awarded a retrial on procedural grounds. He lost his gamble. This time, he was sentenced to die in Sing Sing's electric chair in September 1937. Just five hours before his execution, New York governor Herbert Lehman commuted his sentence to life.

Ironically, for someone whose case contained the seeds of the rackets' eventual undoing, Meyer Luckman never made the cut in any of the countless chronicles of organized crime in New York or the history books about Jewish gangsters. In Ron Aron's 2008 deeply researched book *The Jews of Sing Sing*, he mentions dozens of obscure inmates, but Meyer Luckman doesn't make an appearance.

6

A Good Future in Trucking

George Halas, the crusty owner-coach of the Chicago Bears, was in the market for a quarterback. On December 12, 1937, shortly after Sid Luckman finished his junior year at Columbia, Halas had seen the future, and its name was Sam Adrian Baugh. Unfortunately, the future played for the Washington Redskins.

Halas was prowling the west sideline at Wrigley Field during the Bears' championship game against Washington. The two teams were evenly matched on paper. The Bears had finished the season 9–1–1 and given up the fewest points in the league—just nine a game. The defense of the 8-3 Redskins was almost as good. The teams had scored virtually the same number of points. Yet Washington had gained 300 more yards than the Bears, all of it through the air. The Bears actually threw more touchdown passes than Washington, but the Redskins' highly regarded six-foot-two-inch rookie quarterback from Texas Christian University, two-time all-American Sammy Baugh, had thrown for the most yardage in the league. Soon enough there would be stories, perhaps apocryphal, about Baugh's lack of sophistication. When the Redskins called to congratulate him on being the team's first-round draft pick, it's said that he had no idea what they were talking about, since he had heard of neither the draft nor the Washington Redskins. Then there were the stories about his accuracy, perhaps equally apocryphal. During his first day in training camp, one went, Redskins coach Ray Flaherty challenged Baugh, saying, "They tell me you're quite a passer."

"Ah kin throw a little," Baugh replied.

"Let's see how good you are." Flaherty motioned for a receiver to take off downfield. "Let's see you hit that receiver there in the eye."

"Which eye?" Baugh asked.

Yet nothing quite prepared Halas for what happened on December 12, especially considering the treacherous condition of the field. The 23-year-old Baugh later called it "the worst field I've ever played on in my life." Another game in the rain the week before had badly chewed up the turf, which then froze. At game time, the temperature was 15 degrees Fahrenheit; fewer than 16,000 diehards had shown up, less than half a full house. "There were all these little frozen balls of mud, hard and sharp as rocks, all over the damn field," Baugh remembered. "A lot of people got chewed up pretty bad that day." The Bears defense tried its best to intimidate Baugh, stepping on his throwing hand in one pileup and kneeing him and grinding his face into the gravel-pocked ice in others. In the second quarter, the Bears' Bronko Nagurski, playing linebacker, tried to knock Baugh out of the game but succeeded only in sidelining him for most of the second quarter.

The *Washington Post*'s Shirley Povich filed a story that day about "the beefy Chicagoans" burying Baugh whenever possible. "Somewhere, somehow in the pile, somebody gave his leg an awful wrench," he wrote. "Baugh was the last to arise."

From the opening kickoff, the players were having trouble gaining traction. Backed up on their own eight-yard line early in the game, the Redskins lined up in punt formation on first down, not an unusual strategy in those days when a team's back was against the wall. Up until that point in the history of football, as Halas would write, "Smart quarterbacks never passed on first down, and seldom on second down. Usually they passed only on third down, and then only if they were in scoring territory and needed more than five yards for a first down." There was no sense in Baugh's either passing or risking a fumble on the icy turf and handing the Bears an easy touchdown.

Chicago dropped a man back to receive the kick. In the huddle, though, Baugh had told his team to line up in punt formation, "but we're gonna pass." For a rookie, this was an aggressively overconfident thing to do, but Baugh was a hard-nosed country Texan. As he would tell an interviewer half a century later, "When you're on the field, you've got to feel like you're the best son of a bitch out there." He called a short screen pass, and as the Bears' defensive line fell for the ruse, swarming through the Washington line to block the apparent punt, Baugh flipped the ball over their heads to Cliff Battles, waiting on the five-yard line with a convoy of blockers. Battles skittered 42 yards before the Bears brought him down. Still, the Bears took a 14–7 lead into the locker room at halftime, and the prospects looked good for the Bears to make up for their most recent championship appearance, in 1934, when the New York Giants put on sneakers at halftime to improve their footing on another icy field, in the Polo Grounds, and beat the previously undefeated Bears, 30–13.

The third quarter, however, proved disastrous for the Bears. Three times, the loose-limbed Baugh, operating out of the standard single-wing formation, took the ball five yards behind the center, retreated a yard or two, and flung long touchdown passes over the slipping and skidding Bears' pass defense, two of them to Wayne Millner. Baugh made the tosses look easy, like effortless javelin throws, hitting his receivers perfectly in stride, and Washington went home with a 28–21 victory and the championship.

Baugh's statistics that day were something out of the future: 18 pass completions out of 33 attempts for 335 yards, more than three times his regular-season game average. The team gained 398 passing yards overall, compared with the Bears' 207 yards. The Bears' 26-year-old quarterback, Bernie Masterson, was only 4-for-18. The salt in Halas's wounds came from the knowledge that he had had a chance to trade up in the 1937 draft and possibly select Baugh, but the Redskins' George Preston Marshall had taken Baugh two picks earlier, and Halas had selected Nebraska end Les McDonald. It would not be Halas's last lapse in assessing quarterbacks in his storied career.

During the regular season, Baugh and the Redskins had thrown for 30 percent more passing yards than the Bears, who had finished fifth in that category and would finish sixth the following season. This did not bode well for the Bears, especially considering that Halas, alone among pro football's coaches, continued to believe in, and tweak, a rudimentary version of the T formation. Halas was wedded to the T and its enhanced potential for the forward pass.

What he needed was his own Sammy Baugh, in part to take advantage of a major change in the most basic aspect of the game, the football itself. Until 1912, the ball had been a rounder 27 inches in circumference, three inches fatter than a rugby ball. Between 1912 and 1934, the circumference was reduced to 23, then 22 ½ inches, which was still fat enough that quarterbacks couldn't manipulate the ball easily with one hand and snap off passes with an overhand motion. Beginning in 1935, the ball was reduced to 21¼ to 21½ inches around—still its measurement today—just in time for quarterbacks like Sammy Baugh and Green Bay's Cecil Isbell to demonstrate to the world what a difference an inch makes. The thinner ball started a revolution. In 1932, 1933, and 1934, with the old ball, teams averaged, respectively, 45, 50, and 59 passing yards a game. In 1935, that number jumped to 80 yards a game, and it increased, with a few minor exceptions, every year after that.

The personification of this shift was an elusive six-foot-one-inch end from the University of Alabama named Don Hutson, whose rookie season for the Green Bay Packers, 1935, coincided with the introduction of the smaller football. He was the first man to run pass patterns with any precision. In his 11 years with the Packers, he revolutionized pass catching, leading the NFL in receptions for eight of those seasons, in receiving yardage for seven, and in touchdowns catches for eight. Hutson's record of 99 career touchdowns wouldn't be surpassed until Seattle's Steve Largent caught his 100th in 1989, but Largent needed almost twice as many games to achieve it.

By 1939, teams would begin averaging more yards in the air than on the ground. By 1943, teams would be averaging 141 passing yards a game, almost 100 more than in 1932, and completions would rise from 35.6 to 44.4 percent. But if quarterbacks in the 1940s occasionally looked as if they were having trouble gripping the ball, and as a result throwing more sidearm than modern quarterbacks, the ball's smooth surface, not its size, was the cause. Not until 1955 did Wilson, which manufactured the Duke, begin using a product called Tanned in Tack cowhide leather, also known as Grip-Tite, made by the Horween Leather Company, one of the many companies that sprang up to profit from the Chicago meatpacking industry's primary by-product. The new ball maintained most of its tackiness even when wet.

The year after Baugh embarrassed the Bears in the 1937 NFL championship game, the Bears slipped to 6–5, the team's second-worst record since Halas had organized it as the Decatur Staleys back in 1920. To complicate matters, Halas's miserliness had cost him his star fullback and main attraction, Bronko Nagurski. One of the league's biggest attractions, Nagurski had not received a raise from Halas since he had signed for $5,000 a year in 1930, but when he asked for a thousand dollars more, Halas stood firm, and Nagurski, at the age of 29, retreated to International Falls, Minnesota, to pursue professional wrestling and open a service station, where for years to come he would dispense size 19 souvenir rings to customers.

During the 1938 season, Halas's scouts in the East had alerted him to a kid on Lou Little's Columbia team, even before Luckman had shown up on the cover of *Life* as "Best Passer" that October. With advisory coach Clark Shaughnessy, a man whose football ideas he was smart enough to recognize as groundbreaking, Halas watched film of a couple of Columbia games with growing excitement. Shaughnesssy was about to revolutionize football by exploiting the old T formation's potential with an arsenal of deceptions—quick-hitting running plays, trap blocking, play-action passes, and man-in-motion. This T formation would be like guerrilla warfare compared with the undisguised frontal assault and blunt force of the single- and double-wing offenses that had dominated football for years. The T was a form of football jujitsu that would keep the defense off-balance in a game that had been more akin to sumo wrestling.

As they watched Luckman maneuver in films of his mediocre Columbia team in action, Halas and Shaughnessy exchanged looks. Not only did the kid run, pass, block, punt, and tackle, but Halas had been assured he had brains as well. And quiet leadership qualities. And fast feet. The ideal quarterback, they both knew, needed to be a bit of a ballerina in shoulder pads to perform the new T formation's repertoire of pivots, spins, sleight of hand, and bootlegs, not to mention the evasive maneuvers he would need to get off passes ahead of closing defensive linemen.

And Luckman was durable; he was not rangy like Baugh, who had spent his boyhood punting and passing in the wide-open spaces of the Texas panhandle, but a stocky young man who had first learned his craft on the streets of Flatbush, sending his friends running between rows of parked cars on Cortelyou, Lott, and Beverley Streets to haul in his well-placed heaves.

As luck would have it, the Chicago Bears traveled to New York to play the Brooklyn football Dodgers on the Sunday before Thanksgiving, 1938. It was only a few weeks after Luckman had appeared on the cover of *Life*. The day before the Bears game, Halas sneaked into the press box at Baker Field on the northern tip of Manhattan to watch Columbia host Syracuse in the penultimate game of Luckman's college career. It had rained for the previous two days. The field was such a mess that when Luckman and his teammates came down the ramp from the field house before the game, swaddled in waterproof sheepskin cloaks and hoods, they not so secretly hoped the game would be called on account of the apocalyptic weather. Luckman could barely hold on to the ball, but neither could Syracuse and its talented tailback, Wilmeth Sidat-Singh,* and the two teams flopped and slid around for 60 minutes of what could only vaguely be called football. Players were unrecognizable in their muddy uniforms; one Columbia player threw a perfect block on his own teammate. Against a defense that had little traction, Luckman ran the ball 15 times for 125 yards, and the Columbia team gained 256 yards to Syracuse's 98, but Syracuse won, 13–12.

In the press box, Halas turned to Bob Harron, Columbia's sports publicist, and said, "There's a boy I'd like to have on my club."

Luckman's nose, which had been broken the year before against Stanford, was broken again in a third-quarter pileup, when a Syracuse

---

* Sidat-Singh, an African American athlete who had taken his Indian stepfather's name, was hailed by sportswriter Grantland Rice as the "greatest forward passer" of the 1930s, but he was banned, because of his race, from both professional football and basketball. After graduation, Sidat-Singh became a Washington, DC, policeman and then a member of the all-black US Army Air Force unit the Tuskegee Airmen. He died when his plane failed on a training mission over Lake Huron, in Michigan, in 1943.

player's cleat smashed into it. Adrenaline dulled the pain for a while, but in the locker room the trainer could only shake his head after gently washing away the mud and blood. Coach Little took one look at the damage and almost broke into tears. Luckman himself was pretty emotional at the thought he might miss the last football game of his college career, and possibly his career, a Thanksgiving Day affair in Providence, Rhode Island, against Brown, only four days away. When the locker room had finally cleared, and Luckman was about to be driven down to Columbia Presbyterian Hospital to have his nose set, Coach Little approached his star, an incident Sid recounted in his autobiography.

"The Bears' George Halas was in the press box today."

"How come?" To Luckman, it seemed like little more than an effort to cheer him up.

"Oh, he wanted to have a look at you. One of the other pro bosses—Dan Topping of Brooklyn—drove him up. I had a little chat with Halas before the game and told him that you probably wouldn't be interested in pro ball, though you'd make a good prospect. Finally, I told him that I'd just as soon you gave up football after Columbia. Of course, that's solely up to you."

Luckman wondered what Halas could possibly have seen in him, given all his losses as the Columbia Lions quarterback.

"Apparently, Halas isn't interested in whether you're winning or losing now. But let's not worry about it before the Brown game, although you're really in no condition to face them four days from now."

In the press box that day, Halas and Topping had both decided they wanted Luckman. Halas had seen right past the rain and mud and slippery ball, and Columbia's less than mediocre record during Luckman's three years, to the thing that he coveted. "I saw him play a game in the rain in Baker Field," Halas told a reporter many years later, "and he did so many tricks with the ball I said, 'We have to have this man.'" He had felt the same thing on another rainy November day 14 years earlier, watching Red Grange of Illinois run through the entire Iowa team.

Luckman's nose made headlines in the *Times* over the subhead "But Columbia Star Will Play Against Brown on Thursday." Fitted with a face mask, Luckman met Brown on a cold but dry football field in Providence and watched Brown run up a 36–7 lead. In heroic style, he took over in the fourth quarter, throwing two touchdown passes and scoring himself off-tackle after completing a pass to John Siegal on the one-yard line. Brown prevailed, 36–27, but one sports reporter was moved to call Columbia's star "Luckman the Great."

On the three-hour train ride back to New York that evening, the Columbia team was too beat up to enjoy the special turkey dinner in the dining car. Coach Little sat down next to Luckman, saying, "I must have holes in my head for sending you in at all. I thought Irving Hall and those guys were going to break your neck on some of those tackles in the fourth quarter."

"But I threw for two touchdowns, and got a satisfaction I might never realize again. It's all over now, but at least we didn't go down quietly. And these new kids of ours; they should give you some hope for next year." Luckman was all too aware that Little deserved better than what his teams had given him the last three seasons.

Little said he wished the seniors had more to look back on. "With a few breaks, we could have saved a few of those games." The coach asked Luckman what it had meant to him—the crowds, the losses, the bruises. Later, Luckman would recall it was as if Little was suddenly talking to him man-to-man, no longer coach to tailback.

"I'm not sure," Luckman told him, "but I do know how to battle for each yard now. Remember, I came here a little spoiled from those winning years at Erasmus. Today, I've got a sounder outlook on things. No, it hasn't all been disappointing. I think I've got sight of a future now. Managed to nick off a B average in my business course and physical ed. I might be equipped to enter two fields."

When Little sent Halas the film of the Columbia–Brown game, Papa Bear continued to be impressed. Luckman ran the offense from the tailback position, trying to carry the team himself, then played defensive halfback against a better Brown team. But his valiant recovery from a 29-point deficit was the stuff any football coach loved. Luckman's fourth-quarter performance was strangely reminiscent of Sammy Baugh's third-quarter barrage 11 months before in the 1937 NFL championship game.

As the 1938 draft approached—the third NFL draft ever—all eyes were on Heisman Trophy winner Davey O'Brien, who had broken all of Sammy Baugh's records at Texas Christian University. Halas, though, had his hunch about Luckman. For starters, Luckman was several inches taller and many pounds heavier than the five-foot-seven, 150-pound O'Brien, although a new rule change would protect quarterbacks of any size. Quarterbacks could no longer be hounded and roughed up after they had thrown a pass, when they were "obviously out of the play." More to the point, the T formation needed a quarterback who could see receivers over much taller linemen in a game increasingly about passing. On the eve of the draft, Halas called Pittsburgh Pirates (later Steelers) owner Art Rooney, who had the second pick in the draft, and made a deal: he lent Chicago Bears end Edgar "Eggs" Manske to Rooney in return for the second pick, with which he chose Luckman. Then, with his own draft picks, Halas selected Holy Cross's fullback Bill Osmanski and Western Michigan guard Ray Bray, both of whom would become mainstays of the team during the 1940s.

Halas had the rights to Luckman the player, but not the man; Luckman just wasn't that interested in playing professional football. On the eve of Columbia's last home game, the loss to Syracuse, one local columnist eulogized his career:

> Saturday at sundown Sid Luckman will unhook his kidney pads, skin off his canvas knickers, unsling his leather shoulder harness and pile them in a heap on the concrete floor of the clubhouse. He will slip into the shower room and lather, rinse and towel himself. Then he will dress and go into the autumn evening and pass down the gravel walk out of Baker Field for the last time as a Columbia player.
>
> Then one more game—with Brown at Providence on Turkey Day—and the most distinguished Lion of them all will call it a college career. What he will do after that he isn't sure. . . . He's quite sure that he won't play pro ball.
>
> "All I know is that I'm going to work," he said today as he and other Lions continued preparations for Saturday's last home game with Syracuse, "perhaps with my brother, who's in the trucking business in Brooklyn. I'd like to coach very much, of course, and maybe I'll get the chance. I'm readying myself for the opportunity, anyway, with a course in physical education."

As good as Luckman was, he didn't have an accurate sense of his own value to the game. In a 1958 column titled "Football Meant Nothing Before Sid Luckman," Jimmy Cannon, once the highest-paid sportswriter in America, put him in historical perspective: "The kids who grew up in my neighborhood were not impressed by football," he wrote about Greenwich Village a few years before Luckman's own childhood:

> It was a game as remote as cricket to us and we knew more about soccer because old-country guys played that in the cobbled streets. . . . One of us generally was given a football as a Christmas present, but, after

a few games of touch, it was neglected. . . . When I began to cover
football, the Ivy League got the play. It was good football, but it was
an assignment I didn't like. . . . The reporters cowered from the elements in the open press boxes at Hanover, N.H., and the Yale Bowl
and the wind always blew with a savage restlessness when Harvard
played in Cambridge. . . . Football was drudgery for a cub reporter,
but Sid Luckman changed all that. . . . He was thrilling to watch and
he labored with a team that was small for its league. They tried to
protect him, but they didn't succeed very well because, after a couple
of games, they were exhausted for the rest of the schedule. He had
to do it himself and that was exciting to see. You had to be there to
realize how great Luckman was because the statistics didn't measure
his true worth to a team that didn't help him much.

However, even for the best college players, professional football
was far from a high-status career choice. As the title of a 1936 newsreel, "Pro Football, Major New Sport," suggested, the sport wasn't
so much trying to justify its existence as merely assert it. Irving Hall,
Luckman's opposite number at Brown and a two-time all-American
honorable mention in 1937 and 1938, never stepped foot on a professional football field. Luckman, who was never a first-team all-
American and came in a distant third in the 1938 Heisman voting,
didn't have any reason to believe his chances of success in the pros
were especially good. He knew he was not fast enough to be an NFL
ball carrier, and every team but one, the Bears, was using the same
exhausting single-wing offense that had left Luckman beat up and
bruised after three years at Columbia. And that was playing against
200-pound defenders, not the better, bigger, stronger, 230 and 250
pounders in the pros. Moreover, the pros played offense and defense
in the "single-platoon" system. If you came out of the game, you

couldn't go back in until the next quarter. Pro football was far from a secure livelihood, and that was if you made the team.

Sid's older brother, Leo, had taken over the trucking business with his cousins, the sons of Meyer's brother and ex-partner Ike. They had renamed it E & A Transport Company, but questions clung to it. A year before, the firm had been in the news during a strike of flour truckmen who were members of Teamsters Local 138, the same local that the renegade William Snyder had been head of before he was murdered in the presence of Meyer Luckman in 1934. Of all the flour haulers in the city, only E & A appeared to be exempt from the strike. "What we want to know," the president of another trucking company complained to the press, "is why the Luckmans get preferential treatment—that's all. Their trucks are hauling flour and ours aren't." Why, indeed, was the company suddenly untouchable?

"You've got a good future in trucking," Leo told his younger brother, "if you can apply the stuff they instilled in your noggin at Columbia. Business is improving generally. This year alone I've done ten percent better than last year."

But George Halas had sent Sid a letter, inviting him to check out the Second City. At one of the frequent dinners he enjoyed at the Luckman house, Coach Lou Little asked Sid how he had responded to it. The coach had become almost part of the family; when Sid's mother had fallen ill recently, Little sent an excellent doctor to the house to examine her and had taken care of the bill.

"I told Halas he shouldn't waste his money," Sid replied.

"Dear Mr. Halas," Luckman had already written back on March 16, 1939, on Columbia University Department of Physical Education letterhead, "It is very considerate of you to invite me to Chicato [*sic*] and I should like to be able to make the trip, if no other reason than to talk some football with you.

"But I don't feel that it would be quite worth your while for the outlay in expense because Mr. Halas, the situation as regards my participation in professional football has not changed. As things look now, I don't plan to play and in the circumstances, I don't think it would be worth your while to have me come out just for the ride.

"Again, let me tell you how much I appreciate your interest in my case. I'm sorry that our plans don't seem to fit together more closely than they do but that is about the situation, as I see it now.

Sincerely yours,

Sid Luckman."

"I don't know what makes him think I'd fit in," Sid told Little. Ethel nodded in agreement.

"He's looking for ball handlers who can fake," Little said.

What Luckman didn't know is that Halas had been in touch with Little, convinced that Sid was the one man who could drive the Bears' brand-new model T offense. Then Sid's old idol Benny Friedman showed up at 2501 Cortelyou Road one night on the pretext of discussing new football trends, and the conversation turned very quickly to the T formation, "the coming thing."

"Listen," explained Friedman, "the system's ideal for you." Luckman wouldn't have to take a pounding running the ball. All he had to do was squat over center, take the snap, and distribute the ball to the other workhorses. "The scheming is so effective," Friedman went on, "that you'll have more time than ever to get the ball away. Then, too, you'll be throwing more at a prescribed spot than at a receiver. You'll find plays in which your receiver appears from out of nowhere to grab the ball."

Surprised and impressed by Friedman's sudden familiarity with the Bears' offense, Luckman began to see the outline of a conspiracy. It occurred to him that the various football men around the city who had been weighing in on the subject of his favorable prospects in pro football might all be accomplices in a plot against his trucking career. Looking back, he would refer to it as "Operation Luckman."

Luckman protested again, arguing that calling signals at tailback for a middling college team was one thing, but calling them for the Chicago Bears was another.

Friedman suggested that Halas might know something Luckman didn't. He emphasized that the NFL's new rules would make Luckman "untouchable as soon as you get rid of the ball."

When Halas heard that Luckman wanted to ignore his emissaries in favor of joining the family's trucking business, he called Luckman and let him have it, without the usual quota of expletives for which he was justly known. "Since when does a fine prospect for pro ball take up trucking?!" he barked. "But if that's your aim, my boy, why, we've got a load of good solid delivery trucks right here in Chicago, and you could take over the whole caboodle if you'll join the Bears."

Of course, Halas had to know by now what else was tearing at Luckman. Famous, throughout his life, for his exhaustive background checks on prospective Bears, particularly before the advent of scouting operations that supplied this information, Halas would have learned from Little, if he didn't know it already, that Sid's father was in Sing Sing. Halas must have known that, as genuine as Luckman's doubts were about his abilities, he had to feel the pull of remaining in New York to help support the family. But Halas figured that Sid Luckman might also not mind putting roughly a thousand miles between him and this family tragedy for a while. Between Lou Little and George Halas and her own children, Ethel Luckman would have everything she needed.

Halas had to make two more trips to New York to close the deal. Finally, in July, on the eve of training camp, Halas finagled a dinner invitation to Sid's cramped Manhattan apartment, where he now lived with Estelle on the eve of their marriage. Wanting to impress Halas, the couple asked the woman who lived next door to impersonate a housekeeper and serve them dinner. Over Estelle's homemade meal, Halas argued his case. He promised both of them that Sid would make the team.

George Halas was hardly the kind of man to let a detail like a family trucking company stand in his way. The athletic eighth child of a Bohemian tailor in the Pilsen neighborhood on Chicago's Southwest Side, he had become a force of nature, devoted to family, Catholicism, hard work, and sports. At the University of Illinois, while studying engineering, he had been a slightly built benchwarmer for freshman football coach Ralph Jones, who, along with legendary varsity coach Bob Zuppke, used the early T formation, which had been around since football's infancy in the 1880s. As a six-foot, 170-pound junior, Halas warmed the bench as a right end, but he excelled in baseball, playing all three outfield positions, and in basketball, where he captained the university's 1917–18 Illini team, which won the Big Ten title. When the United States went to war in 1917, the navy sent Halas to the Great Lakes naval training center in Waukegan, Illinois, where the Great Lakes Sailors team he coached became the best military service football team in the Midwest, even beating his old coach Zuppke's team 7–0. Against the marines from Mare Island, California, Halas was cheated out of a touchdown by a referee's bad call, an experience that laid the groundwork for his tirades at NFL officials during the rest of his life.

After his discharge in 1919 and a promise to his mother that he would quit football, Halas took a train to Jacksonville, Florida, to try out for the New York Yankees. He made the team but again rode the bench, a perch from which he taunted Ty Cobb one day when the Yankees hosted the Detroit Tigers in the Polo Grounds. Cobb said he would be waiting for him after the game. When Halas emerged from the Yankees' locker room, Cobb was indeed waiting for him and Halas wondered what the notoriously belligerent Cobb had in mind. However, Cobb simply extended his hand and said, "I like your spirit, kid, but don't overdo it." A grateful Halas walked back to the Tigers' hotel with Cobb, and they struck up a friendship. Halas's gift for abusive language was greater than his ability to hit major-league pitching—he hit .091 in a dozen games for the Yankees—and manager Miller Huggins sent him to a farm team, St. Paul of the American Association, for seasoning. Halas went, but quit baseball after the season and returned to Chicago to take a $55-a-week job designing bridges for the Chicago, Burlington, and Quincy Railroad.

The country was crawling with former college football players who had nowhere to put their love of the game, and at the beginning of their peak years physically, so playing football for money was gaining a little momentum. A group of men in Canton, Ohio, had just attempted to organize a pro football league, the American Professional Football Association. Halas's old navy buddies, including the talented Paddy Driscoll, were playing for an independent team, the Hammond (Indiana) Pros, and when Halas joined for $100 a game he realized that his overriding love was for football, not building bridges. Providentially, his name had been proposed to the A. E. Staley Manufacturing Company in Decatur, 170 miles south of Chicago, a company whose owner loved sports and wanted to recruit Halas for his athletic skills and gift for organizing and coaching, as well as his help boosting the company's cornstarch production. Halas promptly assembled a team that included his old Illini teammate, halfback Ed "Dutch" Sternaman, ex–University of Notre Dame players, and men he personally scouted around the Midwest. Staley put the players to work in his mill while Halas put them to work on the football field, drilling them daily in Zuppke's T formation, in which the quarterback took the snap a few yards behind the center, in front of a fullback and flanked by two halfbacks.

Pro football at the time was played without a real schedule—and without helmets—so only a few months after joining Staley, the fiercely entrepreneurial and visionary Halas asked to meet with the men of the loosely organized American Professional Football Association. Halas took a train to Canton, Ohio, for a meeting, on September 17, 1920, at Ralph Hay's Hupmobile showroom, and his Decatur team joined the association. It was too late to draw up a schedule for 1920, so the new association's teams—the Akron Pros, Columbus Panhandles, Dayton Triangles, Rochester Jeffersons, and now Decatur Staleys—spent the fall playing an assortment of nonleague teams in games that featured a certain amount of extracurricular violence and rampant gambling.

Halas's team was proving too expensive for A. E. Staley, who suggested Halas move the team to Chicago, with his blessing, and gave him $5,000 in seed money, in exchange for the team's retaining the Staley name for at least one season and including Staley ads in the program. Shortly thereafter Halas incorporated the old Decatur Staleys as the new Chicago Bears with former teammate and now partner Sternaman. He prevailed on the other owners to change the name of the American Professional Football Association to the more succinct National Football League. The Bears soon became the first of the teams to play in a professional stadium, Cubs Park (renamed Wrigley Field in 1927), the home of the Chicago Cubs.*

Halas struggled financially, owning a pro team in a sport that ran a distant second to college ball. Over the next 10 years, most of the

---

* It was, however, at the expense of a regulation football field. Because of Wrigley's configuration, one corner of the south end zone was clipped off by the park's brick retaining wall along the first-base line. Over the years, until the Bears moved to Soldier Field in 1971, pass receivers were protected by various pads and curved barriers, an irregularity that the NFL tolerated, attesting to Halas's clout.

crowds were in the four digits, and the Bears came close to filling Wrigley Field only once. Even before the stock market crashed on October 24, 1929, the league was suffering. Halas wrote press copy himself, spread free game passes far and wide, and begged sports editors for every inch of newspaper coverage for the fledgling team and league. What he really needed was a big gate attraction—someone fans had to see. And that's when he saw University of Illinois half back Harold "Red" Grange at Memorial Stadium. Halas signed the national sensation in 1925, and arranged for a Chicago Bears barnstorming tour with him that winter. The grueling exhibition schedule—traveling around the country, they played 10 games in 17 days—made 22-year-old Grange a wealthy man and put professional football on the map.

It never stopped being a struggle, though. Red Grange, the "Galloping Ghost," was long retired by 1939, Nagurski was pumping gas somewhere near the Arctic Circle, and Halas would not be denied the services of the next big thing.

Over dinner, Halas appealed to Estelle, extolling Chicago's culture and excellent shops and restaurants, and offered her husband $4,000.

When Estelle interjected, "Sid, we're not moving to Chicago for four thousand dollars," Halas offered $5,000 and told Luckman that the only man he had ever paid more had been Red Grange—it would be years before Luckman learned that Halas had offered the same to Bronko Nagurski back in 1930 (the same Nagurski who had quit football a few months earlier when Halas refused to give him his first raise in eight years).

"Luckman Is Signed for Pro Football," the *New York Times* reported on July 25, adding that he "had said repeatedly he would pass up the pro game to help his brother run a trucking business in New York." "Sid Luckman Pulls Surprise," the *Brooklyn Eagle* reported the same day: "Decision to Become Pro Gridder Kept Even from Family."

Four days later, Sid and Estelle were married before a rabbi at Brooklyn's Elite Club on Ocean Avenue. The wedding was announced on the front page of the *Brooklyn Eagle*, the newspaper that had assiduously covered Meyer Luckman's crime and trial. The headline that day concerned layoffs in President Franklin D. Roosevelt's Works Progress Administration, but pretty Estelle Morgolin got the front-page photo. "Sid Luckman Quietly Weds School Chum," read the headline, under a picture of Estelle admiring a large publicity photo of her husband straight-arming an imaginary adversary that was hanging in her parents' home. Not all parents were lucky enough to have a Jewish son-in-law whose action photo was suitable for framing in their living room. "Sid, tall and broad-shouldered, towered over his bride, a wisp of white, in the flower-decked setting," the article went on to report. Her attendant was Sid's sister, Blanche, while Sid's younger brother, David, "acted as best man for his famous brother.

"The rough and tumble game of professional football holds no peril for the bride," the article said. "She knows her new husband is as good as any of them. When he finishes out his sports career, Sid will join his older brother, Leo, in the trucking business."

When Sid had gathered the family together to announce— "grandiose-like," he remembered—that he had signed with the Bears for two years, he did not receive a standing ovation. Blanche and David were losing their stalwart sibling; and Leo, according to Sid, almost fainted at the finality of it. He was losing a chance to restore two Luckman brothers to the helm of the family trucking concern. Uncle Ike, Meyer's old partner, who had collected the bribery funds used to fix the case back in the spring of 1935, had been a fugitive from justice for the previous three years. There was a $1,000 reward for his capture. Leo had had to give up a promising academic career at Syracuse in order to take over the business—and working with Sid would have taken the sting out of the unwelcome turn of events. He never complained about having to sacrifice his academic ambitions to pay for his father's crime, but Sid's departure inevitably colored their relationship and that of their children.

The wedding coverage made no mention of Sid's father, although, three columns to the left of the photo of the new Mrs. Sid Luckman, the *Eagle* ran a story that was a reminder of the mob's accelerating violence and an eerie echo of the groom's father's connection to Brooklyn's underworld—an underworld whose landscape was rapidly changing, as indicated by the story's initially confusing headline, "Police Guard Enemies from Lepke's Purge." By July 1939, Lepke Buchalter had been a fugitive from justice for two years, the subject of a global manhunt costing state and federal agencies almost $200,000 a year. His crime organization was beginning to crumble under district attorney Dewey's crackdown, and from his hiding place Lepke was deploying his contract killers to dispose of any individuals thought to be in danger of squealing. In a little less than a year, his campaign of killing, which would come to be known as Murder, Inc., had eliminated at least 11 threats to the mob's operation.

Eliminating real and imagined traitors was not, however, a precision game. On July 25, four days before Sid and Estelle's wedding, on the day that a Lepke associate named Philip Orlovsky was scheduled to make a "secret" appearance in Dewey's office for questioning, five men arrived in a sedan at Orlovsky's apartment building on East 178th Street in the Bronx at eight in the morning. When a short, fat man in a suit emerged from the building, Gioacchino "Dandy Jack" Parisi emptied his .32-caliber pistol into the man's back. Unfortunately for all involved, it wasn't Orlovsky, but a 42-year-old law-abiding citizen named Irving Penn, who worked at G. Schirmer, Inc., the classical musical publisher, and lived with his wife and daughters in the same building as Orlovsky. The mob seemed to be losing its cool and its touch. The police couldn't afford to lose many more prospective witnesses. The reward for Lepke, who was wanted dead or alive, was bumped up to $25,000, and 100 New York City detectives were assigned to guard around the clock "any persons connected in any way with the Lepke and Gurrah rackets in the fur and garment industries." The reward offer made more headlines than Lou Gehrig's retirement.

Sid Luckman was about to put all that behind him, at least for a little while, and leave for what he considered the hinterlands. When he expressed surprise to Halas that Chicagoans knew about his football exploits, Halas replied, "You must remember, Sid, we read newspapers here too. We do a lot of things that New Yorkers do, and play some damned good football to boot."

Before departing, Sid must have taken care of some last-minute business. The Chicago Bears first-round draft choice probably threaded his way through the summer crowd in Grand Central Terminal and boarded a train for Ossining, New York.

7

Up the River

In 1939, Sing Sing was a more humane place than it had ever been in its 100-year history, which wasn't saying much. The medieval corporal punishments of the 19th century had been abolished—the brutal flogging with the metal-tipped cat-o'-nine-tails, the early form of waterboarding called the "shower bath," and the painful metal cage for the head called the bishop's miter. Gone too was the daily horror of claustrophobic, windowless cells, each measuring just seven feet by a tad over three, barely roomier than a coffin. The regimented, zombie-like lockstep marching, every man's hand on the shoulder of the convict in front of him, had been discontinued, along with the dingy striped uniforms made famous by Hollywood, and the strictly enforced silence among inmates broken only by the screaming of flogged prisoners, a few of whom died of their punishment. Gone was the stench of the buckets, in lieu of toilets, that inmates emptied every morning into the Hudson River. No longer could tourists pay a quarter to observe the inmates through peepholes. And yet, even then, Sing Sing had been an improvement over some 19th-century prisons, where prisoners could never leave their cells at all or were left to rot in underground pits.

By the turn of the century, windows were installed in Sing Sing's common areas, parole was instituted, and the reins were loosened. In 1914, a humanitarian warden named Thomas Mott Osborne allowed self-policing in the workshops, created an inmate court to mete out justice, and supplied Sunday movies. He lasted only two years, although that was pretty good as tenures went; between 1860 and 1880, Sing Sing had gone through 13 wardens. Between Osborne's resignation in 1916 and 1920, there were four more.

Then came Lewis Lawes, a warden who, like Osborne, had the distinction of being opposed to capital punishment while presiding over the only state prison with a death house, and a reasonably efficient electric chair called Old Sparky. Lawes allowed radios and initiated rewards for good behavior, from picnics to sentence reductions. Most controversially, he staffed his mansion on the grounds with prisoners, even murderers, who had earned the privilege. Inmates too were living better; the old cell block down by the Hudson had been emptied in 1926 when the new, roomier A and B cell blocks opened. The cells even had windows. A staunch advocate of prison reform and defender of the parole system, Lawes tangled with J. Edgar Hoover, whose FBI kept a file on the renegade warden. But Lawes and his wife, Kathryn, engendered such trust and earned such devotion from the inmates that, when Kathryn died in an accident, in 1937, a thousand inmates insisted on joining the funeral procession to the nearby cemetery, and Lawes agreed, opening the gates. As Ralph Blumenthal writes in his biography of Lawes, *Miracle at Sing Sing*, "A thousand prisoners went out and a thousand returned."

Lawes had abundant compassion for prisoners but also abundant passion for the spotlight. His primary job was to run the biggest prison in the state, but mining the experience for his own artistic enterprises came in a close second. He was smitten by cinema. He even arranged screenings for inmates who were awaiting execution in the death house. When John Ford showed up at the prison in 1930 to shoot a short film called *A Day in the Life of Sing Sing*, the director was charmed by the warden's eight-year-old daughter Cherie and had her come to Hollywood for a role in a flop called *Up the River*, a prison comedy starring Spencer Tracy and Humphrey Bogart, in which she played—not surprisingly—a warden's daughter.

Her father, however, became the celebrity, writing best-selling books, radio plays, newspaper articles, and movie scripts. Lawes's book *20,000 Years in Sing Sing* was made into a Warner Brothers film, also poorly received and starring Spencer Tracy. Another of his books, *Cell 202—Sing Sing*, a novel based on the lives of the four prisoners who occupied the same cell successively between 1826 and 1911—was a critical success. Lawes coauthored a theatrical drama, *Chalked Out*, which closed after 12 performances. In his column, Walter Winchell quipped that "the jury found it guilty." Lawes turned around and sold the film rights to Warner Brothers, which released it in 1939 as *You Can't Get Away with Murder*, starring Bogart again. That same year, Warner released another movie based on a Lawes book, called *Invisible Stripes*, starring George Raft, a young William Holden, and Bogart. Warner was also set to remake *20,000 Years in Sing Sing* with John Garfield. "To Hollywood," Lawes's biographer Blumenthal wrote, "Lawes's Sing Sing was an inexhaustible quarry of prison scripts."

Far more important to Sing Sing's 2,000-plus inmates, however, was Lawes's passion for sports. He believed sports could best sublimate prisoners' sexual impulses, not to mention the aggressive ones that had landed them in prison in the first place. During a previous job at the Elmira Reformatory, Lawes had introduced games of catch between guards and prisoners. Under Lawes's predecessor at Sing Sing, baseball had become part of prison life, with the better prison teams welcoming a string of amateur and semipro teams that included squads from the New York Stock Exchange and the Metropolitan

Life Insurance Company. During the 1920s, the New York Giants baseball team paid several visits to Sing Sing, and in the late 1920s Lawes arranged for the New York Yankees to come upriver and play the prison's Mutual Welfare League team, the Sing Sing Orioles. After lunch at Warden Lawes's mansion, the Yankees toured the prison, while inmates strained to glimpse Lou Gehrig and Babe Ruth, the latter seeming almost to satirize prison garb by wearing a white golf shirt and knickers, black stockings, and black-and-white shoes. Ruth, an orphan who had once done time himself in a Baltimore reformatory, acknowledged everyone with a wave and a "Hello, kid." After he changed with the rest of the team and took the prison field, Ruth proceeded to hit four home runs during the game, including a tape-measure job.

In 1931, Lawes got his hands on some used leather football helmets and jerseys, and organized two prison teams to play on Sundays against visiting teams such as the Ossining Naval Militia and the Port Jervis Police Department. Sing Sing's inmates were no strangers to secondhand uniforms; in 1915, the New York Yankees had shipped 28 of their 1914 uniforms, plus gloves, bats, and balls, to the prison to outfit the teams. The football team, which went by the nickname the Black Sheep, was initially coached by a middle-aged kidnapper named Hope, whose lack of football experience didn't prevent him from using something he modestly called "the Hope system." The prison football field was barren of grass, but 2,000 inmates cheered on the Black Sheep, while the Sing Sing band, which included a former member of John Philip Sousa's famous band, played rousing fight songs such as "Throw Him Down, McCloskey."

A former captain of Notre Dame's undefeated 1929 football team, now a budding politician, John Law, volunteered to coach the Black Sheep in 1932, attracting others to the cause, including a former Harvard coach, who gave a kicking clinic, and none other than Columbia's Lou Little. In the team's third season, 1933, Lawes installed a concession stand for the Black Sheep games, selling hot dogs and soda pop to the prison population, though not to the segregated ticket-buying public, 250 strong.

When Meyer Luckman arrived in March 1936, Lawes was still warden, although in the early 1940s he would resign after an escape attempt by three inmates resulted in the death of two policemen, and everyone wondered whether the "coddling" had backfired. The football program had already fallen victim to New York State's new hard-line corrections commissioner, a former New York City police commissioner named Edward Mulrooney, who denounced the practice of charging spectators to see games, arguing that it was the state's job to underwrite the football program. Since everyone knew that would never happen, and given that the ticket revenue was the primary funding for the program, Mulrooney's edict amounted to the game's death knell.

Football was no longer being played within the prison, but Meyer Luckman had the most intriguing connection to the football being played outside it. Any file kept on Meyer Luckman's incarceration was lost long ago in a fire, so we can only wonder whether the indulgent Lewis Lawes allowed Meyer to keep the cover of *Life* magazine's October 24, 1938, issue taped to the wall of his cell. It is a safe bet that Meyer's relationship to Sid was no secret,

There is no record then of any of Sid's visits. While his sister Blanche once told sportswriter Dan Daly that Sid never visited Sing Sing, it's hard to believe, given the extraordinary lengths he later went to in order to get his father out. Let's assume he occasionally made the short journey and talked football with Meyer, the once powerful father who bought him his first football, who took such pride in him, who had now joined these other men, reduced to a number, condemned to listen to the slow ticking of time. Let's imagine that Sid promised his father he would return to see him in late October, when the Bears were scheduled to play the Giants in New York.

Afterward, as Sid Luckman walked back down the hill to the little Ossining train station, looking at the sailboats sparkling in the sun on the sluggish Hudson, perhaps his thoughts turned to what Chicago would be like, or how hard the hitting would be in professional football, or how it had all managed to come to this—how a father and son had taken such different forks in the road to the American dream.

What we do know for sure is that Sid's siblings did visit Meyer in prison, but that his mother Ethel never spoke to her husband again after his conviction, let alone made the trip to see him.

8

Captive City

If Sid Luckman thought he was escaping New York City's climate of organized crime when he arrived in Chicago, he was in for a surprise. "He thought Chicago was cowboy and Indian country," George Halas said of Luckman, but it had never been cowboy country, and the Indians were long gone, commemorated by countless street names, the Chicago Black Hawks hockey team, and the city's name itself—a Native American word for the wild onions that grew all over the region. It wasn't the Wild West, but it was wild. Chicago was more closely identified than even New York with lawlessness, civic corruption, and gangsters. As the visiting English writer E. M Forster would say of the city a few years later, it was "a façade of skyscrapers facing a lake, and behind the façade every type of dubiousness." All the depredations of New York's organized crime world still couldn't compete with the legendary Al Capone or with two of Chicago's momentous criminal events—the Saint Valentine's Day Massacre of 1929, on the North Side; and the famous killing, in 1934, of gangster John Dillinger as he left the Biograph movie theater on North Lincoln Avenue. The underworld slang for a cement coffin, after all, is "a Chicago overcoat," not a New York garment.

The city, the fourth largest in the world, had been hit hard by the Depression—it experienced twice as many suicides per capita as New York during the 1930s—but Chicago was fearlessly creative when it came to music, architecture, and moneymaking, and would become wildly innovative when it came to theater, television programming, cheap hamburgers, upscale men's magazines, and in the very near future, winning professional football games.

As in New York, Jews were a robust presence in the shadows of the city's power structure, which consisted of three corruptly intertwined institutions: the Cook County Democratic Party, the Catholic Church, and the mob. It was probably inevitable that Luckman, as the Bears' celebrated new addition, would be embraced by the city's Jewish power brokers, but that it happened so quickly was Halas's doing, however unintentional.

To show the young quarterback around, Halas called on young sports reporter Irv Kupcinet, another child of Russian Jewish immigrants. Four years older than Luckman, Kupcinet had also been an attention-getting high school student, on Chicago's heavily Jewish West Side. Kupcinet had been the school newspaper editor, senior class president, and a good enough tailback to win a football scholarship to Northwestern University. There, a fight with the coach's brother resulted in Kupcinet's transfer to the University of North Dakota. He was good. He played for the collegians in the 1935 Chicago College All-Star Game at Soldier Field, on a team that included president-to-be Gerald Ford and future Green Bay star Don Hutson. Signed by the Philadelphia Eagles as a blocking back, Kupcinet played only two games for the team before a shoulder injury ended his NFL career and jump-started his journalistic one, which began at the *Chicago Daily Times*, soon to be renamed the *Sun-Times*. His father was even a bakery truck driver. Irv married Essee Solomon, the chain-smoking daughter of a wealthy drugstore and liquor store owner, Joseph Solomon, who had once earned a living as a rum-running bootlegger.

In 1939, Kupcinet was just a sports reporter, four years away from being awarded the paper's gossip column, which was to become one of the first things Chicagoans read in the morning for decades to come. To quote Thomas Dyja's description in *The Third Coast: When Chicago Built the American Dream*, Kupcinet turned the column into

> a civic institution, a chronicle of the world as it passed by his roost in Booth One at the Pump Room. A Midwestern Walter Winchell connected to major figures in Hollywood, Washington, and the Mob, Kup made nightly rounds of the city's clubs with his wife, Essee, on his arm, then wrote it all up the next morning into a surprisingly intelligent column blending flack tips, paid quips, and starlet sightings with actual reports on politics and entertainment. Parsing his ethics was impossible—he had brains and good taste, was ahead of the curve in matters of race, but he loved trading favors and cherished his access to the rich, famous, and beautiful. That city had no greater chauvinist than Kup.

Or greater freeloader, as restaurateurs and car dealers alike showered him with merchandise so he could shower them with priceless column inches. With his expensive suits, deferential manner, and silky, precise enunciation, Kup would have his own local television talk show by 1952, one of the first, and later filled in for Steve Allen on *The Tonight Show*. From 1953 to 1977, he was WGN radio broadcaster Jack Brickhouse's sidekick for Bears games.

Kupcinet was only a fledgling institution in 1939, but as a well-positioned journalist he already operated in Chicago's immense, and largely unavoidable, vast gray area, where large favors were exchanged and the immovable objects of legitimate business met the levers and pulleys of the underworld. This was nothing new. Important business—moving and managing great amounts of goods and people and money, consolidating financial and legal power—could not be done outside that area. As muckraking reporter Ovid Demaris wrote in *Captive City: Chicago in Chains* in the 1960s: "From the moment of its incorporation as a city in 1837, Chicago has been systematically seduced, looted and pilloried by an aenonian horde of venal politicians, mercenary businessmen and sadistic gangsters. . . . Today it is nearly impossible to differentiate among the partners—the businessman is a politician, the politician is a gangster, and the gangster is a businessman."

Many of Kupcinet's friends were, by his own admission, "bookies, gamblers, and unsavory people." On the moral map of the times, being a bookie carried little, if any, stigma. "I knew some men who were bookies in the old days who were well-respected—real estate operators, capitalists, and very accepted in high society," Chicago's powerful Democratic ward boss and kingmaker Jake Arvey once wrote. "They weren't demeaned by the fact that they were doing an illegal act. . . . This was a different sense of morality."

One bookie, a handsome protégé of Arvey's named Charlie Baron, took such a liking to Luckman that he invited the Bears' rookie to live with him until he got settled. Luckman accepted. Any qualms he might have had about consorting with a bookie were allayed by Baron's total lack of interest in the game of football.

However, it wasn't long before Luckman received a call from the National Football League's president, Carl Storck, notifying him that he was being investigated "for associating with the wrong people," and strongly recommending that Luckman make other living arrangements. "No charges were brought," Kupcinet wrote after Luckman's death, "but he was warned to be aware."

Although no longer roommates, Luckman and Charlie Baron became good friends. Most likely through either Baron or Kupcinet,

Luckman also became acquainted with the already powerful but scandal-plagued Sidney Korshak. Like Kupcinet, Korshak was a West Side Russian Jew, but he had once been an Al Capone associate and was now an imposing and dapper young lawyer for the Chicago mob. He was fast becoming the city's reigning fixer—an invaluable and highly paid bridge between organized crime, Chicago politics, and the highest echelons of legitimate businesses. Korshak would eventually go west to keep peace between the mob-controlled Teamsters and the movie industry in Hollywood, where, coincidentally, he would have among his many famous friends the actor who would play Lepke Buchalter in a forgettable 1975 movie: Tony Curtis.

Korshak had a genius for secrecy and discretion and was never indicted for any crime. Unlike the elusive Charlie Baron, however, the ubiquitous and powerful Korshak did not escape negative publicity forever. A 1976 exposé by then *New York Times* investigative reporter Seymour Hersh detailed Korshak's role as what the Justice Department called "a senior intermediary for and adviser to" organized crime groups. Although his universally recognized influence meant he did not need to threaten others with violence, Korshak was not above resorting to the language of mob reprisal. Hersh reported that one prominent businessman who had fired Korshak as his labor counsel was warned by him not to "walk alone at night." In 2006, a decade after his death, Korshak was the subject of a comprehensive book by investigative reporter Gus Russo, titled *Supermob: How Sidney Korshak and His Criminal Associates Became America's Hidden Power Brokers.*

Korshak would become a lifelong friend of Irv Kupcinet. As Russo writes in his book, "The relationship between the two former Lawndale Russian Ashkenazim was symbiotic: Kup made certain Sidney and the rest of the Korshaks were portrayed in a good light in his daily 'Kup's Column,' while Sidney, after his eventual move to Beverly Hills, helped Kup gain access to Hollywood celebrities and gossip.

'Irv Kupcinet was always kissing Sidney's ass,' said former Chicago FBI man Fran Marracco."

This was the world in which Sid Luckman landed in 1939. As a man, he may have fallen far from his father's tree, but fame and fate had dropped him in the same orchard. He developed lifelong friendships with Baron, Korshak, and Kupcinet. When his son, Bob, was born three years later, Luckman made Baron the godfather. When he needed to help a restaurant-owning relative achieve labor peace with a union years later, he called on Korshak. Yet, with the same genius he demonstrated for eluding tacklers, Luckman would elude any public suspicion of mob connections or hint of wrongdoing.

As for Kupcinet and Luckman, Halas's instinct had been right. The two men got along famously. Beginning in the late 1960s, Luckman would live in the same luxury apartment building overlooking Lake Michigan as the Kupcinets; at the time, this was one of a few buildings on Chicago's Gold Coast that accepted Jews. Their lives seemed almost destined to intersect, yet never more unexpectedly than a year after Sid Luckman's arrival in the Windy City, when he led the Bears to the most lopsided victory in NFL history, in the 1940 championship game against the Washington Redskins. When Luckman took the field in the nation's capital, there, of all people, was his buddy Irv Kupcinet, who, as an experienced football man, had been hired as head linesman for the game, although he was also a sports reporter who would write about it. Talk about gray areas. If you look closely at the film of the game, you can see Kupcinet barely get out of Bill Osmanski's way during the fullback's 68-yard touchdown run on the second play from scrimmage.

Luckman had his hands full learning the Chicago Bears' playbook, which was an imposing document. According to Ken Kavanaugh, soon to become Luckman's favorite receiver, there were 2,300 plays in the Bears' playbook, though that number included many slight variations of the playbook's core, which Luckman estimated as "about 380 plays." Memorizing them would have been a daunting challenge for any rookie, let alone an insecure one who wasn't sure he belonged.

Fortunately, Luckman's insecurity was accompanied by a conscientious streak; he took it upon himself to learn not only his responsibilities on a given play but also the job of everyone else on offense. Halas was astonished when Luckman first demonstrated his almost photographic memory for everyone's assignments. Halas had counted on Luckman's "brains," in addition to his agility, when he traded for the rights to him the previous December, but he had no idea he had acquired the equivalent of a Talmudic scholar with an extremely strong right arm. Many years later, Halas would say of Luckman's intellectual diligence, "He spoiled us."

At first, Luckman struggled. "A headache," he would say of his indoctrination after watching Bears veteran quarterback Bernie Masterson run a few plays from the T formation at the Bears' training camp in Delafield, Wisconsin. "I'd never seen the likes of it." Unlike the single wing's tailback, the T's quarterback handled the ball on every play, and the responsibility intimidated Sid. The T-formation quarterback "might never run a yard forward, but he was key man, flipping, faking, spinning. And in most cases he appeared to have no interference at all," he wrote in his 1949 autobiography.

> It didn't take long to realize that the whole T-formation system was based on split-second timing. . . . My first glimpse of the Bears showed me a quarterback crouching behind center, and three mates five yards back of him, crosswise, like the crossing of a letter "T," but ready to shift into any number of alignments. It didn't look to me like one formation or another—instead, it reminded me of a dozen formations

rolled into one. Then on a given signal the men seemed to run in different directions, and the quarter would take the ball, and fake it to two or three men and finally fade back for a pass.

One of the coaches, a former Bears quarterback named Carl Brumbaugh, who had run Halas's earlier version of the T during the 1930s, told Luckman and his fellow rookie, fullback Bill Osmanski, "Halas has picked you birds because he felt you had the special talents to fit into this picture. You've got to prove it by studying the system in your spare time. And you, Sid, do you realize the job expected of a Bear quarterback?"

"Realize it?" Luckman replied. "I'm worried sick over it." He stayed up late in his training-camp dorm room, "trying to unravel the potpourri of plays, which were given such queer names as 'Crackback,' 'Running Swing Switch,' 'Crossbuck,' and so forth. There were plays designed for every possible situation on the field. Plays to cross up the linebacker and plays to throw an end off-balance." During one of the final preseason scrimmages, Luckman got his signals mixed up, sending a halfback in the wrong direction. The play was a bust. Huge veteran guard George Musso, already in the seventh season of a 12-year career that would send him into the hall of fame, turned on Sid.

"If you can't call signals right, then get off the field and let someone else do it!"

Out of a combination of exasperation and pride, Sid stood his ground. "Listen, Musso," he said. "Halas is paying you to play guard. I'll take care of this position. You take care of yours."

Everyone was stunned into silence by the rookie's outburst, not least of all Luckman himself, a natural conciliator. Musso just glared at him. A fight looked possible, one in which Luckman would not fare well.

After a moment, Musso relaxed his fists and said, "All right, fella, take another crack at it."

That night, after the team meal, Luckman knocked on the door of Clark Shaughnessy, Halas's advisory coach, who was primarily responsible for the modern T formation Luckman was trying to master. A prickly, professorial teetotaler, Shaughnessy laid down the stack of diagrams he had been studying and invited Sid in. Although he was only 47, the handsome Shaughnessy was already one of football's gray eminences and deepest thinkers. As a boy, he had conjugated Latin while delivering milk and later used artillery range-finding terminology to describe pass trajectories. One of his daughters recalled him jumping up from the dinner table to scribble down some epiphany in X's and O's before sitting back down, muttering, "Good play." His lack of natural charm was summed up by Bob Zuppke: "The world lost the greatest undertaker when Clark Shaughnessy decided on football coaching instead." Temperamentally, Shaughnessy was not really cut out for football, but few people understood the game better.

Luckman complained that he didn't seem to be clicking with some of his teammates. "Either they don't trust me, or something. I guess they want a combination mastermind and mystic to be playing quarterback."

"Tell me," Shaughnessy said calmly, as Luckman remembered the conversation. "Did you have any trouble with the men at—at—what was the name of that college?"

"Columbia. But the boys there were my classmates, and we lived together even before the season began."

"Well, let's forget all that and concentrate on the Bears. With this club, you and I have a real chance to get the feel of winning ball for a change." Shaughnessy was coping with the demise of the University of Chicago's football program, where his job as head coach was in danger. He advised Luckman to expect "a few natural prejudices" on a team of such disparate temperaments and backgrounds. "They may be pros, but they are still boys at heart with the ordinary tendencies of boys."

Luckman moved on to the real purpose of his visit. "Halas says that anything I'd have to know about the T, you can tip me off."

Luckman didn't know it yet, but he had been recruited for one of those moments when a game's paradigm was about to shift. Clark Shaughnessy was in the process of deconstructing, and reimagining, football's offensive conventions. Power running through the line—symbolized in the 1930s by Bronko Nagurski carrying the ball behind tightly massed blockers, or pile-driving the defensive line as a blocker to open a narrow hole for a teammate—would soon no longer be at the center of football's universe.

9

A Fast Passing Game

Clark Shaughnessy didn't create the modern T out of whole cloth. Amos Alonzo Stagg had invented it at Yale in the 1880s and the formation had been football's basic offense in the 19th century. The quarterback would take the short snap a yard or two behind the center while, behind him, two halfbacks and a fullback lined up in a straight line, forming the T. But it was merely a formation, good mostly for running between the tackles.

Until 1906, teams had had three chances to gain five yards for a first down (the rule wasn't changed to four downs until 1912), and passing was prohibited, so the college contest was essentially a game of brutal mayhem in which a ball carrier, once tackled, could crawl forward until an opponent pinned him, forcing him to yell "Down!" (Into the 1950s, players in the NFL, could still crawl for extra yardage.) Until 1929, it was legal for college players to hit an opposing lineman on the head, neck, or face with the palm of the hand. The largely unchecked violence of the game resulted in as many as two dozen deaths a year, at both the high school and the college level, and continued to do so even after the forward pass was legalized in 1906 by the rules committee of the forerunner of the National Collegiate

Athletic Association (NCAA). Teams were allowed one pass per set of three downs, but the pass had to be thrown five yards to the right or left of the "snapper," as determined by the lines, parallel to the sidelines, that ran the length of the field. If the pass touched the ground before being touched by any player, it was ruled a turnover, and the other team took possession. Thanks to Walter Camp, the conservative "Father of American Football" and a vigorous opponent of passing, the game was forced to accept limitations on passing that would stifle offenses for years to come. When Glenn Scobey "Pop" Warner introduced the single-wing offense early in the century, it liberated the running game by introducing unbalanced lines and deception, but the forward pass remained a second-class citizen.

The young Clark Shaughnessy had not even seen a football game until 1908, when, as a 16-year-old University of Minnesota freshman, he bought a ticket to a game between the university's Minnesota Golden Gophers and Pop Warner's Carlisle (Pennsylvania) Indians, which featured Jim Thorpe. Inspired to give the game a try, Shaughnessy made the Minnesota team as a benchwarmer, but within three years had turned himself into a star, thanks to his curiosity about a report he read, during the summer of 1911, that some Canadians were experimenting with the rounder football of the era by throwing forward spiral passes with it. Stagg had discovered in the 1890s that a football could be snapped backward with a spiral, but few had bothered to throw a spiral in the other direction, since the forward pass hadn't become legal until 1906—and even then, heaving the melon-like ball was awkward and therefore rarely attempted. The young Shaughnessy bought a two-dollar football, began practicing the forward pass, and discovered he had a knack for hitting his target. A year later, Minnesota coach Henry Williams was calling him one of the best forward passers in the Midwest, and Shaughnessy was named to several all-star teams.

A postgraduate year as an assistant coach at Minnesota was followed by a stint as head coach at Tulane University, where his early innovations—a complex single-wing attack using multiple backfield shifts—propelled his perennially small teams to a 58–27–6 record between 1915 and 1926. He was lured away to Loyola University (of Louisiana) with a lucrative offer, and after impressing Knute Rockne in a six-point loss to the far superior Notre Dame squad, Shaughnessy had his pick of head coach jobs. He landed at the University of Chicago, then a powerful member of the Big Ten Conference, where he succeeded football's great innovator Amos Alonzo Stagg, who had coached the team for 40 years and been forced into retirement at the age of 70.

In Chicago, Shaughnessy began talking about a new kind of quarterback with "brains" and about his plans for "a fast passing game." However, University of Chicago president Robert Maynard Hutchins was in the process of killing off the football program by raising academic standards. The university's vaunted "Monsters of the Midway" were being cut down to size—leaving the nickname available for the Bears, who didn't play anywhere near the South Side's Midway.

Shaughnessy fished around for a new challenge. After spending a few Sundays at Wrigley Field watching Halas's version of the T formation, he found himself at the same civic dinner event with Halas and hastened to introduce himself. He ingratiated himself with Halas over dinner, drawing some of his favorite plays on napkins and informing Halas that he was developing a new type of offense based on the T formation, with some hidden ball tricks that defenses hadn't seen before.

Halas was intrigued. When the NFL started in 1920, he was the only coach to stick with the T, which he had learned from his old freshman football coach at Illinois, Ralph Jones. The T was widely considered outmoded, and all the other teams embraced the single-wing or double-wing formation, or a variation called the Notre Dame Box, and would continue to use those formations into the 1940s, when the Bears' example became too compelling to ignore. In truth, Halas's T had more in common with the single wing than with the expanded T with which he, Shaughnessy, and Luckman were about to revolutionize football in 1939.

Prior to 1929, interior linemen still lined up only a foot apart, with the ends separated from the tackles by only a yard or two. The quarterback took the snap a yard or two behind the center, allowing the center to keep his head up and be a more effective blocker, but the clumping of players on offense meant the defense did the same. Almost all the action took place in that small area, with the occasional attempt to send a ball carrier around the end.

In 1929, Halas had hired Ralph Jones away from Lake Forest Academy, north of Chicago, where he had been coaching football. Jones promised to deliver a championship in three years with a revamped T, in which the lineman were spaced more widely, the ends were split, and the flourish said to have been accidentally invented by Red Grange, the man-in-motion, would be used to better effect. Jones added short passes in the flat and deceptive counterplays, in which most of the team flowed one way while the ball carrier slipped the other. Jones made good on his promise: in 1932 he delivered a championship, and a record of 7–1–6, before returning to Lake Forest.

The six ties exposed the limitations of Jones's system; indeed, the first three Bears games that year ended scoreless. Despite Jones's innovations, the Bears weren't moving the ball, and pro football remained a constipated affair. In those four years from 1929 to 1932, the Bears averaged only 10½ points a game.

In 1932, Halas had the foresight to hire a man to streamline the game of football, Hugh "Shorty" Ray. Although he would be elected posthumously to the Pro Football Hall of Fame in 1966, Shorty Ray remains perhaps the greatest unsung, and at times strangely disrespected, hero of the sport. At the time, Ray had already rewritten old rules and devised new ones to codify the game at the high school and college levels. "I needed his help and badly," Halas recalled 40 years later. In that precomputer era, Shorty Ray was a born data analyst who wielded a slide rule, a stopwatch, and an unmatched obsession with making the game safer, more rational, and higher scoring—and therefore more popular.

After earning an engineering degree in 1907 from the University of Illinois—where, at only five foot six, he played four sports and captained the basketball team—Shorty Ray became the assistant to Oak Park High School football coach Bob Zuppke, future coach of George Halas and Red Grange at Illinois. In 1912, while still in his twenties and teaching mechanical drawing, woodworking, and metal shop in Chicago's public high schools, Ray organized the Chicago Public High School League and civilized football with rules that outlawed, among other customs, hidden ball tricks, irregular and dangerous equipment, unnecessary roughness, clipping, and delaying tactics that ran down the clock. Ray's rules standardized penalty calls, tested officials on the rules and rated their performance, allowed freer substitution, allowed coaches to confer with players during time-outs, created hash marks to make sure offenses always operated toward the middle of the field, and legalized passing from anywhere behind the line of scrimmage.

When Halas hired Ray to work behind the scenes for him, the Bears were in trouble—in 1932, the franchise had won its first championship in 11 years but had lost $18,000—and so was the NFL. Games averaged a paltry total of 16 points. There were only eight teams, and when the average attendance at NFL games started to be kept officially in 1934, the number was just 8,211. Tickets were given away liberally to paper the house. Ray worked behind the scenes to speed up the game, conceiving the 30-second rule, the two-minute warning, and limited substitution. It worked. By 1936, the average point total increased to 23.8 per game and attendance to over 15,000. In 1938,

Halas thrust Ray on the league, whose officials he would supervise for the next 15 years. "I made my greatest contribution to the National Football League," Halas said later, "when I convinced President Joe F. Carr in 1938 to take on Shorty Ray as a technical adviser to the National Football League and to be in charge of officials." He added, "Without him, there would be undue confusion in the sport today."*

When freelance sportswriter Harry Sheer profiled Ray as "Football's Mr. Einstein" in the early 1940s, he wrote, "Officially he is an obscure little teacher of mechanical drawing at Harrison High School, Chicago. Technically, he is technical advisor to the National Football League. You would never believe it, sitting in the stands as the Chicago Bears play for the world's pro championship, for example, that Hugh Ray's pencil is behind every play, every rush, every touchdown, almost every step taken by the Baughs, the Luckmans, the Hutsons, the Waterfields and even the Officials with the whistles."

By 1939, the Bears would score more than 27 points a game, and in two more years, they would average 36 a game, more than three times their scoring proficiency less than 10 years earlier. Throughout the league, games featured more plays, more pass plays, more scoring, less dead time than ever before, and less average elapsed time to complete a game that had formerly been bogged down with delays. However, the Bears had been inconsistent during most of the 1930s—careening from nearly perfect in 1934 to mediocre, then back to first place and mediocrity again. They lost two championships, to the Giants in 1934 and to Sammy Baugh's Redskins in 1937.

In 1938, the team had lost five games. Something still wasn't right and Halas hired Shaughnessy as an adviser. Shaughnessy's radical

---

* Nonetheless, according to Hugh Ray's grandson James W. Stangeland in his book about his grandfather, *Hugh L. Ray: The NFL's Mr. Einstein*, Halas, the NFL, and the Pro Football Hall of Fame have at times in the years since done their best to deny Ray's seminal contributions to the game.

plan for a revamped T formation owed its inspiration to a source so unlikely and so unsavory that he wouldn't even reveal it until 1986, a few years before his death. A student of military strategy, Shaughnessy had been attracted to the ideas of Nazi military strategist General Heinz Guderian, who became leader of the *Panzer* (tank) units that would soon overwhelm the Polish and French forces in World War II. Guderian's advocacy of mechanized warfare between the world wars resulted in a 1936 book, *Achtung—Panzer!* which Shaughnessy had had translated at his own expense into English at the University of Chicago. An opponent of trench warfare and of reliance on slow-moving infantry, Guderian built on Germany's World War I strategy of bypassing the enemy's strengths in favor of surprise attacks at its weak points, using massed tanks, motorized infantry and artillery, and airpower in support. "What we want to do," Guderian wrote, "is, for a short period of time, dominate the enemy's defense in all of its depth."

Shaughnessy's ears perked up. Guderian's *Blitzkrieg* tactics struck the intellectually curious Shaughnessy as eminently transferable to the activities of a handful of men on a football field. The parallels between trench warfare and the single wing's grinding ground attack were obvious to Shaughnessy; the blunt, three-yards-and-a-cloud-of-dust offenses in favor with virtually every football team in America were as primitive a tactic as Pickett's Charge at Gettysburg.

Following the Nazis' example in 1940—deceptively drawing the Allies north by sending Army Group A toward Belgium and Holland, allowing Guderian's tanks to pour through the relatively undefended Ardennes Forest—Shaughnessy would use wider spacing and men-in-motion to spread the defense, then breach it with quick strikes and misdirection plays, all the while concealing the ball as long as possible. The T formation's sleight of hand was controversial, requiring not only the right quarterback but also, some thought, more indulgent fans. Illinois coach Bob Zuppke once teased Halas, saying that he had invented the T after seeing two fellows in the stands surreptitiously pass a flask back and forth between them so quickly that, "I never knew who had it. Then it dawned on me how deceptive it would be to pass a football around that way. I put it in the T, and it worked so well that even the spectators never knew who had the ball. So they stopped coming to the games, because they never got a chance to see the football anymore. There was nothing left for me to do except abandon either the T or all thoughts of future gate receipts." In reality, of course, the modern T was Shaughnessy and Halas's brainchild and the ticket to more exciting football games and bigger crowds.*

Luckman might never have agreed to play pro football had it not been for the T's great appeal for a quarterback: the possibility of self-preservation. Benny Friedman had impressed this fact upon him in the spring of 1939. In the single wing, every back, including the quarterback, was a ball carrier and had to block as well. "I was completely shocked by what I saw," Luckman said of his first exposure to the T. "I didn't realize it could conceivably work, where you had no blocking in front of the ball carrier. Then, when I saw it in operation, I knew right there it was the most wonderful thing that could happen to me because I wasn't fast enough to be a good ball carrier."

Three years of hard knocks at Columbia had worn him out; he wasn't convinced he could physically survive more abuse, especially from much bigger professional players. Bigger men than Luckman were unprepared for the pros' physicality. Just before joining the Bears, Ken Kavanaugh, the six-foot-three receiver from Louisiana State University, had his comeuppance during the 1940 charity game at Soldier Field between 1939 NFL champion Green Bay and a team of recently

---

* Some football historians think the only reason the enigmatic Clark Shaughnessy isn't in the Pro Football Hall of Fame is that he eventually crossed the powerful George Halas by breaking his contract a year early and resigning, in 1962. By then he had not only invented the T but also devised new defensive formations to counter it.

graduated college all-stars. Buford "Baby" Ray, the Packers' six-foot-six, 250-pound tackle, knocked Kavanaugh down and proceeded to sit on him, like a wrestler. "Later we became good friends," Kavanaugh remembered, "but in that game . . . I felt like a fool out there on Soldier Field, and I tried to get away from him as much as I could. I hadn't run into anything like that. The pros were so much bigger and better. There was no comparison."

In the T, Luckman would be the orchestrator of a complex offense, but he wouldn't be untouchable; Shaughnessy cautioned him that his brainchild formation, by spreading the offensive ends, would give the defensive ends on six-man lines a clear shot at a quarterback retreating to pass, unless the halfbacks and fullback blocked them. In practice, after watching the halfbacks risk their lives to shield him from marauding defensive linemen, Luckman wasn't convinced it was a viable plan.

"I don't see how our halfbacks can avoid getting killed the way they come busting in for the ball," he said to assistant coach Luke Johnsos, who had been a Bears receiver earlier in the 1930s. The backs would also take all the punishment on many running plays as they hit the gaps on quick openers and traps without big teammates leading the way.

"Sid," Johnsos assured him, "as fast as each one is murdered, we'll send another one out on the field."*

It is said that George Halas won the true affection of just two of his players in his 63 years as coach and owner of the Bears. One was Gale Sayers. The other was Sid Luckman, and with good reason: Halas

---

*The quip contained more than a kernel of truth. Quarterbacks were about to become valuable merchandise while running backs were about to become, if not expendable, more easily replaceable. By 2017 they had the shortest average career of any players, 2.57 years, while quarterbacks averaged 4.44 years. But a first-round draft pick—which Luckman had been—could expect a career of more than nine years.

stood by Sid in that fall of 1939 when every veteran on the team seemed to resent the Jewish kid from Flatbush. Luckman had been ambivalent about becoming a Bear, and many of his teammates were deeply skeptical about having him there. Echoes of his teammates' doubts appear even in their later reminiscences. Hall of famer Clyde "Bulldog" Turner, Luckman's center throughout the 1940s, never thought Luckman was in Sammy Baugh's class and noted that he often threw behind receivers, who were talented enough to make him look good. Ed "The Claw" Sprinkle, whom Halas called the greatest pass rusher he had ever seen, questioned Luckman's technique: "Sid probably was one of the worst [-looking] passers in the league because he threw sidearm. . . . But Sid got the job done. He could play." Ken Kavanaugh said, "He didn't throw a real long ball, but every ball he threw was catchable and it was soft."

In 1939, the team's grizzled veterans couldn't begin to see what Halas saw in the bookish outsider (Sid's favorite author in those days was Dashiell Hammett) who was earning more than any of them. "Sid Luckman and Biggie Goldberg may be the big noises in the coming pro football campaign," the *Brooklyn Eagle* reported that August, referring to the Chicago Cardinals' rookie fullback Marshall Goldberg, "but right now Davey O'Brien"—whom Halas had passed on—"appears to be the turnstile kid. Large crowds are actually paying money down in Philadelphia to see the Texan pitch passes during the practice periods."*

Luckman's lack of confidence didn't help matters. He was, by his own admission, "a nervous, sensitive ballplayer." He was looking ahead to an illustrious career in trucking. Fifteen years later, another gifted

---

* Unanimous first-team all-American Davey O'Brien, picked fourth in the 1939 draft by the Philadelphia Eagles and given a $12,000 signing bonus, led the league in several passing categories that season; he would set an NFL record for most pass completions, 21, in a loss to the Bears in his rookie season. But the Eagles were a bad team and O'Brien quit football after two seasons to become an FBI agent.

Jewish athlete, a baseball player named Sandy Koufax, a bonus baby who had pitched in only four college games and considered himself a better basketball player, was deeply resented at the beginning of his career by the Brooklyn Dodgers' veterans. Manager Walter Alston didn't quite know what to do with Koufax for the first half of his career. But Luckman had one thing Koufax lacked: the full support of management. Halas knew Luckman wasn't the league's best pure passer, but with Shaughnessy on his team, Halas didn't need the best. "Sammy was the better passer," Halas said later, "but Sid was the greatest all-around quarterback."

Luckman's disgruntled teammates were relieved when newspapers reported that Dan Topping, the wealthy owner of the NFL's Brooklyn Dodgers (descendants of the Dayton Triangles, an original NFL franchise) and later an owner of the Yankees baseball team, offered to buy Luckman and take him off Halas's hands. Several Bears, who hoped some of the cash would find its way into their poorly paid hands, went to Halas and urged him to unload the kid. Halas turned all complaints about Luckman aside.

Topping, who had with Halas watched Luckman playing against Syracuse in the rain at Columbia's Baker Field the year before, did not go away. He knew that Luckman would be a great box-office draw in his hometown. When the press announced in October that he had made another offer, Topping called it "the biggest offer in the history of the National Football League," reputed to have been $50,000 (in reality, it was $15,000). The *Brooklyn Eagle* headline the next day read, "Luckman Not for Sale, Bear Boss Declares." "Not a chance in a million of us letting Sid go," Halas told the *Eagle*. "He's a great player and he fits in very well with our scheme of things. Besides, he seems to like the city of Chicago very much."

Three months later, after the 1939 season, Topping complained to the *Eagle*—delusionally, it seems: "I'll say now that we might have had Sid Luckman for less than the $15,000 I offered for him in mid-season, if I had used my own judgment." At the league's annual meeting in New York in April 1940, Topping was still at it, hoping to land Luckman after he had given up on trading for Marshall Goldberg.

No wonder Luckman adored Halas when so many others resented his tightfisted abrasiveness. But although Halas had had a sixth sense about Luckman, in 1939 his belief in him was inescapably a matter of some faith, since the criteria for success at quarterback in the NFL have always been frustratingly unquantifiable and elusive. Even in more recent eras, with more analytic data available, the NFL's football fields have been littered with the husks of can't-miss star college quarterbacks, let alone men of Luckman's less predictable promise. In 1983 the Detroit Lions passed on future hall of famers Jim Kelly and Dan Marino; in 1991 many teams had Browning Nagle (who eventually played in only 24 NFL games) rated higher than hall of famer Brett Favre; and, of course, Tom Brady, one of the most effective quarterbacks in NFL history to date, was drafted 199th in the 2000 draft. The college game then was, as it is now, much slower than the pros, and a quarterback's assets in college, such as arm strength and toughness, can easily be nullified.* Halas's judgment would prove as fallible as anyone's in the late 1940s, when he would be flush with

---

* As NFL scout Dan Shonka told *New Yorker* journalist Malcolm Gladwell in 2008, in regard to quarterback Chase Daniel, the highly regarded University of Missouri prospect, "In the spread [offense], you see a lot of guys wide open, but when a guy like Chase goes to the N.F.L. he's never going to see his receivers that open—only in some rare case, like someone slips or there's a bust in the coverage. When that ball's leaving your hands in the pros, if you don't use your eyes to move the defender a little bit, they'll break on the ball and intercept it. The athletic ability that they're playing against in the league is unbelievable." Quarterback may be the most complex and intellectually demanding position in sports; the passing play we enjoy from the stands or our armchairs is, at ground level, an indecipherable and continually changing tangle of bodies, vectors, random phenomena, and constantly altering possibilities, all of it perceived under threat of personal annihilation by blitzing linebackers and safeties.

good quarterbacks—the veteran Luckman and two first-round picks, Johnny Lujack and Bobby Layne—and end up with none.

Today, the pressure to win often inhibits coaches from nurturing young quarterbacks, but Halas didn't have to please the boss; he owned the team, which hadn't had a losing season since 1929. In addition, he believed in a new system, in which his quarterback would play a teachable role rather than be seen as the team's savior.

Knowing that he was anything but a sure thing when the 1939 season got under way, Luckman spent his off-hours in training camp peppering Shaughnessy with questions.

"What about a 6–3–2 defense?" he recounted asking Shaughnessy, in *Luckman at Quarterback*. "How do I handle it?"

"Be conservative with end-arounds. They've got you covered on each side. Here's where the man-in-motion will prove valuable—he'll toss a scare into the enemy."

"And when they send charging tackles at us—good tackles?"

"That's the time to slip around end, and catch those tackles flat-footed. Have one of our backs come across unexpectedly to handle a charger; block him into the line."

"But what about a roving linebacker?"

"Cross him up by feinting ordinary over-scrimmage passes to a halfback, while letting a fast end slip behind the rover boy to take longer flings. You might need two or thee plays to cross the guy up."

When he practiced his spins and bootlegs with Bears assistant coach Carl Brumbaugh, he was grateful to Lou Little for having told him to focus on his footwork at Columbia. Brumbaugh called out plays and watched as Sid tried to figure out which way to go. Brumbaugh had been the team's quarterback in the run-crazy days of Bronko Nagurski, when the pass was still the offense's last resort. In his entire nine-year NFL career, the slight Brumbaugh had completed just 34 of 121 passes—28 percent—for only 656 yards and nine touchdowns.

That was then. In just his first year with the Bears, Luckman would complete 45 percent of his passes for only 20 yards less than Brumbaugh had in his entire career—and Luckman wouldn't even play quarterback for most of the season; he was eased into the Bears lineup at the position most similar to his old tailback position in college, halfback.

Halas, in his wisdom, was hardly about to throw Luckman into the deep end or ram him down his suspicious teammates' throats.

10

Runaround

While Sid Luckman prepared for his first season of professional football, a grisly epoch was coming to an end in New York. Shortly before winning the 1937 election for Manhattan district attorney, 35-year-old Thomas Dewey had likened Louis "Lepke" Buchalter and his mob to the city's venerably corrupt Tammany Hall Democratic machine, and said, "I intend to see the grip of the underworld broken in the next four years."

By the summer of 1939, Lepke had been a criminal for most of his life and a fugitive from justice for two years. After Dewey had managed to convict him and his partner, Gurrah Shapiro, in 1936 for violating the Sherman Antitrust Act—for conspiring to fix rabbit-skin prices through their control of the Protective Fur Dressers Corporation—Buchalter and Shapiro skipped bail in 1937. There was talk that the two top mobsters were in Canada, Cuba, Puerto Rico, Vermont. Or they were in Warsaw, Poland, plotting to kidnap the fiancée of Prince Radziwill. The press couldn't get enough of the geographical speculation.

In 1938, Shapiro, who was in bad health, turned himself in, telling FBI special agents that Lepke was determined to remain at large, "to see how he made out." For another 16 months, while agents scoured the earth for him, Lepke never left Brooklyn, moving frequently, from the Oriental Palace dance hall in Coney Island to a Brooklyn waterfront flat to an apartment in Flatbush, where he played the "paralyzed" husband of a Mrs. Walker, wearing a mustache and going limp in his armchair whenever anyone came to the door. Albert Anastasia, Lepke's equally ruthless counterpart in the Italian Mafia and partner in Murder, Inc., helped arrange logistics, staying ahead of both the cops and nosy neighbors.

From seclusion, Lepke ordered the deaths of at least a dozen men in a position to compromise the operation of his lucrative rackets. The authorities distributed a million circulars offering a $25,000 reward for him; by contrast, in the 1932 Lindbergh baby kidnapping case, a mere 20,000 circulars had been printed. The feds then offered an additional $5,000 for Lepke. Citizens hoping to grab the reward "informed" the police that Lepke had gone to Russia on a fake passport and was now in the Lubyanka prison, or that he lived in a Catskills cabin protected by a machine gun, as Jack "Legs" Diamond had done several years before.

Why Lepke Buchalter finally surrendered to J. Edgar Hoover after federal and local authorities had spent two years looking for him is not documented. Certainly, he was tired of not seeing the sun and of trying to keep his fraying empire together. Perhaps he could finally identify with the lower-level men he was afraid would testify against him; he had ordered them to leave town under penalty of death, go where prosecutors couldn't find them, but they would sneak back to New York, unable to tolerate exile. On the other hand, a federal study of his psychological traits had established that he was extraordinarily well adapted to a life of sensory deprivation. "Give him some books and magazines," Major Garland Williams had pronounced, "and he's content to hole up in one room for six months."

There were rumors that Lepke was lured out of hiding by a false promise from the syndicate's Meyer Lansky, Lucky Luciano, and Frank Costello: if he turned himself in to the feds, he would never be handed over to Dewey, and after serving a short federal sentence, he would be back in business. To strengthen the case for surrender, Lepke's trusted lieutenant Morris "Moey Dimples" Wolenksy assured him that a deal had been made with the feds that would keep him out of Dewey's hands and therefore nowhere near Sing Sing's Old Sparky. But it was far more likely that the mobsters had been promising the opposite: to hand Lepke over to Dewey, while pledging organized crime's and labor's full support for Dewey's run for governor of New York; in exchange, they wanted the freedom of Lucky Luciano, who was doing 30 years for running a prostitution ring.

In any case, the truth was that Lepke knew not only that the heat on him would never let up, but that the heat was bad for everyone's business and would eventually make even him a marked man. "The suspicion seeped into his mind," Burton Turkus wrote in his and Sid Feder's book *Murder, Inc.: The Story of the Syndicate*, "that the ever-increasing counsel to give up was really only a lightly disguised decree; that if he did not move voluntarily, the board of governors was going to call a kangaroo court on him." As Harry Anslinger, the commissioner of the U. S. Narcotics Bureau, would later write of the combined efforts of his agency, the FBI, the New York police, and Thomas Dewey's office, "We made it so hot in fact that the syndicate bosses decided they wanted no more of shielding Lepke. The word spread over underworld channels: 'Tell Lepke to give up or we'll kill him ourselves and dump his body on the steps of the courthouse in Foley Square.'" Under the circumstances, a federal prison sentence began to look pretty good. He might be a free man again before he turned 50.

So, after almost two years in hiding, Louis "Lepke" Buchalter, the most wanted man in America, surrendered to FBI director J. Edgar

Hoover. At 10:17 p.m. on August 24, 1939, Lepke climbed into the back seat of Hoover's limousine at the corner of Fifth Avenue and 28th Street in Manhattan. He took off his dark glasses and told Hoover, "I would like to see my wife and kid, please."

The choreography of Lepke's surrender, the interminable security arrangements involving the powerful syndicated newspaper columnist Walter Winchell as the go-between, had been as complex and full of misdirection as anything in the Chicago Bears' playbook. The oft-told tale varies only in small details. On August 5, 1939, Winchell got a phone call at the Stork Club. "Don't ask who I am," the caller said. "I have something important to tell you. Lepke wants to come in. If he could find someone he can trust, he will give himself up to that person." Winchell volunteered for the job. The caller rang back to say Winchell had been checked out, and they wanted him to broadcast that Hoover guaranteed Lepke's safety.

"Your reporter is reliably informed," Winchell said on his radio broadcast on August 6, enunciating slowly, "that Lepke, the fugitive, is on the verge of surrender. If Lepke can find someone he can trust, I am told, he will come in. . . . I am authorized to state by the G-Men that Lepke is assured of safe delivery. . . . No part of the $35,999 reward"—it had grown again—"[is] to be claimed by me."

Now Winchell began getting phone calls simply telling him to await further phone calls. Late one night, a caller directed him to drive his car through the Holland Tunnel to a deserted swampland in New Jersey. When he arrived, at 3:30 in the morning, no one was there to meet him. He sped back to Manhattan, wondering whether maybe he shouldn't have volunteered for this assignment. Next came a call from a different person, ordering him to a bar near the George Washington Bridge in upper Manhattan, where another man instructed him to ask Hoover what the possible federal narcotics rap sentence would be if Lepke surrendered. Once he had the answer in hand—12 to 15 years—Winchell was told to be at one spot, then another, in Manhattan, and then to wait at a certain pay phone for yet another call.

By now, Hoover was irate at the cat-and-mouse game, and dressed down Winchell at his home court, the Stork Club. FBI associate director Clyde Tolson told Winchell that if Lepke didn't turn himself in within 48 hours, Hoover would order him shot, to which Winchell replied, "You people haven't been able to find him for two years. How you gonna find him in forty-eight hours?"

More calls followed, the last directing Winchell to drive to a theater in Yonkers, north of the Bronx. En route, he was pulled over, and a man with a handkerchief tied over the lower half of his face got into Winchell's car and told him to be at a drugstore at 19th Street and Eighth Avenue at nine that evening, then exited the car.

At the appointed hour, Winchell nervously sipped a Coca-Cola at the drugstore's lunch counter when another stranger motioned him outside to tell him that Hoover should be in his car at 28th Street and Fifth Avenue between 10:10 and 10:20 that night. Winchell phoned the information in to Hoover and then got back in his car with the stranger, who, observing that Winchell was shaking too much to get the key into the ignition, took it from him and drove with Winchell around the city for the next hour. At 10:15, the stranger stopped Winchell's car near Madison Square Park, at Fifth Avenue and 23rd Street, handed him a small Star of David, and told him to give it to Lepke. At this point, having been jerked around for two-plus weeks by Lepke's cronies, and having jeopardized his priceless credibility with J. Edgar Hoover, Winchell had had more than enough; the gossip columnist who knew everyone had lost his taste for meeting the head of Murder, Inc. He asked the stranger why Lepke couldn't be driven directly to Hoover's car and was told that it wasn't possible, that no one would ambush Lepke for the reward if Winchell was with him.

At that moment, 37-year-old Albert Anastasia, waterfront rack-eteer and the most feared Italian hit man in organized crime—he had justly earned his nickname, "Lord High Executioner"—was driving into the city from Brooklyn. He looked for all the world as if he were merely chauffeuring a married couple holding a baby in the back seat. The "wife," however, was thug Louis Capone's sister-in-law, the poor infant had been borrowed from a friend, and the "husband" was none other than Lepke Buchalter.

At Madison Square Park, the stranger climbed out of Winchell's car and a moment later a short, well-dressed man in dark glasses and a little Hitleresque mustache climbed in beside the columnist and said, "Let's go."

The two men—both 42 years old, both children of Jewish refugees from pogroms and shtetls—drove slowly up to 28th Street. In America's new celebrity culture, amplified by radio, they were the stars of their respective realms. The insecure Winchell could destroy reputations from behind a shield of newsprint or a microphone, while Lepke ruthlessly ordered the literal extinction of other men from behind a hedge of professional killers. Winchell's slogan, embla-zoned on *New York Daily Mirror* delivery trucks, was "He sees all . . . He knows all"—but Lepke had seen and knew things Winchell could only fantasize about.

Winchell, badly rattled, maneuvered his car behind Hoover's and parked. For all he knew, with so much at stake, both Lepke and Hoover had men stationed on nearby rooftops, lining him up in their telescopic sights. He opened the passenger-side door for Lepke and led him into the back seat of Hoover's chauffeur-driven limousine. Following Lepke inside, he introduced the two men at last. They were three of the most powerful men in America. Winchell rode with them downtown toward the Federal Building. On the way, according to a report five days later in Winchell's column, Lepke surprised the other two by complaining about his celebrity—"Lepke, Lepke, Lepke! Everything is Lepke. All of a sudden I'm a big shot!"—but such an outburst would have been wildly out of character for a man who rarely said more than necessary. Near Union Square, Winchell jumped out and phoned in his scoop, then called his wife, June, who still wanted to know why he was risking his neck with gangsters.

Hoover offered Winchell the reward money after all, but he refused it. One of the movie studios wanted to know if he would write the story for the silver screen, but when he did tell the story, which he did often, it was only for smaller audiences of friends.

Lepke's surrender earned a beneath-the-fold front-page story in the *New York Times* on August 25, 1939—"Lepke Surrenders to FBI"—but only because the headlines about rackets and rubouts that had enthralled New Yorkers for the previous few years were already being trivialized by news of an incalculably bigger threat to peace at home. The Lepke story was dwarfed by the grim banner headlines that day, stacked three high: HITLER ACTS TO TAKE DANZIG, ORDERS ARMY BE READY; CHAMBERLAIN GETS WAR POWERS; LONDON, PARIS DARK; ROOSEVELT APPEALS TO GERMANY, POLAND AND ITALY. In a week, Hitler would invade Poland.

The battle for jurisdiction over Lepke started immediately. The feds wouldn't even let Dewey's men talk to Lepke, claiming he was "too tired," although rumors abounded that Dewey was considering indicting Lepke for ordering the murder of Teamsters official William Snyder in 1934. Nonetheless, Lepke soon realized there was no deal with the feds to keep him out of Dewey's hands. Moey Dimples had lied to him. How he ever believed for a minute that he could control his fate once he turned himself in, he would never understand. Suddenly, he was just another sucker. Moey Dimples would get what was coming to him, but it would take four years before Albert Anastasia took care of that. (In 1957, the Lord High Executioner himself would be taken care of while sitting in a barber's chair in Manhattan's Park Sheraton Hotel, a victim of the wars for control of the Cosa Nostra.)

By December, Lepke and accomplices were convicted in federal court of running a multimillion-dollar narcotics ring. Three Bronx gangsters—Yasha Katzenberg, Jake Lvovsy, and Samuel Gross—had partnered with Lepke to buy "clearance stamps" from crooked customs officials, allowing them to smuggle heroin-filled trunks into New York from China without being questioned. In little more than a year, the gang moved 1,465 pounds of drugs through customs in New York, on to a processing plant in the Bronx, and out to the streets. In exchange for his capital and influence, Lepke received half the profits.

The moment Lepke was sentenced to 14 years in federal prison, Dewey grabbed him and hustled him over to the state court a block away to be tried for racketeering in the baking industry. Numerous union officials, having been granted immunity, were willing to testify against Lepke, although the prosecution stopped short of trying to prove he was behind the 1934 murder of Teamsters official William Snyder at a table at Garfein's Restaurant—the murder that Meyer Luckman had watched, seeing nothing.

11

Rookie

"Knowing how these boys operate should enable you to feed 'em the ball with proper precision," George Halas told Luckman that fall, inserting him in the lineup at halfback, where he could see for himself how critical it was for a running back to get the ball in the right spot and in the right rhythm.

For the first five games of the season, Luckman blocked and carried the ball into defenses more formidable than any he had ever faced. Sid was right about his limitations as a ball carrier in the pros. For the season, he would gain a paltry 42 yards on 24 carries for a 1.8-yard average, while his fellow rookie Bill Osmanski led the league with 699 yards and an outstanding 5.8-yard average. With Bernie Masterson at quarterback, the Bears were tearing up the league on offense, scoring an average of more than 27 points a game, losing only once, in week two, to their chief foe, the Green Bay Packers.

Then came week six, when the Bears faced the undefeated New York Giants in upper Manhattan. A crowd of almost 59,000 filled the Polo Grounds, many hoping for their first look at hometown hero Sid Luckman's debut in Chicago's navy-and-white uniform with orange trim. It was the second-largest crowd in NFL history, after Red

Grange's New York debut in 1925. There was a reason Dan Topping wanted Luckman for his Brooklyn Dodgers.

For most of the game, the Bears could do nothing, except for another local New York product, Fordham University alumnus Joe Maniaci, who ran for 102 yards. In the third quarter, with New York ahead 16–0 and Masterson having completed just three of 15 passes for 67 yards, Halas decided to give the fans what they wanted and tapped Luckman to relieve Masterson. So much for easing the rookie into the fray. It was a baptism by fire for Sid, to say the least, given the size of the crowd, the presence of so many friends and family members, and the shadow cast by his father, sitting in his cell 30 miles to the north. At least Sid couldn't be held responsible for losing a game they had little chance to win.

"The first time I played quarterback for the Bears was the single most emotional time in my life, as far as playing was concerned," Luckman recalled toward the end of his life. "Boy, was I a wreck. Everyone from my past was there that day to watch me: Coach Lou Little of Columbia, my college teammates, my brothers, even my mother, who only saw me play three or four times. I went in, my knees shaking. What did I do? I spun the wrong way, I delayed signals, I fussed around with the ball for twenty-seven minutes, unable to compose myself. But I guess I had the blessings of someone in the football world."

It would hardly be the last time the football gods smiled down on him. End Dick Plasman, the last man to play in the NFL without a helmet—he would finally put one on in 1941—told Luckman in the huddle he could beat his man on a long pass pattern. "Sure enough," Luckman remembered, "he faked the Giant defender out and was ten yards behind him in the open when I threw him the most beautiful pass—for the Giants, that is. The ball didn't even come out of my hand as a spiral. I don't think I'd *ever* thrown a pass that looked this bad." The end-over-end pass was about 10 yards short of Plasman, who put on the brakes, came back for it, outfought Giants defender Ken Lunday for the ball, then outraced him to the end zone for a 68-yard touchdown. It should have been an ignominious interception, although in the next day's box score of the Giants' 16–13 victory it looked picture-perfect.

"Will someone tell me how the hell we roll up over four hundred yards on offense and still lose to those cocksuckers?" Halas roared in the locker room after the Luckman-led comeback failed to catch the Giants. The Bears had almost four times as many passing yards as the Giants. "We muffed six chances to score on them. They don't pay off on chances in this league, only victories. So who can tell me why we lost out there when we battered the Giants' line to shreds?" Luckman had acquitted himself well, completing four of eight passes for 166 yards, with one interception, and set up a second Bears' touchdown with another couple of long passes. But he wasn't fooled by his performance; he had spun the wrong way, had botched signals, and hadn't felt composed for a minute. He figured he would be skewered along with the rest of the team, but once Halas ran out of steam, he looked at Luckman and said, "You'll learn, Sid. Just have patience."

He needed it the next week in front of 31,000 fans at Wrigley Field. The Bears played poorly against the Detroit Lions, who unveiled a new defensive alignment: just before the snap, the entire Detroit defensive line would slide one way or another to confuse the Bears' blocking assignments. The Bears' scouts had previewed the new wrinkle for the team, and the offense was ready with plays that consisted in quarterbacks Masterson and Luckman faking handoffs to Detroit's strong side before they pivoted and shoveled a lateral to another back going to the weak side. But Luckman's timing was off, his signal calling still left something to be desired, and he even hurt his own fullback, Joe Maniaci, by handing him the football late after a slow pivot, stranding him in the backfield, where he was crushed between two Lions. Luckman saw the real damage he could do by being a beat too slow.

After the 10–0 loss, in which the Bears managed only 138 yards of total offense and completed just two passes, Luckman sat in Clark Shaughnessy's sedan outside Wrigley Field, and he and the coach discussed the game for two hours, by which time all the fans had disappeared and the streets had been swept clean of programs, empty paper cups, and hot-dog wrappers. Luckman was disconsolate. The team's 4–1 start had melted into a 4–3 record with four games to go and Green Bay sailing along with a single loss.

Shaughnessy reassured him. "You'll make the grade. I've watched you in two games now and I know what I'm talking about. You've got to believe you're good, and forget all these mistakes. In another year, there isn't a quarterback in the business who'll be able to touch you."

"But my signal calling. . . . It's been fine in practice lately, but during a game no one seems to understand what I have in mind, except maybe the other team."

Shaughnessy told him he was calling plays too mechanically, without detecting the changing situation on the field. Moreover, he was calling the signals too softly, not much above a whisper. "Make up game conditions in your room at night, just like we did in training camp," Shaughnessy said. "Pretend you've got ten men with you in that room, and go through an entire game. So far you've just been studying the signals. Now start out on your twenty-yard line. Gain five, lose two, pick up three, and then punt. When you get the ball back," he said, "you should know what kind of defensive schemes they like to use, how they played you, and there's no reason to make the same mistakes again."

By the way, Shaughnessy told Luckman, he needed to shovel those laterals to his backs as soon as he touched the ball.

The Packers, with the league's premier receiver, Don Hutson, came to town the next Sunday, and Luckman again alternated with veteran quarterback Bernie Masterson, but he played with increasing confidence. He tried his hand at complex play-action passes, in which he pivoted twice, faking handoffs to not one but two halfbacks before dropping back to pass. The Bears regained the lead two times, but a touchdown pass from Arnie Herber to Don Hutson gave Green Bay a 27–23 lead late in the game, with the sun now well behind Wrigley's stands along the third-base line and the field in shadow. Halas left Luckman in the game. Sid responded with an 18-yard completion and then a 45-yarder to Bob MacLeod—two of only six passes the Bears completed that day—to set up Bill Osmanski's winning touchdown.

Luckman was beginning to get the hang of it. The following week, in a rematch against the Lions in Detroit, he varied his signals, took more chances, and lateraled the ball to Osmanski so fast that the fullback was past the scrimmage line before Sid knew it. Osmanski ran for 111 yards in the game; Luckman and Bob Swisher, who had played for Northwestern University, collaborated on a second-quarter 85-yard touchdown; and the Bears nullified the Lions' sliding defensive line. Chicago won, 23–13, earning a 6–3 record for the year, with two games to go.

After the Detroit game, Halas pulled Luckman aside to ask whether he'd been talking to Shaughnessy lately.

"I've got to," Luckman replied. "He's been a sort of psychiatrist to me."

"He's pretty much done the same for me," Halas told him. "Many times I was ready to give up the damn T, and Clark would show up to assure me that I only needed the right material to make the system go. Too bad Clark can't get material himself at the U of C. They're about ready to discard the game. You know, they're basically phasing out football."

"He must envy you, Coach."

"No, Clark's philosophical about such matters. He's content to remain in the background, as a sort of man of mystery. He gets a quiet satisfaction out of watching his theories work."

During the season, the Bears improved on their rudimentary method for getting suggestions to Halas from assistant coach Luke Johnsos, who was observing the game's big picture from high in the stands. "I remember having Luke Johnsos in the upper deck," Halas told Shorty Ray's grandson in the 1970s. "We didn't have telephones, so we used to write on a piece of paper and wrap a stone in it, throw it down, and send one of the players to pick it up. Oh Christ! Then we got the phones, and there was nothing to it." To Johnsos's "eye in the sky," patterns and problems that were indecipherable at ground level were glaringly obvious. Soon visiting coaches were demanding the Bears provide them with a phone as well, Halas recalled. He obliged, installing a system for the Redskins, but he stationed the band behind the Redskins' bench, and the music drowned out the message. When the Giants came to Wrigley, their phone line mysteriously went dead.

In the season's last two games, nothing would have helped the Bears' opponents, the two weakest teams in the league. In the penultimate game, against the Philadelphia Eagles (0–7–1 for the season), Masterson threw for two scores in a 27–14 victory, even while the Eagles' acclaimed rookie quarterback Davey O'Brien set a new NFL record for completions. The final score didn't reflect the Bears' offensive domination; while holding the Eagles to an excruciating negative 36 yards on the ground, Chicago ran for 285 yards and passed for another 246. Then the Bears crushed their feckless crosstown rivals, the Cardinals (1–9), racking up more than 400 yards of offense and seven touchdowns, two of them thrown by Luckman.

The Bears missed out on the playoffs, finishing 8–3, one game behind the Packers—who shut out the Giants for the championship—but something good was happening. The Bears' offense had gained 1,100 more yards than in 1938—100 more yards a game. Not everyone in the league was paying attention yet, but Clark Shaughnessy's master plan was working. Sid Luckman, who had just turned 23, had thrown five touchdown passes, accounted for a third of the team's passing yards, and even finished third in the league in punting, averaging 42 yards from scrimmage, behind Sammy Baugh, whose 51.4-yard average still stands today as the record.

More significant, Luckman was winning the respect and confidence of his teammates. It hadn't been easy. Early in the season, Jumbo Joe Stydahar, the six-foot-four-inch, 233-pound two-way tackle from a small Pennsylvania coal-mining town, who would become his lifelong friend, had had to come to Luckman's defense when another son of a coal miner, guard and team captain George Musso, taunted Luckman while the team was reviewing some game film in the locker room. Between plays, the cameraman had tilted the lens up beyond Wrigley Field and lingered for a moment on Temple Sholom, several blocks away on North Lake Shore Drive. "Why the hell we panning up to a goddamn Jewish temple?" Musso had complained. It was a less than good-natured gibe at the rookie Luckman, who was then, as he would be now, one of the league's few Jewish players. Luckman picked up a metal folding chair, looking as if he was about to hurl it at Musso's head. Stydahar, doubtful about Luckman's chances of survival in any tussle with the six-foot-two-inch, 262-pound lineman, intervened and quickly brokered a peace.

But by mid-November, even Musso was coming around. During the team's 23–13 win in Detroit, something extraordinary had happened. On the sidelines, Musso had cut a griper short. "Sid's the boss on the field," he told everyone. "Do as he tells you!"

As he relaxed, Luckman's natural charm began to emerge. As tough as Joe Stydahar was—he would end up in the hall of fame—he often vomited before games from nervousness. After a few plays on offense, Luckman would mutter in the huddle, "Joe, has your stomach settled yet?" To which, as if it were part of a deadpan comedy bit, Stydahar would say, "Much better, thank you, Sid."

Luckman was, by the end of his first season, one of the boys. "If there was any remnant now of the Luckman of Columbia," he wrote ten years later, "it was only that big No. 42 on his jersey."

By the following season, the guy who didn't think he would ever make it in the pros would be mentoring rookies barely younger than himself. "He looked out for everyone," George McAfee would recall about his first year as a Chicago Bear in 1940, "helped them fit in, adjust to the pros. He was a terrific fellow as well as a great quarterback."

12

They All Laughed

A week after the end of the 1939 season, Sid was in New York, picking up a trophy awarded to him back in 1938 as the most valuable college player in the city. While he was in Manhattan, he dropped by the *New York Herald Tribune*'s sports department, where he had worked for two months after graduating the previous summer.

"In his first six months out of Columbia a lot had happened in Sid's life," reporter Jesse Abraham wrote in a column about his visit, titled, "Of Cash and Joy in Pro Football." "He had married and he had banked several thousand dollars in the first year of his contract with the Bears as a professional football player. And he had a share in a trucking business with his brother Leo, which will keep him occupied between now and next August, when he reports to the Bears again." Sid told Abraham that the next year, the second of his two-year contract with the Bears, would be his last. "We aim to win the championship next year for sure," he said. "I think we had the best team this year, but we had some tough luck in spots."

Asked about the difference between college and the pros, Luckman told Abraham, "They are bigger and tougher, tackle harder, run harder, block harder. But you play only thirty minutes instead of sixty and that offsets the other, I'd say. Then you have great players all around you, and you get real protection when you pass."

"Luckman declined a bid to play on the All-Star league team under Steve Owen against the Green Bay Packers in Los Angeles next month," Abraham wrote. "He wanted to get home and get into the trucking business."

Aware of his brother's sacrifice, and no doubt fully intending to join him for real in a year, Sid inscribed a copy of the column to him, writing, "Brother Leo, Love you so much, Regards to Leona," and signed it "Brother Sid."

Other Luckmans besides Sid were once again in the news. After having been convicted in December of running a narcotics ring and sentenced to 14 years, Lepke Buchalter faced further charges in New York of running a racket in the flour and baking industry. He was found guilty and given another 30 years, to commence when he had served his federal term. On February 2, 1940, the first of the prosecution witnesses against Lepke Buchalter and his codefendants, Aaron Held of the United Flour Trucking Company, testified that Lepke's gang had extorted money from him for six years, between 1930 and 1936. "Through his testimony," the *Times* reported the next day, "ran a thread of names—that of William Snyder, who was murdered; of Meyer Luckman, a flour trucker, who was involved in the Brooklyn murder of Sam Drukman."

The most damning report showed up six days later on the front page of the *Brooklyn Daily Eagle*, where the Luckman family couldn't miss it. It was a fuller account of Meyer Luckman's criminal activity, headlined "Calls Luckman Lepke Mobster," over the subhead "Drukman Case Figure Was His Contact Man, Says Borough Baker." Abraham Schornstein, of the Klappholz-Schornstein Baking Corporation of Brooklyn, testified that Meyer Luckman had been the go-between for the mob, which demanded the nonunion company pay $2,500 to Lepke's "labor adjusters" or be put out of business. Luckman, who handled the flour trucking for the baking company, accompanied Schornstein when he delivered $1,500 in cash "to a man identified only as a former driver for Luckman." A year later, while Luckman was in jail after his first arrest, Lepke's representatives demanded the other $1,000 in "back dues"; when Luckman was released on bail pending the first grand jury, he advised Schornstein "how much money to take" and where to go. Another witness, the president of a flour trucking company, testified to having paid the Flour Truckmen's Association dues since 1933 and of having met Lepke twice, once at Meyer Luckman's office at Brooklyn's Pier 4 on the East River.

The terrible public stain of Meyer's crime kept spreading, five years after Sam Drukman's murder. No one could blame a scandal-mongering press; the story kept growing on its own merit. The bold-faced linkage of the Luckman name to Lepke's made the rounds of the Jewish community. Leo, the eldest of Meyer's children and 50 percent owner of the reconstituted family trucking business, no doubt recoiled at the continuing visitation of his father's past. For two years after he and Uncle Ike's two sons had taken over the business in 1936, Leo's wife, Leona, a college graduate like Leo, had bodyguards to protect her from the mobsters who were trying to pry the business away from this younger, criminally uninfected generation of ownership.

Sid had to have been devastated. From the family's perspective, he was simply indulging a whim called professional football while family and financial security waited for him in New York. But whatever his loyalty to his family and its fortunes, it must not have been easy for Sid, fresh from his promising rookie season in Chicago and the object of new attention, to reenter the orbit of the five-year-old Drukman murder and the intricacies of the various Luckman relatives' involvement in it.

A month later, on March 6, 1940, after being a fugitive from justice for nearly four years, Ike Luckman, Meyer's brother and former partner in the Luckman Brothers Trucking Company, surrendered to his lawyer in Brooklyn to face the music in the Drukman case. His name, the *Times* wrote, had "virtually studded the court record in the first Drukman conspiracy trial in the Summer of 1936." By the time Ike was charged that year with collecting the slush fund to bribe officials and jury members not to return an indictment against his brother Meyer, he had already disappeared. Also vanishing then was Ike's son, also named Sidney Luckman, who had become Leo's partner in the trucking company. When this other Sidney Luckman was found by investigators living less than a mile from his mother, who had repeatedly told authorities her son had left the city, he "protested sullenly that he had not known the investigators were looking for him." He was considered a key material witness, one who transacted "much of his father's business and also knows where he is hiding"; accordingly, the "swarthy thick-set young man," as the *Times* described him, was held on $50,000 bail as a material witness. However, he denied he knew his father's whereabouts and was released. Now, four years later, Ike had suddenly surfaced, although no one was saying where he had been keeping himself. He had lasted two years longer in hiding than Lepke Buchalter. Ike would plead guilty to conspiracy to fix the Drukman case and receive a slap on the wrist—a $500 fine and a suspended one-year sentence.

However, the seemingly endless aftermath of the Drukman case proper was overshadowed by news of the larger events it had helped set in motion: the further dismantling of Lepke's empire—the finely tuned machine in which Meyer Luckman had been a reliable cog. Soon after taking over the infamously corrupt office of Brooklyn district attorney in 1939, William D. O'Dwyer pledged to drive the mob out of the borough. Murder, Inc., was desperate to eliminate anyone who might testify against it, but O'Dwyer preempted Murder, Inc.'s plans to take out at least two of its own, Anthony "the Duke" Maffetore and Abe "Pretty" Levine. To get them off the street and preserve them for future testimony, O'Dwyer had them arrested in early 1940 for a 1934 murder, along with Martin "Buggsy" Goldstein and a hired killer who would turn out to be the biggest game of all, Abe "Kid Twist" Reles. They would all sing sooner or later, and their testimony would lead to the arrests of mob executioners Harry "Happy" Maione, Harry "Pittsburgh Phil" Strauss, and Frank "the Dasher" Abbandando. Reles and Maione were not mere "schlammers" but high-ranking men in Murder, Inc., and therefore priceless to the authorities—Reles in particular, with his photographic memory, gift of gab (he wore out stenographers during 12 days of talking to the authorities), and desire to cop a plea. He had been to Sing Sing in the mid-1930s on an assault conviction, and the time away had eroded his reputation. When he got out, he said, "I was a bum." Like Joseph Valachi's testimony before the U. S. Senate several years later, Reles's epic, copious 12-day-long confession—"He had the most amazing memory I have ever encountered," Brooklyn assistant DA Burton Turkus said—exposed organized crime's national scope. It led another notorious hit man, a glib Jewish boy gone wrong named Albert "Tick-Tock" Tannenbaum, to raise his hand in Clinton state prison in Dannemora, New York, where he had been sent for seven years of hard labor, and volunteer to talk. Like Reles, Tick-Tock delivered enough information to earn his release and immunity.

With his expanding reputation, Sid could not keep his name out of the papers, but all his mentions were honorable. In New York, he was bona fide column fodder. Shortly after the 1939 NFL season ended, he was feted by the men's club of the East Midwood Jewish Center, in Brooklyn, and later in the year he emceed the center's annual box-ing and wrestling sports show. The *Brooklyn Daily Eagle* ran a publicity photo of him demonstrating how to grip a football for eight-foot-tall Dave Ballard, billed as the world's largest man, who was appearing as Gulliver at the Abraham and Straus department store. There was an item about Sid losing a bowling match to his father-in-law by one point, and the paper took note when he went to Florida on vacation. He spoke at an "interfaith goodwill rally" at Erasmus High, where he also addressed the student body at the football team's annual dinner. "You can't eat headlines," Sid, ever suspicious of his own success, cautioned his audience. "Once you step from the striped arena for the last time you are forgotten in the game out in the business world." Dur-ing the summer of 1940, as the combined forces of Mayor Fiorello La Guardia, Manhattan DA Dewey, and Brooklyn DA O'Dwyer and his attack dog Turkus toppled one gangster after another, Sid could be found at Brooklyn's Manhattan Beach, where he worked under famed Long Island University basketball coach Clair Bee, the beach's director of recreation.

When he reported to Chicago Bears' training camp in Wisconsin later that summer, he was a different man from the Sid Luckman of a year before. And the team he reported to wasn't the same, either. The disappointing loss to Baugh's Redskins in 1937 and the mediocre 6–5 record in 1938 were buried beneath the 1939 campaign, when the team took Luckman's training wheels off and finished a single game behind the Packers. There was a new emphasis on speed, conditioning, and agility, and there was a new Bear tamer to enforce it. Halas had hired Heartley "Hunk" Anderson, a Knute Rockne mentee and Notre Dame alum who had played offensive line for Halas in the early days, when his five-foot-11, 190-pound frame was not considered Lilliputian. As the new line coach, he instituted daily weigh-ins and sprints for the overweight. Fundamentals were in; complacency was out. Nothing was taken for granted. Anderson barked at the high-priced talent as though they were a group of unschooled rookies. "Where did you learn your football, son?" he would bellow. "If you ever worked under Rockne, he'd have you sent home the first day!" Luckman, not yet 24, tried to keep his mouth shut. Anderson actually showed up at practice with a small paddle, which he said he had picked up downtown at a very good price.

"He may look as if he spanks dogs and old women," Halas told Luckman, "but I was told of a day when Hunk broke out in honest-to-goodness tears during a ball game at South Bend. A halfback had to be carried off the field and Ol' Hunk cried because he had whipped the boy into such fine form, only to have him lost for the season."

Fullback Joe Maniaci, the team's class clown, a New Yorker who had averaged an almost unheard-of 7.1 yards a carry in 1939, tested Anderson, who responded by whacking him on the ass. Maniaci protested that the players were no longer in high school, even though he, more than any other member of the team, often acted like a high schooler. For instance, he and his brother had an Italian restaurant in New York, and just minutes before an exhibition game at the Polo Grounds, Halas found him in the stands, handing out leaflets proclaiming, "If you enjoy this game, you'll also enjoy feasting at Maniaci's Grill in Manhattan. Delicious spaghetti dished out by the best fullback in the National League."

But Hunk Anderson was all business, and it wasn't the restaurant business. Halas had applied a few more finishing touches to a roster that already included veterans such as Maniaci, Ray Nolting, Dick Plasman, Bill Osmanski, Joe Stydahar, and Danny Fortmann. Luckman's old Columbia target John Siegal had just arrived as a rookie and would have a negligible five-year career, but Halas had drafted three other rookies who would all play significant roles from the start and spend their entire playing careers with the Bears: halfback George

McAfee from Duke University; center Clyde "Bulldog" Turner from a little Baptist school, Hardin-Simmons University, in Abilene, Texas; and a rangy receiver from Louisiana State University, Ken Kavanaugh.

Kavanaugh would go on to catch 162 of Luckman's passes in his eight-year career, almost a third of them for touchdowns. Of Luckman's 137 career touchdown passes, Kavanaugh would be responsible for 50. "One-Play" McAfee was a slightly built game-breaker; while at Duke he had been the fastest collegiate sprinter in the nation, and he could do just about everything on a football field—pass, receive, punt, play pass defense, and return kicks—but nothing quite as well as elude tacklers. He was also fashion-forward, pioneering the use of low-cut football cleats, saying, in describing the experience of wearing them, "It was almost as though I didn't have any shoes at all." When Halas first saw the whippet-thin McAfee in training camp, he worried the rookie wouldn't survive, but he stopped fretting after he watched McAfee give defenders a hip or a leg and then disappear downfield. Taking three years off to fight the Germans, McAfee would last 11 seasons and go to the hall of fame. Halas wouldn't have McAfee's equal in the backfield until Gale Sayers arrived in 1965.

By all rights, Bulldog Turner should have ended up in Detroit, which had the seventh pick in the first round of the 1940 draft, but for some reason the Lions' coach, Elmer "Gloomy Gus" Henderson, defied his owner's wishes and drafted University of Southern California tailback Doyle Nave. Halas immediately shouted, "Clyde Turner, Hardin-Simmons," and the Bears ended up with a fierce future hall of famer who would snap the ball on offense and sparkle on defense for the Bears for the next 13 seasons. George Connor, the Bears' hall of fame lineman who is credited with being the game's first real linebacker, paid Turner the same sort of compliment Halas would frequently pay Luckman: "Bulldog Turner was the best football player and smartest player I ever knew in my whole life. He knew everybody's position on every play." Luckman would say Turner was "a rare combination of muscles and brains." Congeniality, however, wasn't part of that mix. To Luckman, Turner was one of team's "hillbillies"; we can only guess what kind of big-city slicker Luckman seemed to him. At first, Turner was wary of Luckman, but he soon warmed up, both to his quarterback and to the T, which he had never encountered before.

Drafting Bulldog Turner was a prime example of Halas's shrewd scouting skills. There was something a bit contrarian in taking a center from little Hardin-Simmons University, just as there had been in drafting George Musso from Millikin University in 1933, or preferring Luckman, from a losing football program at Columbia, to Davey O'Brien from a winning major college power like Texas Christian. "By his own peculiar—but effective—scouting methods," Luckman wrote 10 years later, "George Halas had plucked from the collegiate ranks a bunch of competent unknowns, chosen for talent alone—the Bears' kind of talent. They come from St. Anselm's, and West Virginia, and Western Michigan, and Millikin, and Hardin-Simmons, and other unballyhooed campuses. College reputations weren't discussed much. Nobody cared how or why a guy came up. He was here—a pro, making his living—and that's what counted."

One important piece that wasn't there for the 1940 season was Clark Shaughnessy. With no program to speak of anymore at the University of Chicago—the Maroons had managed to win only a third of their games over three years—and having finished laying the groundwork for the T with the Bears, Shaughnessy took a job as head coach at Stanford University. Stanford president Ray Lyman Wilbur had been impressed by a Bears game he had seen during the 1939 season, and also by Knute Rockne's view that Shaughnessy "was one of the two best coaches in America." Wilbur signed Shaughnessy for five years, at an annual salary of $9,000, with a professorship thrown in. It was not a popular hire, however, since Shaughnessy's remodeled

T formation had not yet begun to pay dividends for the Bears, and an observer had to understand the man and his ideas to look past his record at the University of Chicago.

"We thought he was crazy," one of Shaughnessy's Stanford lineman wrote 60 years later, remembering the team's first look at the cockamamie scheme. Former Stanford coach Pop Warner, the creator of the single- and double-wing formations and then almost 70 years old, minced no words: "If Stanford ever wins a single game with that crazy formation, you can throw all the football I ever knew into the Pacific Ocean." The *San Francisco Examiner* chimed in wittily, "We have heard it said that Shaughnessy has developed the knack of losing to the point where, with him, it is an exact science." For Shaughnessy, of course, losing wasn't an exact science; designing football plays was. He was the first to study the game microscopically. When he watched game film of Stanford's 1939 season, he picked out a single man in every game and watched him straight through. "You can figure how many times I had to go over each picture," he said.

For the 1937 Fred Astaire and Ginger Rogers movie *Shall We Dance*, George Gershwin and Ira Gershwin had confected the song "They All Laughed," containing a litany of disrespected scientific innovations, including the phonograph, radio, steamboat, airplane, and cotton gin, and the discovery that the entire world happened to be round. The list also included "Ford and his Lizzie," a nickname for the Model T, produced from 1908 to 1927. Now Shaughnessy's model of the T formation was running into the same kind of ridicule on the part of many otherwise informed, intelligent people.

In four short months, however, no one would be laughing.

13

Whiners, Crybabies, and Quitters

It would be a mistake to assume that, because 1940 ended for the Chicago Bears with the most lopsided victory ever in professional football, the team dominated the league for the entire season. The Bears were very good, but hardly great. They ranked only fifth among the 10 teams in passing yardage. For the nine years from 1940 to 1948, Sid Luckman's Bears would lead the league or rank second in passing yards every year but one, and it was this one. Three teams were better defensively.

In 1940, Luckman started seven of the 11 regular-season games, appeared in all of them, and did the bulk of the team's passing. But passing was still a sideshow—a strategy for keeping the defense honest. Luckman completed only 45 percent of his passes—48 of 105—for less than 4.5 completions a game. In contrast, Sammy Baugh completed 10 a game and an impressive 63 percent of his passes. Luckman threw only four touchdown passes—one fewer than he had thrown in a part-time role in 1939—and nine interceptions. Overall, the team threw only 10 touchdown passes, six fewer than the year before. The Redskins passed for almost 500 more passing yards than the Bears.

The genius of the T formation consisted in how it opened up the rushing game. No team ran for more yardage than the Bears in 1940—165 yards a game, compared with Washington's 127. The Bears ground it out, to be sure, gaining a respectable though hardly impressive 3.7 yards a carry, but that was better than any other team's. They scored 60 fewer points than they had in 1939 and were a team in transition with an inexperienced quarterback but were proficient enough to win eight of their 11 games.

No one could have predicted at any point during the regular season what was going to happen in the nation's capital on December 8, even if, on opening day at Green Bay, it looked as if the Bears had been reborn as a juggernaut. "One-Play" McAfee and veteran Ray Nolting both ran kickoffs back for touchdowns. McAfee ran for another and threw a touchdown pass on a halfback option to fellow rookie Ken Kavanaugh for another in the Bears' 41–10 cakewalk. Yet the Packers held a decided statistical edge on offense. The following week, the Bears held their own offensively against the Cardinals at Comiskey Park, but lost 21–7 to a team that had gone 1–10 the year before. Then the Bears won their next five games, including a 37–21 victory over the New York Giants at the Polo Grounds, in which Luckman tossed his first touchdown passes of the season to little halfback Ray "Scooter" McLean.

Meanwhile, 2,000 miles away, Clark Shaughnessy was having better luck with his T formation at Stanford. He unveiled it on September 28, at Kezar Stadium in San Francisco, when his Stanford Indians faced a heavily favored University of San Francisco team and beat them 27–0. Shaughnessy's left-handed quarterback, Frankie Albert, who would play seven years for the San Francisco 49ers after the war and lead the league twice in touchdown passes, exclaimed, "This stuff really works!"

"Without Luckman, I still think I have the best team in the league," Halas told reporters, "but with Sid in there I don't worry about winning, even if the breaks go against my team. Besides being a mechanically good football player, he is a smart quarterback and has the knack of holding the team together." Leadership and brains meant more than ever with new rules allowing, for the first time, limited substitution of players. This removed the pressure of having to survive 60 minutes playing both offense and defense, but it meant that players came and went as never before, which constantly altered the team chemistry. "What puzzled you most," Luckman would later write, "was the way [Halas had] been sending certain men in as runners, others as defenders, whenever conditions allowed. We had become a team of specialists." Pro football was no longer an endurance event for 11 men who played both offense and defense. Like Lepke's mob in that other highly competitive and much higher-stakes realm, with its "finger men," "wheel men," "hit men," and "evaporators," football could now exploit individual expertise.

On November 3, in a home game against Green Bay in which the Bears did all their damage on the ground, throwing only 10 times, the team made a 14–7 half-time lead hold up, bringing their record to 6–1. But they were not quite as good as their record suggested, and the next two weeks proved it, as they lost 17–14 in Detroit and 7–3 in Washington, DC.

The Washington game would have lasting implications for both teams and the league as a whole. In a flawed and chippy contest, the Bears gained almost twice as many yards as the Redskins, but they were penalized 80 yards and completed only nine of 29 passes. The *New York Times'* Arthur Daley, who had been following Luckman since college, wrote that the blocking and tackling "were far beneath the usual Chicago standards." So was the pass catching: Ed Manske dropped an almost certain touchdown pass from Luckman in the fourth quarter. More than anything else, the game was a punting contest between the Redskins' Sammy Baugh and the Bears' McAfee, who shared punting duties that season with Luckman.

With 20 seconds left in the game and the Redskins ahead 7–3, the Bears' third-string quarterback, Bob Snyder, rifled a pass from midfield to McAfee, who was caught from behind by Dick Todd at the one-yard line, but the Bears were out of time-outs. When McAfee feigned an injury to stop the clock, the officials weren't impressed and penalized Chicago five yards, back to the Washington six, with 10 seconds left on the clock. Luckman came in and threw an incomplete pass. With time for one last play, Luckman faked to McAfee and Nolting and fired a pass to Bill Osmanski in the end zone.

"Sid's pass was perfect," Osmanski would recall. "Someone grabbed me from behind and pulled my arms tight against my sides. The ball hit my chest and flopped to the ground. The gun went off. I shouted a protest to the referee. Mr. Halas came running."

"I was furious!" Halas remembered. "I was ready to tear the referee limb from limb. I knew his ruling of no interference must stand, but I wanted to make my feelings known. He popped into the dugout. All I could do was shout abuse after him. I probably used all of the words I had learned on the Chicago streets and in ball parks and training camps and maybe even made up a few new ones."

While Halas and the Bears screamed foul, the players had only themselves to blame for squandering their offensive superiority in the loss. Washington had the victory and an insurmountable two-game lead in their division. With questionable judgment, Louis Effrat of the *Times* called the game "a titanic struggle" that would go down as "one of the most thrilling ever witnessed" in Washington, while the local press slammed the Bears as "rulebook weepers" and worse. Redskins owner George Preston Marshall, resorting to schoolyard epithets he would come to regret, told reporters that Chicago's players were whiners, crybabies, and quitters. The national sports press loved it. Halas could do nothing but post clippings of the slurs in the Wrigley Field locker room as the team prepared for its last two games, both at home.

At this point in the season, the Bears were as likely to sabotage themselves as to dominate opponents. "All season," Luckman remembered, "we'd been telling one another that this Sunday or that we would have the danged thing really mastered. We'd been sliding back and forth between overconfidence and anxiety."

After their two straight losses, the team recovered and dispatched two weak opponents, the Cleveland Rams and the Chicago Cardinals, to seal up first place in their division and a date with the Redskins for the championship in the nation's capital. However, they struggled with overconfidence in their last game, almost frittering away a 31–0 lead over the Cardinals.

Out west, Shaughnessy's Stanford Indians, playing solid defense and applying the T formation, finished the season undefeated, 9–0. A team that had gone 1–7–1 the year before and hadn't been a contender since 1935 had now beaten everyone in its way and was chosen to face the University of Nebraska's Cornhuskers in the Rose Bowl on January 1, 1941. Despite the Shaughnessy-engineered turnaround, the T-formation haters wouldn't go away. Nebraska's coach, Lawrence "Biff" Jones, a staunch advocate of the single wing and the Notre Dame Box, told the press he couldn't wait to see the Redskins shut down the Bears' T in the championship game. The implication was that his own club would do the same to Stanford three weeks later in Pasadena.

With a little time on his hands before preparing for the Rose Bowl, Shaughnessy called Halas to see whether he could use some help protecting their shared investment. Unlike Stanford, the Bears had been a model of inconsistency and had just one week to prepare for their return engagement with Washington. Before boarding the *California Zephyr* in early December, Shaughnessy lied to reporters, saying that he was going to Chicago to see friends and then up to Minnesota to see his family. En route, he studied the latest triumph of his favorite military thinker, General Heinz Guderian, an architect of the Nazis' invasion of France the previous May. As the British Expeditionary Force and France's best divisions rolled to the northeast toward Belgium—exactly where Hitler hoped they would be lured—1,222 tanks made their way through the Ardennes forest to puncture the Allies at their weakest point. It had been the military equivalent of the fullback counterplay with man-in-motion.

Shaughnessy arrived several days before the game and went right to work with Halas at the Bears' downtown offices, watching film of the team's earlier 7–3 loss to Washington long into the night, studying the adjustments the Redskins had made late in that game to stop the Bears' quick openers. The men called in Luckman, and they all decided what plays to use this time to penetrate Washington's defense.

The anticipation building around the NFL championship game was sharp-edged, perhaps exacerbated by the climate of conflict created by a real war taking place in Europe, and the increasing tensions at home between isolationists and interventionists. "The buildup was like preparation for a war," Luckman would recall. "We were going to fight and we were going to win. You could feel the emotion, the stress and strain." One creative sportswriter portrayed the game as a battle between Baugh's "bombers"—a reference to Washington's superior aerial attack—and the Bears' "tanks." George Marshall fired a telegram at his friend George Halas: "Congratulations. I hope I will have the pleasure of beating your ears off next Sunday and every year to come. Justice is triumphant. We should play for the championship every year. Game will be sold out by Tuesday night."

Frigid weather in Chicago forced the Bears to practice on the hardwood floor of an armory before moving to the dirt floor of the University of Chicago field house. On the Friday before the game, Halas named his starting backfield: Luckman would get the nod, with rookie McAfee, second-year man Osmanski, and veteran Ray Nolting behind him. In Washington, Redskins coach Ray Flaherty was hoping for good passing weather, not the rain or mud that would help the Bears' punishing ground attack.

Halas took 33 players to Washington, and for once they were all glued to their playbooks on the overnight train instead of their gin rummy hands. The approaching game marked a turning point in the league's coming-of-age. The Mutual Broadcasting System bought the radio rights for the 1940 championship game for $2,500, making it the first NFL game to reach a coast-to-coast audience. Thirty-two-year-old Walter Lanier "Red" Barber, the clipped, lyrical Southerner who had recently become the Brooklyn Dodgers' play-by-play radio announcer and had also broadcast the first televised major-league baseball game, would be at the microphone. Well over 100 sportswriters would crowd the press box. Fifteen hundred Bears fans boarded special trains to travel to the nation's capital. Ticket scalpers were having a heyday.

George Marshall had been right about selling out—36,034 seats were snapped up to the tune of $102,280—and the press had stoked the event into a confrontation of epic proportions. On Saturday,

Baugh and Luckman turned up the heat with a joint radio interview. The two passers were treated as mortal rivals, and in fact there was little common ground between the Texas rancher and the Brooklyn Jew beyond their athletic gifts and genial natures. However, the two men were already friends, having first met in 1937 when Baugh, in his rookie year for the Redskins, visited a football practice at Columbia, where Luckman was in his junior year. Coach Lou Little promptly phoned Benny Friedman, urging him to drive over, intrigued by the prospect of seeing a retired NFL great, a current one, and maybe a future one all together. When Baugh demonstrated his passing form to everyone, Luckman had been stunned to see him use only his thumb on the laces, not his fingers.

"Ah just feel better holdin' it this-a-way," Baugh had explained. "Coaches have tried to change me, but they decided that so long as a fellow kin toss 'em seventy yards, well, who cares how he does it?" At the time, Baugh warned Luckman against the pro game—too big a gamble with too little payoff—but fate, talent, and Halas's powers of persuasion had thrown them together, and in 1940 the two men played up their rivalry for all it was worth.

Baugh, known for not getting his own uniform dirty, once teased Luckman about playing the T formation. "No quarterback ever had less labor than you," he chided him, "squattin' there behind center all day. Why, Sid, if Ah had nothin' more to do than that, Ah swear Ah'd last in this league twenty years."

Luckman exacted a kind of revenge when he saw Baugh signing autographs for a bunch of kids before a Bears–Redskins regular-season game. Luckman ambled over with a football and got in line.

"Well," Baugh said, "Ah see y'all have finally recognized a real passin' man."

Luckman laughed. "It's just that I bet George Wilson five bucks that I could collect your signature on this football." Wilson apparently wasn't aware that Baugh had, in Luckman's words, "a natural weakness for scribbling his name."

"Anything to help a friend fatten his bank account," Baugh said, signing the ball. However, Luckman had the last laugh, using the ball later that day to beat the Redskins.

Both men appreciated professional football as a breeding ground for better understanding among young men of different regions, who rarely mixed in a country where the majority of people never ventured far from home. "Ah like to think," Baugh once said, "that this business has done a whole lot to bring Southerners and Northerners together—to give a better understanding, a more genuine appraisal of one another's little habits and peculiarities." Down the road, Luckman thought he could have been referring to their own relationship off the field and "the many times we've talked over old clashes in a genial spirit, giving the lie to people's notions about sectional animosities."

The animosities were not racial. Few photos bring that home as clearly as a publicity photo taken during a Bears' practice at Griffith Stadium the day before the game. Chicago's starting offensive lineup is poised in position, all players in pads and uniforms but without helmets, wearing their game faces. They are the picture of vengeful determination, but also a snapshot of America's great racial divide. Football had begun as a testing ground for the white males of the elite Ivy League colleges. As late as the 1920s, when Amos Alonzo Stagg was asked by an African American newspaper for his views on black men playing football, he replied—incredibly, given what an enslaved race had endured—that they lacked the courage and bravery. The handful of African American players who had played in the early NFL, such as hall of fame halfback Fritz Pollard, were all gone by 1934. The racism of the influential Redskins' owner George Preston Marshall, the acquiescence of Halas and other owners, and the scarcity of jobs during the Depression all contributed to the league's unwritten segregation.*

The photo of the Bears' starting offense, however, is a picture of lily-white diversity, beginning with the team's Jewish quarterback. Luckman is flanked by fullback Ray Nolting, from the University of Cincinnati; fullback (and future dentist) Bill Osmanski of Holy Cross; and halfback George McAfee from Duke, who would return after his playing days to North Carolina to run a Shell Oil distributorship. The offensive line included the indestructible center Bulldog Turner, of Plains, Texas; guards George Musso, a coal miner's son from downstate Illinois, and Colgate's Danny Fortmann, valedictorian of his high school class and future team doctor for the Los Angeles Rams; left tackle Joe Stydahar, another coal miner's son, from West Virginia, who later coached the Rams; rookie right tackle Lee Artoe of Tacoma, Washington, an alum of the University of California; and, finally, ends Bob Nowaskey, a rookie out of George Washington University, and George Wilson of Northwestern, who became the head coach of the Detroit Lions and the Miami Dolphins, an expansion team formed in 1965.

The weather at game time was clear, sunny, and a balmy 49 degrees. Baugh would have no trouble gripping the ball to throw it to receivers who would have no trouble running their patterns and holding on to the ball. Among the 36,000 in Griffith Stadium was Speaker of the United States House of Representatives Sam Rayburn, along with

---

*That segregation ended only when the Cleveland Rams moved to Los Angeles to play in the publicly funded Coliseum. The venue's commission refused to let the Rams play there without adding a black player to their roster. They signed two in 1946, Kenny Washington and Woody Strode. The Detroit Lions and the New York Giants were the only other teams that signed African Americans before 1950. By 1952, every NFL team had signed a black player except for Marshall's Redskins, which held out until 1962.

TELLS HIM HOW—Coach Paul } to Sid Luckman, capable quarter-
Sullivan points out a thing or two } back. Luckman is a high scorer.

The teenage Sid Luckman with Erasmus Hall High School coach
Paul Sullivan in 1933. *Courtesy of the* Brooklyn Daily Eagle

Luckman Scoring for Erasmus Hall

Sid Luckman, star back of Erasmus Hall, crossing Alexander Hamilton's last stripe for his team's third touchdown.

Luckman scores again for Erasmus Hall, this time against Alexander Hamilton
Technical and Vocational High School. *Courtesy of the* Brooklyn Daily Eagle

The Luckman home on Cortelyou Road in Flatbush, Brooklyn, where Sid learned to throw a football in the streets.

Courtesy of Erik Lieber

Meyer Luckman in jail after being arrested for murder a second time in November 1935.

Courtesy of Luckman family

Fred Hull (in light-colored hat) and Meyer Luckman's nephew Harry Luckman (center), accomplices in the murder of Meyer's brother-in-law Sam Drukman, turn themselves in to Brooklyn detectives in December 1935. *Courtesy of Luckman family*

3 SEEK SPEEDY APPEAL IN DRUKMAN CONVICTION; GEOGHAN OUSTER ASKED

3 Drukman Defendants Leaving Court

Defense Assails Verdict—Dismissal of Prosecutor Sought by City Affairs Committee

McGoldrick Praises Todd for Conviction

Drukman Verdict Pleasing to Mayor

Mayor LaGuardia expressed today his gratification at the conviction of the three defendants in the Drukman murder case, congratulating Police Commissioner Lewis J. Valentine and Deputy Commissioner of Accounts Irving Ben Cooper for their work in the investigation and declared that he himself had prevented the case from being tried on the stump in last Fall's election.

Commissioner Valentine hailed the verdict as a vindication of justice, said the Mayor had counselled and assisted him at every step and recalled that he (the commissioner) raised the cry of suspicion to District Attorney William F. X. Geoghan when the April grand jury failed to indict the defendants last year.

The Mayor's statement is published elsewhere in The

The alleged slayers of Samuel Drukman, stunned by their conviction, are shown as they are led from the courtroom early today. Left to right, Harry Luckman, Fred Hull (he is behind the guard and hidden except for his hat) and Meyer Luckman. They got 20 years to life.

The February 20, 1936, *Brooklyn Daily Eagle* headline announcing the men's 1936 convictions and 20-years-to-life sentences.

Courtesy of the Brooklyn Daily Eagle

Publicity photo of Sid at Columbia University, where he first came to the attention of Chicago Bears owner and coach George Halas.

University Archives, Rare Book & Manuscript Library, Columbia University Libraries

After Halas convinced Luckman to come to Chicago, it was the beginning of a beautiful relationship. *AP Images*

Three of America's premier passers posed in a New York City hotel room in 1937: NFL rookie sensation Sammy Baugh, Sid's childhood hero and former New York Giant quarterback Benny Friedman, and Sid himself, then a junior at Columbia.

AP Images

Clark Shaughnessy, the NFL's great intellectual, whose most significant innovation, the modern T formation, was inspired by his love of German military strategy.

The Terrapin *(University of Maryland Yearbook), via Wikimedia Commons*

The Bears' starting lineup on the eve of their historic 73-0 defeat of the Redskins. First row, L to R: George Wilson, Lee Artoe, George Musso, Bulldog Turner, Dan Fortmann, Joe Stydahar, Bob Nowaskey. Second row: George McAfee, Bill Osmanski, Sid Luckman, Ray Nolting. *AP Images*

During the game, Sid Luckman, who like everyone in that era played both offense and defense, tackled Washington's Jimmy Johnston. But it was for his offensive leadership that day that the *New York Times* called him "an inspired genius."

AP Images

On November 14, 1943, playing before his hometown crowd and family members on "Sid Luckman Day," Sid prepares to throw one of his record seven touchdown passes against the New York Giants at the Polo Grounds. *Getty Images*

Later in that World War II-depleted season, in what Luckman considered the best game of his career, he runs for 15 yards in the Bears' 41-21 victory over the Redskins in the 1943 NFL championship game at Wrigley Field. He also threw five touchdown passes. *Getty Images*

Luckman's application to the U. S. Coast Guard in September 1944. He would make three long foreign voyages as a Merchant Marine in the first half of 1945.

Courtesy of the U.S. Coast Guard

Luckman returned in his Coast Guard uniform to watch his alma mater, the Columbia Lions, in action.

University Archives, Rare Book & Manuscript Library, Columbia University Libraries

After two years in hiding, in 1939 head mobster Louis Lepke turned himself in to J. Edgar Hoover—handcuffed to the FBI director—and within months was convicted of operating a multi-million dollar narcotics ring.

Photo by Al Aumuller. New York World-Telegram *and the* Sun *Newspaper Photograph Collection (Library of Congress); Library of Congress Prints and Photographs Division, Washington, D.C. 20540 USA*

Lepke, however, was more notorious for running Murder, Inc., his campaign to eliminate enemies and squealers as the heat on organized crime intensified in the mid-1930s.

Photo by Al Aumuller. New York World-Telegram *and the* Sun *Newspaper Photograph Collection (Library of Congress); Library of Congress Prints and Photographs Division, Washington, D.C. 20540 USA*

Lepke's downfall was the 1936 murder of ex-trucker Joe Rosen at his Brooklyn candy store. In 1941, Lepke was convicted of ordering the hit and eventually executed at Sing Sing in 1944, the only mob boss in history to meet that fate.

Burton Turkus Papers, Special Collections Lloyd Sealy Library, John Jay College of Criminal Justice/CUNY.

Calls Luckman Lepke Mobster

Drukman Case Figure Was His Contact Man, Says Borough Baker

Meyer Luckman, one of the key figures in the Sam Druckman murder case, was consulted repeatedly as a contact man in 1934 and 1935 when the Louis (Lepke) Buchalter mob extorted $2,500 from Abraham Schornstein, president of the Klappholz-Schornstein Baking Corporation of Brooklyn. Schornstein swore today on the witness stand in General Sessions Court, Manhattan.

In 1940, when Meyer Luckman had been in Sing Sing almost four years, this *Brooklyn Daily Eagle* headline confirmed that he had been more than a bit player in the Brooklyn rackets.

Courtesy of the Brooklyn Daily Eagle

To: Sid Luckman.
My QB for all seasons!
George Halas
7-26-82.

Halas was Luckman's surrogate father, Sid his surrogate son.

Courtesy of Luckman family

CHICAGO BEARS FOOTBALL CLUB
55 EAST JACKSON BOULEVARD
CHICAGO, ILLINOIS 60604

GEORGE S. HALAS
PRESIDENT AND
CHIEF EXECUTIVE OFFICER
312/663-5100

May 24, 1983

My dear Sid,

"I love you with all my heart."

When I said this to you last night as I kissed you, I
realized 44 wonderful years of knowing you were summed
up by seven words.

My boy, my pride in you has no bounds. You were the
consumate player. Remember our word, "Now"? Every-
time I said it to you, you brought me another
Championship.

You added a luster to my life that can never tarnish.
My devoted friend you have a spot in my heart no one
else can ever claim.

God bless you and keep you, my son. "I love you with
all my heart."

Sincerely yours,

George

Geo. S. Halas

Mr. Sid Luckman
1040 Lake Shore Drive
Chicago, Illinois 60611

In 1983, Halas wrote Sid a letter that Luckman kept in his wallet for the rest of his life.
Courtesy of Luckman family

A star since his high school days, Sid hobnobbed with American royalty—here with Frank Sinatra, flanked by Jilly Rizzo on the left and Luckman buddy Jack McHugh— but he never lost his touch with people from all walks of life.

Courtesy of Luckman family

Luckman with his old Columbia coach and mentor Lou Little, whom Sid chose to introduce him at his Pro Football Hall of Fame induction ceremony in 1965.

University Archives, Rare Book & Manuscript Library, Columbia University Libraries

Estelle and Sid Luckman. In 1939, when she told George Halas that Sid and she were not moving to Chicago for four thousand dollars, Halas immediately offered a contract for five.

Courtesy of Luckman family

Quarterback Cruise: Earl Morall, Sid Luckman, Sid's son-in-law Dick Weiss, Otto Graham, and Y. A. Tittle on a cruise ship in the 1980s. *Courtesy of Luckman family*

Luckman surveyed his old stomping grounds, Wrigley Field, on a visit in the 1980s.
Courtesy of Luckman family

numerous other dignitaries. Biff Jones, the Nebraska head coach, had flown in to reassure himself that the Redskins' defense would prove that the T formation was no more than a passing fancy.

The Bears were slightly favored to win on the theory that Washington could score in bunches with one weapon named Baugh, but the Bears had many weapons, not the least of them a desire for revenge. Luckman reported to Halas that during his appearance with Baugh on a radio show Saturday night, the quarterback had seemed overconfident. More to the point, Halas had plastered the team's Griffith Stadium locker room with the week-old clippings calling them crybabies.

"That's what the people in Washington are saying about you gentlemen," Halas told his men just before game time. "I know you are the greatest football team ever. Now go out and show the world." Luckman's recollection of Halas's pep talk is more colorful: "You have one great advantage over the Redskins today. An important score to even up. Those boys have been strutting about the past two weeks like half-lit roosters, raving about a flimsy four-point edge. I'm thinking in bigger terms than that—much bigger. I want to show them how a real big-league outfit operates. If I had taken the kind of razzing that you boys did, why, I'd want to whale the daylights out of anyone attached in any way to Washington."

As the team stormed out of the locker room, a stampede of cleats clattering over the cement, Halas held Luckman back for a moment and handed him an index card on which he had written the signals for three plays—plays they had worked out with Shaughnessy in Chicago a few days before.

"Sid," he said, "I want you to call these first, in this order. The first one will show you whether the Redskins are staying with the defense they used in the last game against us. If they are, you should have some success with the next two."

14

Barrage

The Bears needed only the first two plays to make a statement. After McAfee took the kickoff to the 26-yard line, Luckman called the first of Halas's plays. The Bears, in white jerseys and navy helmets and pants with orange trim, lined up against the Redskins, in their industrial-looking uniforms of burgundy-brown helmets and jerseys and gold pants. McAfee took a handoff and sliced off right tackle through a big hole to the 32. As Halas had hoped, Washington was in the same 5–3–3 defense as before.

"OK, men," Luckman said in the huddle. "Spread left-O-scissors-46. On two."

The play called for Luckman to fake to the halfback going right, then pivot and pitch left to Osmanski going around left end. "But something went wrong," Luckman later admitted. "Either I didn't yell the play loud enough, or else Bill misunderstood it." McAfee went in motion to the left and Osmanski, thinking the play was a handoff to him, took the ball from a confused Luckman and headed for left tackle. The Washington defense collapsed toward him. To escape the congestion on the line, Osmanski stiff-armed a Redskin tackle, pushing himself toward the outside—the play's original intention.

Osmanski gave a little ground before beating half the Washington team around left end and sprinting untouched down the left sideline, with Redskins Jimmy Johnston and Ed Justice in hot pursuit, only a step or two behind Osmanski at midfield. In another 10 or 15 yards, they were going to catch him from behind or push him out of bounds.

Normally, on a play around left end, the right end would have been so far from the action that he would have been watching the play unfold, but George Wilson never stopped running at full speed across the field on the off chance that Osmanski might break free and need his help. Coming from Johnston's and Justice's right, Wilson sized the two defenders up and delivered one of the most famous blocks in football history, sending Justice flying into Johnston near Washington's 35. As Johnston and Justice hit the deck like Keystone Kops, Osmanski coasted in for a 68-yard touchdown.

Max Krause returned the ensuing kickoff 50 yards and was caught from behind, ironically, by Osmanski. Several running plays took the ball down to the Bears' 35, at which point Baugh faded back to pass, stepped up in the pocket, and threw a perfect strike to Malone, now playing offensive end, on a crossing pattern toward the left flag. As the ball spiraled toward the wide-open Malone at the Bears' five, it looked like a glorious day for both tanks and bombers, but Malone dropped the sure touchdown pass.

With a relentless barrage of 17 running plays—quick openers, traps, and occasional end runs—the Bears moved methodically downfield against the suddenly porous Washington defense. Luckman's only pass on the drive, to the right flat, took the ball to the one, where the Redskins stopped the Bears twice before Luckman's quarterback sneak put Chicago ahead, 14–0.

Baugh immediately took to the air out of Washington's single-wing formation, but a swing pass went nowhere, he underthrew to his receiver on the next try, and his third pass went right through the receiver's hands. Baugh's punt was partially blocked, and the Bears took over on Washington's 42. In a virtual carbon copy of Osmanski's touchdown, his replacement Joe Maniaci took Luckman's handoff and galloped, barely touched, around left end into the end zone.

A two-touchdown first-quarter deficit could happen to anybody—but 21–0? The Griffith Stadium stands were blanketed with an uneasy silence.

The second quarter featured the first two of Chicago's eight interceptions, but neither team could get near the goal line until Luckman, operating from the Redskins' 30-yard line, pump-faked a pass to the flat, giving double-teamed end Ken Kavanaugh time to get open on a deep crossing route. Luckman dropped the ball perfectly into Kavanaugh's hands just before he ran out of real estate in the end zone. 28–0.

On the last drive of the first half, Baugh completed a long Hail Mary pass to the Bears' five, getting the throw airborne just as he was nearly beheaded by a Bears defender. Two plays later, Baugh inexplicably threw a short pass into a gaggle of Bears and was intercepted again. The Redskins' performance was now officially verging on pathetic.

In the locker room, Halas reminded his players that Marshall had accused the Bears of being "a first-half club." As Halas well knew from the 1937 championship game at Wrigley, Baugh was eminently capable of throwing a bunch of touchdown passes in a single quarter and putting the Redskins back in the game.

However, when the second half began, the Redskins were still in a generous mood. Bears' defensive end Hampton Pool picked off another ill-advised Washington pass and waltzed in from the 15 for the Bears' fifth touchdown. On Washington's next possession, an increasingly desperate Baugh faked a punt on fourth down from his own 33 and missed Malone on a long pass. Two plays later, with veteran quarterback Bob Snyder taking over for Luckman, the Bears' halfback went in motion to the left, stretching the Washington secondary as the Chicago line opened up a big hole for Nolting over left tackle, who streaked to the end zone. "I swear," he reported afterward, "not a man laid a finger on me. They must've been asleep." The score was now 41–0.

A few plays later, McAfee intercepted a pass from Baugh's replacement, Roy Zimmerman, and slithered down the left sideline through several Washington players, juking one Redskin, faking out another with a double move at the ten, and then scoring. It was the prettiest run of the day.

The third period was only five minutes old, and the score was 48–0. Red Barber told his national radio audience that the touchdowns were coming so fast he felt like a cashier at a grocery store.

On the Bears' sideline, Halas smirked and wondered spitefully how George Marshall was taking it. Assistant coach Hunk Anderson was more superstitious. "It's hardly a thing to laugh at, George," he told him, "getting beaten like this. A shameful thing for a pro boss." Halas tried to look compassionate, but Luckman couldn't help noticing that he was delirious with joy.

After Bulldog Turner intercepted another Zimmerman throw and ran 24 yards, unmolested, to make the score 54–0, the officials were concerned about running out of footballs and told the Bears they couldn't afford to lose any more on extra-point kicks into the stands, where lucky fans got to keep them. For the rest of the game, the Bears resorted to passes and runs for their extra-point attempts.

The Washington fans eventually joined in the perverse spirit of the proceedings. Initially, they had booed the public address announcer's tedious refrain of "Artoe will kick off for the Bears," but then, with two minutes left in the third quarter, they began chanting, "Sixty, sixty." When the announcer reminded fans that season-ticket books for 1941 were now available, the crowd really let the Redskins front office have it.

In the fourth quarter, Halas sent in rookie running back Harry Clarke of West Virginia, but refused to show the Redskins any mercy, humiliating them with yet another elaborate deception. All three backs, including Clarke, started toward left end on the snap, taking most of the Redskins with them. Clarke put on the brakes, reversed field, took a short lateral from quarterback Snyder, circled back around right end, picked up a block or two, and rambled 42 yards down the right sideline to give the crowd what they wanted: it was now 60–0. Had the scoring stopped there, the game would still have set a record for the largest shutout in NFL history to date.

Someone on the Bears' bench suggested the team ease up. He was shouted down. In any case, the Redskins made it hard for the Bears to relax; second-string quarterback Frank Filchock fumbled a snap in the shadow of his own goalposts, a huge Bears reserve tackle named Jack Torrance fell on the ball, and Gary Famiglietti ran it in from the two. He was the 10th Bear to score a touchdown.

The Redskins' greatest triumph of the day consisted in their professionalism in simply remaining on the field. After still another Bears interception, Chicago tortured Washington by holding the ball for several minutes, passing and running down to the one-yard line. In the huddle, Snyder asked who hadn't scored yet. Harry Clarke, who had scored just moments before on that 42-yard run, impishly replied, "I haven't," and no one bothered to correct him. Clarke remembered thinking, after scoring for the Bears' final touchdown, "People will remember me now." They don't.

Perhaps strangely, few fans left during the game. Jeering at the home team was to be expected, but many fans were actually cheering for the Bears. Deep into the fourth quarter, the spectators remained in their seats. With a few minutes left in the game, there wasn't an empty seat in the vicinity of the scoreboard, now displaying 73–0. The fans couldn't take their eyes off the spectacle of their team's gruesome, slow-motion execution.

Unlike the Bears' finger-pointing over the 7–3 game three weeks earlier, the Redskins' official postgame reaction was devoid of sour grapes or reproach. "We were awful, but they were tremendous," owner Marshall told reporters. He could hardly have said otherwise. "So far as Chicago having piled it on—well, that's the way it should be in this league." The Bears, meanwhile, had passed for only 138 yards—Luckman was only three for four in his one half of action, but he hadn't needed to do more since the team ran through and around Washington for 381 yards on 53 rushes, an average of over seven yards a rush. In contrast, the Redskins managed a paltry 22 yards on the ground, in addition to passing for 226 yards, with a shocking eight interceptions.

Redskins coach Flaherty told reporters that, had Malone caught that touchdown pass on the Redskins' first drive, "Things might have been different. Maybe not, though." Sammy Baugh had the last word: he became famous for saying that if Malone *had* scored, the game would have ended up 73–6. Arthur Daley's lead the next day in the *New York Times* would become equally famous: "The weather was perfect. So were the Bears." It was as if Chicago, which had shown flashes of brilliance during the season, had been stockpiling its true greatness for this one contest. And as if Washington had saved up a season's worth of dazzlingly poor play. On Monday, a *Milwaukee Journal* headline didn't pull any punches: "36,034 Watch Grid Slaughter: Chicago Scores in First Minute, Then Continues Romp at Will."

From a modern perspective, the game featured innovative play calling but also the era's relatively primitive level of physicality. The players may have been bigger and faster than collegians, but they tended to tackle high. In large part, this was because the scant protection afforded by leather helmets and other padding dictated tackling styles. It was said to be the last game in which a player— six-foot-three, 218-pound Bears end Dick Plasman—went without a helmet, although Plasman still played bareheaded the following season.

In the locker room after the game, the consensus was that George Wilson's block on Osmanski's run, the team's first touchdown, would be remembered far longer than any Bears' play that followed, even if Wilson himself called it "a bad block" and "too high." But it had been a game in which even the team's flaws had a touch of genius, and the players were right—Wilson's obliterating "bad" block would be remembered most, along with the ridiculous score.

When Louis Effrat of the *New York Times* asked George Halas after the game which one of his players stood out, he named Luck- man, even though he hadn't played in the second half. Luckman was the grand strategist who had made Halas look like a magician and a genius. After running the plays Halas had ordained to begin the game, Luckman deftly managed the offense in a time when plays couldn't be sent in via messenger from the sidelines—that would not happen until 1942—and quarterbacks didn't have crib sheets on their wristbands. "If Sid made a mistake or called one wrong play," Effrat wrote, "that went unnoticed by the record crowd of 36,034." The *Chicago Tribune*'s Wilfrid Smith began his front-page article on Monday with the sentence, "This is the story of the man who this afternoon directed the greatest team professional football has ever produced," and went on to call Luckman "an inspired genius."

Luckman found out shortly after the game, when he appealed to Halas for a bonus, that the coach's gratitude had its limits, as Don Pierson of the *Chicago Tribune* revealed on the 50th anniversary of the 73–0 victory. Luckman remembered going into Halas's office and making a speech: "Coach, we have the greatest football team ever assembled. I can't thank you enough for permitting me to be a member. Coach, let's talk a little bit about a bonus. What do you think of a thousand dollars?"

Halas grew pale and took some notes out of his pocket. "You know what happened in the first Green Bay game?" he asked with a straight face.

"I know we won forty-one to ten."

"You threw an interception."

"Coach, I must have done something right."

"Remember the game against Cleveland?"

"We won twenty-one to fourteen."

"You fumbled on the four-yard line." In this manner, Halas replayed all of Luckman's flaws, concluding with, "I'll give you two hundred fifty."

"Coach, if that's all you think I'm worth—"

"Two fifty. It's more than you deserve."

But later on, Halas wrote to Luckman and asked him to come to training camp early to learn some new assignments, offering him $750 to attend. Luckman understood that Halas simply wanted to give him the thousand dollars *his* way—and get something for it.

"Dear Coach," Luckman wrote back. "You really don't have to pay me. It would be my pleasure, and I am very anxious to learn. But, if I do come, make it fifteen hundred dollars."

We don't know whether Halas agreed to those terms, but there is no doubt that, in a single burst of offensive and defensive brilliance, the Bears had changed football fans' concept of what 11 men could do with a football. Luckman—and, on his numerous better days, Baugh—defied the gravity of the game's earthbound traditions. America itself was becoming increasingly airborne. The decade had seen the game of basketball liberated by the innovative idea—thanks to Missouri's John Miller Cooper and Stanford's Hank Luisetti—of players' feet leaving the ground as they shot the ball. The Charleston, tap, and the jitterbug, with their faster-than-the-naked-eye steps and aerial acrobatics, had freed dancing from the floor. And in 1938 the Civil Aeronautics Board had been established to regulate the burgeoning commercial airline industry, which was liberating humanity from conventional constraints of time and distance.

By Monday morning, December 9, 1940, those who weren't now convinced that the T formation was revolutionizing football had to wait only three and a half weeks. On January 1, 1941, Nebraska head coach Biff Jones, still pontificating that the Bears' victory was a result of superior players, not the T formation, sent his seventh-ranked Nebraska Cornhuskers out against Clark Shaughnessy's second-ranked, undefeated Stanford Indians in the Rose Bowl—and lost, 21–13.

Before the 1940s were over, virtually every high school, college, and professional football team would adopt the T formation.

15

Temptations

Sid Luckman had hit the jackpot at 24. He was the right man at the right time with the right team coached by the right coaches using the right system. He was the marquee player of the most powerful team in football, beloved by the NFL's most esteemed figure, George Halas, and by a rapidly increasing number of football fans, who couldn't fail to see his name in headlines all across the country on December 9, 1940.

As so often happens with the suddenly famous, Luckman was immediately considered a candidate for other leading roles. In late January, Arch Ward, the *Chicago Tribune*'s powerful sports editor and columnist, wrote that Luckman was being considered for the leading role in the Chicago company of the new Broadway play *My Sister Eileen*. The column was accompanied by a cartoon of a theatergoer at the show's box office saying, "Give me two on the one-yard line." It was no surprise he didn't get the part, given that the highlight of his stage career had occurred during the spring of his senior year at Erasmus Hall, when he had grown a mustache to play public-relations guru Grover Whalen, inventor of the ticker-tape parade, the 1939 New York World's Fair's official greeter, and a former law-and-order

New York City police commissioner who had been forced to resign after his men had used excessive violence to disrupt an International Unemployment Day parade back in 1930.

In the days following the game, the chameleonic Irv Kupcinet stripped off his officiating uniform and resumed his identity as Chicago's rising, glad-handing nexus of brilliant athletes, entertainers, and politicians. He hosted a party for the Bears and some of his entertainment friends. Some have said that a drawling just-turned-18-year-old from Grabtown, North Carolina, named Ava Lavinia Gardner was among the guests. It's possible, although it wasn't until 1941 that her sister Beatrice's photographer boyfriend took Ava's photo and plunked it in the window of his studio on Fifth Avenue, where it was discovered by an MGM talent scout. Wherever the two may have met, Gardner was very taken with Luckman. A letter soon arrived at the Luckman residence in Brooklyn, where Sid lived with Estelle during the off-season. Sid was still away when the note came, so Estelle, accustomed to opening his mail in his absence, pulled it from the envelope and read: "Dear Sid, I have the hots for you. Best, Ava Gardner." "The hots" was a Briticism that had only recently achieved some popularity in America.

The note would have troubled Sid's young wife even more had she any clue who Ava Gardner was or was going to become. Estelle called her sister-in-law Leona for advice. It's unlikely Luckman and Gardner ever consummated their initial attraction; by her own account she was a virgin before being briefly married to Mickey Rooney. Gardner was in New York City during the summer of 1941 to audition for MGM at its Ninth Avenue offices; after she returned to her home in North Carolina, she learned she was being offered a contract and returned to New York to catch the *Twentieth Century Limited* for Los Angeles on August 23. But there is no evidence she was in Chicago, and in her posthumously published tell-all memoir, the name Sid

Luckman does not appear. Yet Gardner's interest in him must have been real; the fact of it trickled down through the years to pool in unlikely places. Decades later, the wife of Leo Luckman's son, Peter, who works in the garment business, was having lunch with an associate; when he discovered that Geri was related by marriage to Sid, he asked, "Is it true? That he had an affair with Ava Gardner?"

The most dangerous temptations, however, were embedded in the game of professional football itself. George Halas's probity notwithstanding, the history of the National Football League was deeply entwined with America's underworld. In fact, without high-stakes gamblers, the league would never have gotten off the ground. In 1925, a bookmaker, boxing promoter, and horseplayer named Tim Mara had no trouble coming up with the $500 franchise fee for a new New York team called the Giants. In the early 1930s, the Brooklyn Dodgers football team was owned by "Big Bill" Dwyer, a major New York bootlegger and Tammany Hall crony. In 1933, a bootlegger, gambler, racetrack owner, and associate of Al Capone named Charles W. Bidwill bought the Chicago Cardinals, and in so doing had to give up his minority stake in the Chicago Bears, for which he had served as team vice president. That same year, a prominent Pittsburgh gambler and intimate of Tim Mara named Art Rooney, who reportedly once won a quarter of a million dollars in two days at two different racetracks and was thought to be the most powerful "layoff man" in Pittsburgh, bought the Pittsburgh Pirates football franchise (renamed the Steelers in 1940) for $2,500. The very day after Rooney's purchase, in 1933, another horse-race gambler, named Bert Bell, and a partner bought the NFL's Frankford Yellow Jackets franchise for $4,000 and turned it into the Philadelphia Eagles. A year later, another gambler, Detroit investor George "Dick" Richards, bought the Portsmouth (Ohio) Spartans, one of the original NFL teams, for $21,500, moved the team to his hometown, and renamed it the Lions.

It was an impressive history for a league that expressly prohibited not only gambling by any player, coach, or owner but also association with bookies and gamblers. Under those strictures, in 1940 Detroit owner Richards was caught bribing a college star to join the Lions and was forced to sell his team to a Chicago department store owner. But the gamble paid off handsomely; the price was $225,000, a return of almost 1,000 percent on his original investment six years earlier. Numerous NFL owners have been involved over the years in real estate deals that also involved known organized-crime funding.

Despite the regulations, cozy social relationships have always existed among many professional athletes, gamblers, and bookmakers. Sid Luckman's opposite numbers in the 1940 championship game, the Redskins' first- and second-string quarterbacks, would have their own run-ins down the road with the NFL head office over their suspicious activities. In 1943, Redskins owner George Marshall secretly recorded conversations in which Sammy Baugh and other players discussed point spreads, player injuries, inside information, and their bookmaker friends. "Although there is no evidence on the recordings that Baugh or any other Redskins player ever threw a game in 1943," wrote investigative journalist Dan E. Moldea in his exhaustively reported book *Interference: How Organized Crime Influences Professional Football*, "the evidence is clear that Baugh and perhaps as many as four other players had personal and/or financial relationships with gamblers and bookmakers."

Baugh's 1940 backup, Frank Filchock, found himself in much hotter water three years later. On December 15, 1946, Filchock, then the starting quarterback for the Eastern Division champion New York Giants, received a phone call shortly before his team's championship game against the Bears at the Polo Grounds. It was the NFL's new commissioner, Bert Bell, informing Filchock and Giants fullback Merle Hapes that Manhattan district attorney Frank S. Hogan and William O'Dwyer, the mob-busting Brooklyn district attorney turned New

York City mayor, had determined through a wiretap that a 28-year-old gambler, Alvin J. Paris, had attempted to fix the championship game on instructions from a New Jersey bookmaking syndicate. Paris had courted the players after meeting them at a cocktail party the previous month and then proposed that, in exchange for a $2,500 payment to each player, plus a $1,000 bet placed on the game on their behalf and no-show off-season jobs with an unnamed Chicago business, Filchock and Hapes would ensure that the Bears won by at least 10 points—which was what most bookmakers had the Bears favored by. Paris had admitted to the scheme on the Saturday before the game had been arraigned, and was being held on $25,000 bail. When Paris's attorney protested the high bail, city magistrate Joseph B. Glebocki replied, "This matter is of grave and vital concern to the country. When they start to pollute sports it will prejudice the public and hurt the players."

It was the first major scandal involving the National Football League since its founding in 1920. Hauled in for questioning, Hapes admitted that Paris had asked him to throw the game, but denied taking any money. Bell suspended him for the game anyway. However, Filchock, whose name had not been mentioned in the wiretap, denied being approached and was allowed to play. This in itself was mildly suspicious, since Filchock was the most important offensive player for the Giants, the only experienced quarterback on their roster, while Hapes was the Giants' fifth-best rusher that season, and therefore hardly in a position to easily throw a game, even if injuries to other Giant runners had thrust him into a starting role. Why Filchock was permitted to play is even more curious in light of the *New York Times'* report the day after the game that Filchock had in fact admitted before the game to being approached; he definitely admitted it later.

Even more ludicrous, Filchock was the ideal target for game fixing because he was an interception-throwing machine, and nothing can control the outcome of a game like throwing interceptions when you have the ball. Whereas the best modern quarterbacks throw far more touchdown passes than interceptions, it was common for quarterbacks in the 1940s to throw more interceptions than touchdown passes in their careers. Even Sammy Baugh threw more interceptions than touchdowns. Sid Luckman was an exception; he would throw 137 touchdowns in his career, compared with 132 interceptions. But Filchock's inaccuracy was off the charts; he had abysmal career totals of 51 touchdown passes and 92 interceptions. In the 1940 championship game, Filchock had been responsible for five of the Redskins' eight interceptions.

And against the Bears in 1946, in front of a record playoff crowd of over 58,000, Filchock threw six interceptions, one of them returned for a Bears touchdown, all but ensuring that the Bears would win, which they did, by exactly 10 points, 24–14, a win for those who had bet the spread. The newspaper coverage of the game was inexplicably obtuse in regard to Filchock's potential role in a point-shaving scheme. "Filchock played furiously despite his broken nose and the fact that he had been up half the night while the investigation was in progress," the *New York Times* wrote, in a lengthy front-page story about the scandal. "He threw two touchdown passes that represented the sum of the Giants' tallies. The Bears intercepted half a dozen of his passes but that was not unusual as during the season, despite his proven worth as a passer, he held the unenviable distinction of having the most passes intercepted against him." The consensus was that Filchock had played marvelously, all things considered.

According to their testimony, Filchock and Hapes rejected Paris's repeated offers, so there is little reason to believe that Filchock in any way threw the game. Nonetheless, Filchock and Hapes were soon suspended indefinitely by commissioner Bell. Along with Paul Hornung and Alex Karras in the 1960s and Art Schlichter in the 1980s, they are the only NFL players to be suspended for gambling or association with gamblers. Nonetheless, such associations were rampant. In the 1960s, former Bear George Wilson, then head coach of the Detroit Lions, was fined $4,000 for failing to report to the league some of his players' unsavory friendships.

In 1947 Frank Filchock joined the Baltimore Colts, part of a new rival professional football league called the All-America Football Conference, a league also riddled with high rollers until it folded in 1949. The majority owner of the AAFC's Los Angeles Dons, Ben Lindheimer, was "the overlord of Chicago's racetracks," according to Dan Moldea. His personal lawyer was none other than Chicago fixer and Luckman's friend Sidney Korshak. Another short-lived franchise, the Chicago Rockets, was owned by a high-stakes gambler, trucking company executive, and racetrack owner named John L. Keeshin, known to have "loaned" money to Jimmy Hoffa, who at the time was head of the Central Conference of Teamsters. The Cleveland Browns were formed by a crime-syndicate bookmaker named Arthur "Mickey" McBride, who ran the Continental Racing Wire, the mob's gambling-news service, which was described later by Estes Kefauver's congressional committee investigating organized crime as "public enemy number one."

In 1969, Pennsylvania trucking magnate Leonard Tose, whose Russian immigrant father had founded one of the biggest trucking concerns on the East Coast, bought the Philadelphia Eagles for $16.1 million. Known for gambling hundreds of thousands of dollars on NFL games, Tose was nonetheless cleared by the NFL to purchase the team.

It's remarkable that few NFL games have ever been proved to have been fixed, given the great interlocking elite bodies of American business, gambling, politics, entertainment, and sports, and considering that, according to the FBI, the single largest source of revenue for organized crime has come from the $100 billion–plus annual wagers on NFL games (although the Supreme Court's 2018 ruling legalizing sports betting will change that). The NFL owes a significant measure of its own revenue and popularity to millions of betting fans who view its broadcasts. According to a 1983 PBS *Frontline* documentary on the Mafia and the NFL, betting on a game soared 600 percent when it was televised, and that was before all the league's games were easily viewed. One of the more chilling rumors about the NFL still clings to the Colts' dramatic sudden-death overtime victory over the Giants in the nationally televised 1958 NFL championship, a game that rivals the Bears' 1940 victory over Washington in terms of pivotal importance for the league. According to bookmakers at the time, Colts owner Carroll Rosenbloom had bet heavily on his own team to beat the spread—and a three-point victory wouldn't do it, whereas six points would. And so, goes the theory—denied by Baltimore quarterback Johnny Unitas—the Colts didn't settle for a winning field goal in overtime and instead risked a fumble or interception on their way to scoring a touchdown, for a 23–17 victory and a big payday for Rosenbloom. Oddsmaker Bob Martin told author Dan Moldea that Rosenbloom's wager was not theoretical and that, furthermore, he "was involved with players in at least thirty-two NFL games that were dumped or where the points were shaved. I knew a lot of players and then through them I got acquainted with other players and then did business with them."

It's unimaginable that Sid Luckman, whose family tragedy originated with unpaid gambling debts, would ever have put himself in a compromising position with bookies. There is no evidence he ever did, although his name did show up in one inconvenient place. In 1983, Allen Dorfman, the former fiduciary manager of the Teamsters' Central States Pension Fund and a convicted embezzler, was awaiting sentencing for bribery. As a mobster who was also involved in sports-gambling operations, Dorfman knew a lot. Rather than run the risk that he would cooperate with authorities to reduce a maximum 55-year sentence, the Mafia had him murdered by three ski-masked gunmen in a hotel parking lot outside Chicago. Dorfman's address book included the names of several NFL owners, coaches, players, and former players, including Sid Luckman. None of them was ever charged with any illegal activity. By all accounts, Luckman confined his gambling to gin rummy games.

In any case, he now had the right connections, if he should ever need a lot of money in a hurry. And in the early 1940s, he did.

16

High-Priced Help

In the midst of Sid Luckman's sudden good fortune and fame, his father's fate had to haunt him terribly as he felt the tide of celebrity carry him away from Flatbush and a childhood marked by humility and then humiliation. Football talent had excused him, at least for now, from the responsibilities his brother had inherited in New York. Sid did not have to risk feeling the stigma of his father's actions on a regular basis, but for years the rest of his family—Ethel, Leo, Leona, Blanche, and even David, the youngest—couldn't go anywhere without encountering the Meyer Luckman case, whose appearance in headlines persisted through two grand juries, one murder trial, and a protracted bribery investigation. Meyer's name kept cropping up in the coverage of Lepke Buchalter's trials.

Meyer Luckman's children did what they could to make their father's life more tolerable. Daughter Blanche visited regularly, as did David, who brought boxes of food. But Sid did not believe Meyer belonged in prison in the first place, despite having sat in the courtroom during his father's trial, having listened to the testimony, having witnessed his murdered uncle's effigy carried into the courtroom, having heard his grandfather shrieking in Yiddish that his father was the murderer, having seen, several years later, the headline, "Calls Luckman Lepke Mobster." According to Sid's son, Bob, Sid would believe his entire life that his father had been railroaded to Sing Sing by overzealous politicians and prosecutors—Mayor Fiorello La Guardia, Governor Herbert Lehman, Thomas Dewey—who were trying to exert some much-needed control over crime in their city.

F. Scott Fitzgerald famously remarked in *The Crack-Up* that "the test of a first-rate intelligence is the ability to hold two opposed ideas in the mind at the same time, and still retain the ability to function. One should, for example, be able to see that things are hopeless and yet be determined to make them otherwise." Sid Luckman may well have believed in the impossible—that his father was innocent—given that the impossible had already happened: he had emerged from a mediocre Columbia football team to become professional football's darling and help lead the Chicago Bears to a most improbably lopsided victory. Perhaps Sid even hoped against hope that Meyer's release would lead to the restoration of the broken Luckman family, although his mother had not said a word to her husband since he had gone "up the river" five years earlier.

Meyer Luckman wouldn't be eligible for parole for several more years, but the possibility remained that his sentence might be commuted to time served, or that he might earn "compassionate release," as an old man with heart disease, a man who had served his time quietly and wanted only to see his son play football before he died. A decision on a request for commutation or clemency could take anywhere from six months to two years, but Sid felt the right, connected lawyer might do better.

Sid asked around discreetly, and someone among his new friends and acquaintances told him of an individual—a man with powerful government connections—who would be willing to pull some strings and lean on the right people. Hope came at a high price, though; the lawyer required an exorbitant $25,000 retainer—the equivalent of almost $400,000 today—or so Sid's son would remember his father saying.* Sid made another round of discreet inquiries, his appreciation of the fact that he now knew people with money outweighing his mortification at having to ask for it.

Word that Sid was anxious to find this money finally reached his good friend and former roommate Charlie Baron, then serving in the Illinois National Guard as aide-de-camp to General Samuel Lawton Sr. of the 33rd Infantry Division. Baron was on the phone to Luckman immediately, miffed, according to Bob Luckman, that Sid had not thought of him sooner, since he would do anything for Sid. Just like that, Luckman had what he needed.

Charles "Babe" Baron is a name that only occasionally bobs to the surface in the annals of organized crime. He owned a Ford dealership in Chicago, but he had in his youth served some time as an enforcer and was, in all probability, once a hit man. In his 1969 book on Chicago corruption, *Captive City*, Ovid Demaris writes of Baron, whom he characterized as a close associate of Chicago Democratic machine boss Jake Arvey (as well as a mob representative in Las Vegas): "Back in 1929, Baron, while accompanied by Joe Cota and Robert Emmer Ryan, two notorious Capone hoodlums, shot and killed

---

* We'll never know who the lawyer was. Sid Luckman's son, Bob, says his father went to Washington to talk to President Roosevelt, but it's more likely to have been Senator Harry Truman, FDR's future vice president. Later in the 1940s, the Chicago Outfit crime syndicate, which supported Truman and later helped elect him president, successfully pressured him and his parole board to release several convicted *federal* felons. The connection might have been arranged through Paul Ziffren, a close friend of Sid Korshak, who was a close friend of Irv Kupcinet. Ziffren was a protégé of Chicago Democratic leader Jake Arvey and a tax law specialist for the US attorney's office in northern Illinois, who became one of the top Democratic advisers to the Truman administration and the moving force in California Democratic politics after settling there in the 1950s. He was also a lawyer to many entertainment stars (including Chicagoans Charlton Heston and Bob Newhart) and chairman of the city's 1984 Los Angeles Olympics board.

gambler Jimmy Walsh in front of Henrici's restaurant (no indictment); five years later, he was a prime suspect in the machine-gun slaying of Gus Winkeler, a West Side gambler (remains unsolved). A brigadier general in the Illinois National Guard, he was cleared to handle secret communications in 1961, soon after he returned from Cuba, where he had worked in casinos bossed by Meyer Lansky."

To have been a suspect in the 1933 murder of Gus Winkeler was to be connected to the very epicenter of Chicago's colorful gangland history. Gus Winkeler, who had one glass eye as a result of an automobile accident, was widely considered to be one of the shooters (when he had two good eyes) in the grisly Saint Valentine's Day Massacre on February 14, 1929. Al Capone, who controlled the city's South Side, tried to lure his North Side rival, George "Bugs" Moran, to a warehouse on the North Side with the promise of a stolen truckload of whiskey. Arriving late at the warehouse that morning, Moran turned away when he saw a police car nearby, but five of his men and two innocent victims, already in the warehouse, weren't so lucky. Four Capone hit men, two of them dressed as police officers, ordered the seven men to face a brick wall inside and riddled them with shotgun and Thompson submachine gun bullets. Leaving the carnage behind, the two men dressed as cops proceeded to lead the other two shooters out of the warehouse at gunpoint in the pantomime of an arrest, whereupon all four of them disappeared. After Capone's 1931 federal tax-evasion conviction ended his short, violent reign, his successor, Frank Nitti, began to suspect Winkeler of singing to the FBI and had him shot and killed on the street in 1933 by unknown assailants. One of them was likely Charlie Baron.

In 1933, young Charlie Baron was only beginning to climb the ladder of organized crime. He later became a trusted associate of Meyer Lansky, who hired him to manage his Riviera Hotel in Havana in the 1950s. After Fidel Castro came to power, Baron became a

I percent owner of the Sands Hotel in Las Vegas, which was run by Joseph "Doc" Stacher, an architect of the Jewish-Italian national organized crime syndicate, who had been in charge of gambling operations for Lansky. When the FBI bugged the Chicago mob's headquarters in a tailor shop on North Michigan Avenue in the late 1950s, Baron showed up on the tape discussing whether to have a certain gambler killed who had welshed on a large debt to the mob in Las Vegas. It's a rich irony that Baron loaned Sid Luckman money to rescue Meyer, killer of a gambler who had stolen money from him in order to avoid welshing on a debt to the mob.

While growing up, Bob Luckman saw Charlie Baron, his godfather, from time to time with his father. When Bob visited Las Vegas as a young man in the 1970s, Baron, then the "official greeter" at the Sands, "took care" of him, just as he had, years before, looked after Sid when he first arrived in Chicago. Baron happened to mention the old loan, some 30 years in the past, without saying what the loan had been for. But Baron wanted Bob to know that Sid had paid him back every penny.

17

Another Botched Job

In early 1941, Louis "Lepke" Buchalter had been in the federal penitentiary in Leavenworth, Kansas, since the previous April, serving his 14-year sentence for drug trafficking, after which he was due to serve his New York State sentence of 30 years to life for racketeering.

But Thomas Dewey wasn't through with him. Dewey wanted to put a stake through the heart of the rackets and the killing machine that in a few years would be awarded a name so apt and compelling—Murder, Inc.—that, in the future, at least seven actors would get to play Lepke Buchalter on television and the big screen. The accomplices that Dewey and Brooklyn DA O'Dwyer had already put in jail were starting to bite one another, name names, and scramble to get out of jail. The chattiest rat by far was Abe "Kid Twist" Reles, now 35, who in past years had been an ice-pick wielder extraordinaire and author of at least 10 murders, some of which were so deftly committed that coroners were hard-pressed to find the entry wound. He was wasting away in the Tombs in lower Manhattan, when his pregnant wife came to visit and gave him an ultimatum: do whatever you have to do to get out of jail or you'll never see me again. Unlike many mobsters, who kept their mouths shut, the cold-blooded Reles discovered that his love of freedom exceeded both his love of killing and his loyalty to his former employer and colleagues.

Reles had already fingered fellow hit men Harry "Pittsburgh Phil" Strauss, considered the most zealous exterminator of all, and Martin "Buggsy" Goldstein in the 1939 murder of gambler Irving "Puggy" Feinstein. Feinstein's demise had taken place in Reles's own Brooklyn home—and with his assistance. The methods used were similar to the ones employed in the murder of Sam Drukman in 1935, although with the addition of Reles's weapon of choice. Reles's mother-in-law testified that the killers had requested an ice pick and clothesline earlier in the day. Strauss and Goldstein were convicted in September 1940 and sentenced to death in Sing Sing's electric chair. The men had not endeared themselves to the court; Strauss had stopped shaving and feigned insanity during the trial, while Goldstein told the judge after sentencing that he'd like to pee on his leg.

In exchange for immunity, Reles and Albert "Tick-Tock" Tannenbaum, under heavy police guard in the Half Moon Hotel in Coney Island, told prosecutors that Lepke had ordered the 1936 murder of a former trucker named Joseph Rosen and they would gladly testify to that effect. This was terrific news, even if the authorities would have appreciated more reliable witnesses to Lepke's directive than men whose livelihood was disposing of other human beings without due process. Mayoral hopeful O'Dwyer and presidential hopeful Dewey rejoiced—even though, with all the dozens of important figures whose murders Lepke had ordered, a nobody named Joe Rosen might be the one to send him to the chair. In early April 1941, O'Dwyer announced that he was indicting Lepke for the Rosen murder, along with three of his associates—Emanuel "Mendy" Weiss, Louis Capone, and Philip "Little Farvel" Cohen—for participating in it.

O'Dwyer went to Washington, DC, himself to arrange for Lepke's transfer from Kansas to Brooklyn, where Lepke's arraignment with the others, on May 9, became such a chaotic public spectacle that the judge half-joked about sending in the marines. The prosecution's case was precarious. Capone and Cohen hadn't actually witnessed the killing, and Weiss, who had, wouldn't confess to it. The other hit man present at the murder, Pittsburgh Phil Strauss, was unavailable to testify since, by the time the trial got going in the fall of 1941 (it took forever to find 12 jurors who didn't want to shoot Lepke themselves), he and Buggsy Goldstein had been sent to Sing Sing, where they had been executed, one right after the other, on June 12.

Lepke felt it was beneath his dignity to be tried for the murder of someone so insignificant, so forgettable as Joseph Rosen—a "peanut." Rosen had been the owner of a small trucking company in Brooklyn whose customers were assorted garment shops in Pennsylvania and New Jersey—shops Lepke was determined to put under his control. In the process, he put Rosen out of business. Rosen, who had a family, complained, and Lepke found him a new job. Rosen was fired. He went to Lepke's office, at 200 Fifth Avenue, to complain, and Lepke found him another job, driving a truck. Rosen was fired again. He complained of heart problems. After being unemployed for 18 months, Rosen opened a candy store in the Brownsville neighborhood of Brooklyn. Lepke's men even sent union members to the store to buy candy to help Rosen out, but by then Rosen was grousing regularly about the mob's treatment of him.

Rosen made enough noise that Dewey's investigators finally paid him a visit. Lepke was incensed. He gave Rosen an ultimatum he had issued to others before: shut your mouth, leave town, and don't come back. Rosen dutifully left for Pennsylvania with some mob spending money in hand, but got homesick and returned to New York, whereupon the usually imperturbable Lepke lost his cool and vowed that he would take care of Rosen once and for all. Unfortunately, Lepke had made the error of vowing it in front of Tick-Tock Tannenbaum and Max Rubin. Arrangements were made—the casing of the store, the clipping of a kill car, and the conclusion that early morning was the optimal time to take out Rosen. And so the deed was done on the morning of September 13, 1936. Fifteen bullets later, Rosen was sprawled on his back by the Coca-Cola cooler in his tiny store.

That Max Rubin was available to testify in Lepke's murder trial was nothing short of a miracle. A former garment-industry worker who had become a powerful labor adviser to Lepke, he had been vehemently opposed to Joe Rosen's murder and had been observed giving Rosen some money the previous July to help him survive. Now that Rosen was dead, Rubin was concerned that his relationship to Rosen would be misunderstood and implicate him in the crime. Before the DA's people could get their hooks into Rubin, Lepke sent him away to Saratoga Springs, then to Salt Lake City. Each time, when upstate New York and Utah failed to agree with him, he sneaked back into town.

As reported by Brooklyn assistant district attorney Burton Turkus in his book *Murder, Inc.*, Lepke said, "Have you got something in the back of your head?"

"Look, Louis," Rubin replied, "I got no notions. It's just that I'm a lonesome man when I can't see my family."

Lepke next sent him to New Orleans to help with Frank Costello's slot machines. "You'll have money from New York, money from me, money from there," he told Rubin. "You'll be OK."

But he wasn't. He checked out of his New Orleans hotel and returned to the Bronx. Lepke liked the peace-loving, cosmopolitan Rubin, but this was getting ridiculous. Lepke had himself driven up to Rubin's building in the Bronx during a thunderstorm and confronted him.

"Max," he said, "you came back again without permission."

"But Louis, I couldn't take it any more. I had to see my wife and child. You know how it is, Louis. Don't get ideas, Lep. No one knows I'm in town. I didn't talk to anybody."

Lepke pondered the situation for a moment, then asked Max how old he was.

"I'm forty-eight, Lep," the startled Rubin said. "Exactly."

"That's a ripe age, Max, isn't it?" Lepke said blandly and concluded the interview.

In early 1937, Lepke sent Rubin away again, this time on a two-month car trip with another man along the Atlantic seaboard. Rubin grew long hair and a mustache, but his homesickness was again getting to him. An irritated Lepke surprised Rubin in a Washington, DC, hotel room in February 1937, and told him he was now on his own—no more financial assistance, no help if he came back and got into trouble. "Thus," Burton Turkus wrote, "he was allowed to come home, after being on the run for half a year, because of a murder to which he was not a party—which, in fact, he had tried desperately to prevent."

There may be no greater tribute to the charms of New York City than the preference of some mobsters to be murdered there instead of living out their years somewhere else. When Rubin returned yet again, Dewey's men wouldn't leave him alone, and Rubin appeased them with information about Lepke's rackets while scrupulously avoiding any mention of Joseph Rosen. On October 1, 1937, Rubin made a secret appearance before a Manhattan grand jury to tie Lepke more tightly to the flour and bakery racket. Grand jury visits rarely escaped Lepke's notice. He had either a tail on Rubin or an informer on the grand jury, because as Rubin left the aptly named Gun Hill Road subway stop in the Bronx on his way home that day, he was shot in the back of the head. The gunman—one account says it was Kid Twist Reles, giving his ice pick a rest—was so sure of his work that he didn't bother to fire a second shot. In fact, the single bullet entered the back of Rubin's neck and exited between his nose and one eye.

But Rubin was not added to Murder, Inc.'s hit parade. Instead, something extraordinary happened: the bullet severed nerves and muscles and left Rubin closer to death than life for over a month, but he didn't die. When he left the hospital, it was in the company of three police guards. He was never alone without an escort. Try as they might, Lepke's minions couldn't get another clear shot at him.

Four years later, the tables were turned, and Rubin, healed and of sound mind, would have his chance. Lepke's defense lawyers played every nasty card they could to discredit Rubin. They scoffed at the idea that Lepke would stoop to squash a bug like Rosen and even tried to paint Rubin himself as Rosen's killer. Rubin told the court that he had heard Lepke say he was going to make sure Rosen never talked. "That bastard," Lepke had said, according to Rubin, "he's going around shooting his mouth off about seeing Dewey. He and nobody else is going anyplace and doing any talking. I'll take care of him."

But Rubin was not a witness to the murder itself and his testimony would need to be corroborated. At this point, the prosecution led into the courtroom none other than Tick-Tock Tannenbaum, so nicknamed because of his rapid-fire speech, who proceeded to tell the jurors that he was in the room when Lepke had yelled that he was going to take care of Rosen. There had been 52 witnesses at the trial, but none as important as Rubin and now Tick-Tock.

Kid Twist Reles was due to testify at Lepke's trial a few days hence to corroborate Lepke's order of Rosen's death, but he famously fell six floors to his death at the Half Moon Hotel on the morning of November 12, despite being guarded around the clock by six cops. His death was officially ruled a suicide, but no one was fooled. Everyone but the prosecutors wanted him dead, from his boss, Albert

Anastasia, to the crooked cops it was thought Anastasia might have paid to drug Reles and toss him out the window.

Lepke's partner in organized crime, Gurrah Shapiro, was shipped up from the US penitentiary in Atlanta as a possible defense witness, but Lepke's lawyer never called him to testify. However, Gurrah did manage to privately convey a one-sentence written rebuke to Lepke— "I told you so"—referring to Gurrah's minority view in 1935 that Dutch Schultz ought to be allowed to rub out Thomas Dewey, which could have saved them all trouble.

However, Reles's testimony was no longer necessary. It took the jury six hours to find Lepke, Mendy Weiss, and Louis Capone guilty of first-degree murder. Judge Franklin Taylor sentenced the three of them to death at Sing Sing a month hence, during the week of January 4, 1942. It was the first death sentence ever handed to a top-level mobster. The men's lawyers immediately filed an appeal.

Lepke, still a federal prisoner, was returned to the Federal House of Detention in Manhattan. Weiss and Capone were transferred two days later, on December 2, 1941, to Sing Sing. A photo captures them on the train from Grand Central, traveling along the Hudson, both in suits, white shirts, and tightly knotted ties. Under his fedora, Weiss is half-smiling, but Capone is actually beaming, as though it has all been just a crazy game. A detective standing behind Capone wears a small smile too, as if they're all in on the same joke. If not for the handcuffs joining the two convicts, one would think they were celebrating a victory. It was almost a genre, photos of happy-go-lucky condemned men on a train. In the summer of 1941, it had been Pittsburgh Phil Strauss and Buggsy Goldstein smiling on their way to the chair.

Meyer Luckman's murder of his brother-in-law, Sam Drukman, in 1935 may have been an inconsequential loose thread in Lepke's empire, but now the fabric was completely unraveling.

18

Almost to a T

Five days after Mendy Weiss and Louis Capone's train ride to the electric chair, the Bears concluded a remarkable season with a chippy, come-from-behind 34–24 victory over the lowly Chicago Cardinals at Comiskey Park before a crowd of more than 18,000 fans. While the Cardinals were in the lead, the public-address announcer suddenly told servicemen to report to their units and delivered the shocking news that the Japanese had just attacked Pearl Harbor. The crowd fell silent. The coaches and officials conferred and decided to play on. Luckman remembered the shift in the teams' emotional state after the announcement, but George McAfee, who would lose almost four years of his career to the war, didn't break stride; in the fourth quarter, after Halas had been tipped off about a Cardinal defensive weakness by his "eye in the sky," Luke Johnsos, McAfee caught a 39-yard touchdown pass from Luckman, then later burst through tackle to race 70 yards for another score, putting the game away.

The victory left the Bears with a 10–1 record, in a tie with the idle Green Bay Packers for first place in the NFL Western Division, forcing a playoff game at Wrigley Field the following Sunday for the right to meet the New York Giants, who had won the Eastern Division with an 8–3 season. Scouting their likely playoff opponents, the Packers' coach Curly Lambeau and several of his players, including Clarke Hinkle, Don Hutson, and league-leading passer Cecil Isbell, were in Comiskey Park's stands that day, looking like mobsters themselves in overcoats and fedoras, and taking written notes on the action.

On Monday, December 8, President Roosevelt addressed the nation, declaring the previous day "a date which will live in infamy," and the United States promptly declared war on Japan, a courtesy the Japanese had denied America before the attack. Three days later, Germany and Italy declared war on the United States. On Sunday, December 14, more than 43,000 football fans filled Wrigley to see the Bears and the Packers battle each other. Perhaps the 16-degree temperature numbed them to the fact that their nation had been attacked for just the second time in its history.* Isolationism had evaporated overnight. Japanese American citizens were already being arrested on the West Coast, and the front-page cartoons of a few weeks past that had questioned Congress's rush to go to war were gone, replaced by illustrations of men symbolizing American ingenuity and courage, and captions like "We'll Make 'Em Say 'Uncle.'"

In the still impermeable bubble that was the world of sports, after the Packers scored an early touchdown, the Bears tallied 30 straight points in the first half, the first six of them on an 81-yard punt return by one of Clark Shaughnessy's former Stanford stars, rookie halfback Hugh Gallarneau, whom Halas had drafted in the third round that year. Fullback Norm Standlee, Gallarneau's Stanford teammate and Halas's first-round pick in the 1941 draft, ran for two touchdowns in the second quarter, and the Bears went on to win, 33–14, in a game in which Luckman,

---

* The first having been during the War of 1812: on August 16, 1812, the British invaded and sacked Washington, DC, and burned the White House to the ground.

once again, hadn't needed to pass very often to complement the team's rushing attack, which had been dominant all season. Although the Bears ran up 128 yards in penalties, their 277 yards rushing, and a ferocious defense that held the Packers to less than one yard per carry, ensured their second straight division championship.

Strangely, the NFL championship game at Wrigley the following Sunday was played in unseasonably warm 47-degree weather, but hardly anyone came. Only 13,341 fans—less than a third of the previous week's gate and the smallest crowd of the entire season—bothered to show up to see their team dismiss the Giants 37–9, outgaining New York on offense, 389 yards to 157. Film of the game shows points-after in the south end of Wrigley being kicked into eerily empty grandstands. Luckman completed nine of 12 passes for 160 yards, without an interception but without a touchdown either, as McAfee and Standlee combined for 170 yards on the ground. The *Chicago Tribune*'s Edward Prell tried to attribute the low turnout "to the imminence of the Christmas season and the fans' correct premonition that the eastern champions would be no match for the Bears," but it's much more likely that the shock of Pearl Harbor had finally worn off, rendering thousands of pro football fans too preoccupied to think about football.

Although the team came alive for a celebratory group photo, the players seemed unimpressed by their second consecutive championship. They groused less about the small crowd than about their small paychecks for winning—$430.94 for each of them, less than half their take-home the year before in Washington.

It was an unceremonious end to a brilliant season that had begun, in a sense, the previous March 18, when George Halas had signed the once reluctant Luckman for a third year of professional football, giving him a slight raise. Not that his re-signing was ever in doubt. The Luckman trucking business, now reorganized as Tri-Borough Transportation

Corporation under the leadership of Leo and his cousins, didn't look so appealing anymore, even if the defanged Brooklyn mob was leaving it alone. Luckman's re-signing was commemorated in the press by an Associated Press photo of Halas admiring Luckman's right arm with the caption: "George Halas, dropping into Brooklyn yesterday, looked over Sid Luckman's arm, found it full of touchdowns, and immediately signed the quarterback star to his third Chicago Bear contract."

"You can call Luckman the perfect quarterback," Halas told reporters. "When he does something wrong, it's news."

While Luckman's arm did not prove to be "full of touchdowns" in 1941—he threw only nine in 11 games—he passed with far more accuracy than he had the year before, throwing only six interceptions all season and completing 57 percent of his passes, the best percentage of his career. In any case, the point of the T was not to fill the air with touchdown passes but to use the running game to provide the context for a more effective and timely passing game. "Very often," Luckman explained, "an entire game is planned on certain kinds of passes. When they work, they may strike you as long-range gambles. But we can't afford to gamble against the smart defenders opposing us. Our job is to maneuver them out of position by a series of ground plays or laterals, or to get them off the track by sending a clever set of decoys chasing upfield along with a receiver." At the time, this explanation of offensive strategy was a revelation. "I imagine that the old-timers must have been shocked at the first sight of such shenanigans—good running plays used only as a springboard for a pass," Luckman wrote. "The big day for the pro passer was yet to come."

Luckman and the Bears had done very little wrong all season. The Bears opened the 1941 season right where they had left off in 1940, averaging over 40 points a game in their first five contests. Their dominance was an echo of their 73–0 thrashing of the Washington Redskins in 1940, silencing all who suspected that game was an anomaly. As if to serve notice that they meant business, the team wore new, intimidating uniforms, a switch from the orange or white jerseys they had worn throughout their history. Halas, a navy veteran, unveiled the design that, with minor changes, has remained the team's home uniform ever since: deep navy blue jerseys with three orange stripes on the sleeves, reminiscent of the three gold stripes on the cuffs of a naval dress uniform; navy helmets; and white pants with navy and orange piping.

The Bears averaged 36 points a game for the 1941 season—12.5 more points a game than their nearest rival, the Packers—while holding their opponents to 13.4 points per game, fourth best in the league. One of the more anticipated matchups came on November 30, when the Bears, with a 9–1 record, traveled to Philadelphia to play the one other team in the NFL that had adopted the T formation in 1941. The Eagles' rookie coach, Alfred "Greasy" Neale, had spent the summer poring over film of Chicago's 73–0 rout of the Redskins in an attempt to absorb and implement its lessons. It appeared he had succeeded when his Eagles led 14–0 at halftime. But the Bears recovered consciousness and in the second half scored seven touchdowns—two on Luckman's passes—and finished the afternoon with over 500 yards on offense and a 49–14 victory.

Many people had given the T formation only a measure of the credit for the Bears' 1940 shellacking of Washington, but coaches had begun to line up to learn the T's secrets. "There were mysterious strangers slipping into Chicago from Los Angeles and Texas, New York and New Orleans after the Washington job," Luckman remembered. Over the spring and summer of 1941, Halas had taken his show on the road to hold T-formation clinics in Iowa, Kansas, Oklahoma, Utah, and New Jersey, with Luckman and Shaughnessy as copresenters. With the interests of the entire league he had created at heart, Halas took a position that would be unthinkable today. Why would he withhold from others the offensive elixir that would promote the growth and popularity of the entire sport? Even college powerhouses queued up, though with questions.

"Seems to me," one college coach said to Luckman, "there's too many intricate details to expect the average back to carry them around in his noodle."

Luckman jumped at the opportunity for some genuine humility. "I'm afraid you're insulting the intelligence of our football players," he replied. "If a stupid and bruised college man like myself could pick it up inside two seasons . . . " Sometimes Sid would demonstrate the footwork and pivots in a hotel room, crouching behind an imaginary Bulldog Turner while deploying veteran coaches as halfbacks and fullbacks. The collegians were concerned about some of the formation's vulnerabilities, such as the lightning-quick timing required or the offensive line's brush-blocking, which created only split-second holes for the running backs but compensated for that by providing a second wave of blocks downfield. Or they wondered how, when their teams confronted the T, they would defend against it. "How will you stop it?" Shaughnessy would say. "Necessity. It always produces defenses of some sort." The process was already in motion, as more and more teams shifted from the standard six-linemen and two-linebacker defense to five and three in order to handle the T's man-in-motion and its greater variety of options.

Even legendary Notre Dame coach Frank Leahy asked the president and vice president of the university how they would feel if he installed the T—that's how important a decision it was—and he was told they had no objections as long as it was the better formation. The T could probably have had no better advertisement than being embraced by the team that had given its university's name to the

single-wing variation known as the Notre Dame Box. In the fall of
1941, Leahy traveled up to Chicago from South Bend to watch the
Bears in action. The following spring he further studied the T with
Shaughnessy at the latter's spring-training sessions at the University
of Maryland, whose program Shaughnessy had left Stanford to coach.
Leahy summoned Luckman to Notre Dame for a clinic. "We copied
the Bears' offense kit and caboodle," Leahy would recall. "That spring,
I had Luckman come to Notre Dame to coach the T in practice.
Afterward, he told me it was one of his greatest thrills in football—a
Jewish quarterback from Columbia being invited to teach football at
America's leading Catholic University."

The T was starting to democratize the game, altering pro football's traditional dependence on unique stars like Red Grange and
Bronko Nagurski to attract fans. Game-breaking talents like George
McAfee or Don Hutson, and passers like Sammy Baugh or Luckman,
still brought people into the tent, but now fans expected to witness
a cleverly orchestrated team effort. "Prima donnas were on their way
out," Luckman wrote, looking back on the decade. "A coach could
no longer point to a fair-haired hero in the dressing room and advise
the club to give him every ounce of support."

The Bears weren't worried about giving away trade secrets,
because they still had the jump on the league. During Luckman's third
campaign, and his second season as the Bears' starting quarterback,
in 1941, the team would set league records for team offense in eight
categories: total passing yards, first downs, total yards, touchdowns,
rushing touchdowns, extra points, total points, and average yards per
completed pass, an astounding 20.4. Had the Bears not beaten themselves and lost against Green Bay in early November, they would have
been riding a 16-game winning streak going back to 1940.

The T formation was still a curiosity, and the Bears' supremacy
was still something of a mystery. During the season, the *Chicago Tribune*'s

Edward Prell interviewed the team's coaches to find out whether perhaps there was a connection between their dominance and the relative paucity of all-Americans in the lineup. "It is our contention," Halas preached, his past pursuit of Luckman and McAfee notwithstanding, "that the player who is a big shot on a big college team is more or less through after taking the hard knocks for three years. He absorbs a beating every Saturday. All the team's rivals are laying for him." "There are only so many years a man can play good, hard football," assistant coach Paddy Driscoll chimed in, offering as examples the Bears' undervalued assets Bob Swisher and George Wilson, both out of Northwestern and undrafted. "These are the kind of fellows the Bears like to get," Prell told his readers. "Smart and willing and unmarked by the pitiless glare of the intercollegiate sports limelight." As long as Luckman was the leader and linchpin, Halas was confident.*

Halas had more than the prosperity of the Bears in mind. "The failure of pro football for a long time was due to its lack of spirit," he is quoted as saying in *Luckman at Quarterback*. "Today it's got the kind of drive the customers want. Let's keep it up. Talent alone will never add up to the right ball club. . . . Not when that talent rests on its laurels. I need men who are keyed to win; men who are out for victory and nothing else." While Luckman was the exception to the prescription for hiring college players who hadn't been worn out by the time they graduated, Halas saw that Luckman had been uniquely

---

* Almost 80 years later, this philosophy would be echoed in explanations of the dominance of the New England Patriots under coach Bill Belichick and quarterback Tom Brady. In a 2018 *Sports Illustrated* article about "how the Patriots scheme around the varying skills of the personnel who surround their one brilliant constant at quarterback," retired Patriot receiver Brandon Lloyd explained that it was "because so many of the players lack the ability to start on another team, so they just do what they're told to do. The Pats take players like that on purpose. That's the business model." Like Belichick, Halas didn't squander his budget on stars, leaving gaps elsewhere. He understood there was no simple correlation between college stardom and success; it was better to seed the roster with undervalued players.

tempered physically and mentally by his experience. In any case, the Bears' offensive linemen were increasingly devoted to protecting their quarterback from further damage. Luckman acquired a reputation for never getting his pants dirty, even if the pair he donated to the NFL's Pro Football Hall of Fame in Canton, Ohio, is suitably soiled. Neither Luckman nor Baugh played in an era of collapsing pockets, 300-pound headhunters, sophisticated blitzing schemes, and bone-crushing sacks. Both men often threw off the back foot, often to the flat, and quickly retreated from contact. Nonetheless, the Bears were widely considered a "dirty" team; between 1939 and 1947, the bulk of Luckman's career, the Chicago Bears led the league in penalty yards eight times, often by huge margins.

In the wake of the Bears' easy wins over Green Bay and New York in the 1941 postseason, complacency would seem to have been their worst enemy. "We made the T formation appear almost simple, which was one of the illusions produced by success, as I see it now," Luckman would recall. "Our chief trouble was the notion, at times, that we produced 100 percent perfect football. . . . Whenever this attitude developed, we played a brazen, overconfident game, usually playing right into the hands of our opponents."

When the 1942 season opened, the two-time NFL champions were ripe for a comeuppance, having lost much of the offense's nucleus to the war. "There was never a team like this one," Luckman had told the press after the Bears beat a team of NFL all-stars at the Polo Grounds on January 3, 1942. "I'm sorry to see it break up." Fullback Norm Standlee, who had gained five yards a carry as a rookie in 1941 and gone to the Pro Bowl, went to war and wouldn't return to pro ball until 1946, and then with the AAFC's San Francisco 49ers. George

"One-Play" McAfee enlisted in the navy, taking his 7.3 yards-per-rush average with him, and wouldn't return to the Bears for almost four seasons. End Ken Kavanaugh would also return in 1945, beating the odds against survival after running 30 bombing missions. For others, though, the war would mean essentially the end of their careers. End Dick Plasman returned to the team in 1944 but played little thereafter, and halfback Bob Swisher returned in 1945, caught two passes, and was done. Quarterback Young Bussey, from LSU, a rookie in 1941 who backed up Luckman along with Bob Snyder, didn't come back at all; he was killed in combat in the Philippines in 1945, one of 20 NFL players to die in the war. All in all, a third of the players on NFL rosters in 1941 were in the military by the 1942 season.

The Bears' offense was decimated; Standlee, McAfee, Plasman, Kavanaugh, and Swisher had accounted for almost half of the Bears' total offensive yardage in 1941. And now, after the first five games of 1942, 48-year-old Lieutenant Commander George Halas of the US Navy was in Oklahoma with his engineering degree, training aviation mechanics.

Yet, for the second time, a Bears team won 18 games in a row, and the team wouldn't lose again until December. After winning their last seven in 1941, they ran the regular-season table in 1942, winning their games by an astounding average score of 34 to 11.* Only three teams scored more than a touchdown against them, four scored a single touchdown, and four didn't score at all.

But all streaks are temporary, and the Chicago Bears' reign would finally come to an end as well, and not with a bang but a curious whimper against the team, and the quarterback, to which Sid Luckman and the Bears appeared to be connected by fate.

* In NFL history, only two teams have had longer winning streaks: New England won 21 straight in 2003–4, and Green Bay won 19 in 2010–11.

19

With a Thud

Lepke Buchalter was dying a slow death. He was back in the US penitentiary in Leavenworth, continuing to serve his narcotics rap, while awaiting a decision from the seven-member New York State Court of Appeals on his—and Louis Capone's and Mendy Weiss's—New York murder conviction in November 1941. The Chicago Bears were halfway through their undefeated season when the mealy-mouthed decision came down on October 30, 1942, 11 months after the mobsters had been found guilty of Joe Rosen's murder.

Three of the judges agreed that the state's evidence and the prosecutor's and the judge's behavior "left a good deal to be desired, but the trial had been fair and the conviction should stand." Two other judges described the trial as "outrageous" and believed the defendants deserved another chance to defend their lives. A sixth judge called the trial "grossly unfair." Lepke's fate, like that of Capone and Weiss, was in the hands of Chief Judge Irving Lehman (brother of New York governor Herbert Lehman; Governor Lehman was the man who had stepped into the Meyer Luckman mess back in 1935, had initiated the investigation into the bribery of the first grand jury, and had commuted Fred Hull's death sentence at the last minute.)

Judge Lehman agreed with the three judges who considered the trial unfair, writing that all the testimony came from "degraded criminals whose credibility [was] impeached, if not completely destroyed, by the cross-examination, in which they admitted a callous disregard of every law, human and divine." Nonetheless, he thought the convictions should stand and the death sentences be carried out. "One senses from Judge Lehman's muddled and vacillating opinion," historian Albert Fried has written, "that the prospect of giving Lepke and the others a second chance, or, worse, exonerating them outright, was simply unthinkable, that procedural standards had to yield to larger considerations of the public good."

Moderate Republican Thomas Dewey was elected governor of New York the same week as the appeals court decision, and he now had his eye on the Republican nomination for president in 1944. The popular crime buster was riding high, and President Roosevelt wasn't about to hand him any more victories; he rejected Dewey's demand that Lepke be turned over to New York so final justice could be done. The issue became irrelevent when Lepke's lawyers, having read the appeals court's tepid affirmation, appealed to the US Supreme Court to overturn the convictions. Lepke returned to his cell and Dewey bided his time.

In February 1942, Sid Luckman became a father when his son, Robert, was born. Sid rushed a telegram off to the Bear's George Halas, requesting a contract for the 1965 season, the year his son would presumably graduate from college. "OK, if the Bears are still alive then," Halas replied, a reminder that the NFL was still a somewhat shaky proposition. Bobby Luckman was the first boy born to a member of that year's Bears roster, and Luckman's teammates showered the family with "enough gifts—buggies, diapers, trinkets—to get a good-sized family going."

"Estelle has been content to remain in the background," Sid would write later when he was the father of three, "raising a family and maintaining a sane household. It wasn't always easy to put up with a football husband and his many child-like habits." Besides a reference to his coarse dinner-table etiquette, the only childlike habit he dwelled on was his inability to turn down invitations to speak at banquets and to wolf down the meals that went with them.

"Sid," Estelle teased him, "you're getting so you can hardly drink a glass of milk in the house without getting up to offer a toast. I never knew there were so many banqueteers in the country. They don't seem to have anything to do but prepare another party."

In reality, he was too soft-spoken to make a great orator. He was afflicted by the same diffidence that he had needed to correct when it came to calling signals in the huddle. He popped up in the sports pages frequently for little more than showing up and delivering a few remarks. A couple of weeks before his son's birth, he appeared at a dance at the Brooklyn Edison Club to say that he couldn't say much because he was momentarily expecting word of the birth of his first child. At least pro football players, once frowned upon by polite society, were on the map.

"Do you realize that these folks once considered us football bums?" he told Estelle.

"Sid," she said, "the fact is you can't talk about football, much less any other subject, without squirming. You're probably the worst after-dinner speaker in the game. Yet the moment a banquet is mentioned, you're on the spot."

The year had its heartaches off the field. Estelle's mother had died of a heart attack in July, at the age of 59, and Sid's father was in his seventh year in Sing Sing, a man repudiated by his wife, if not banished from her memory, and visited only periodically by his children. Sid now awaited word from the lawyer who was supposedly pulling strings to get Meyer out. In the off-season, Sid did his best to make his brother Leo feel appreciated for all he was doing for the family by running the company, but feelings between them were complicated. While Sid had spun off into another orbit, Leo, Phi Beta Kappa and an all-American himself, remained earthbound in Brooklyn with his uneducated cousins, his fugitive Uncle Ike's children, as partners.

The Bears made it look easy that fall. After their five straight wins to open the 1942 season—over the Packers, Rams, Cardinals, Giants, and Eagles—they shut out four of their last six opponents, outscoring them by an average of 33–2. Their 38–7 victory over the Packers on November 15 was accomplished with what the *Tribune's* Ed Prell called "ridiculous ease" and even featured a 56-yard touchdown run by Sid Luckman after he intercepted a deflected pass.

They were so good that Luckman became playful on the field. In one of their blowouts, with the ball on the one-yard line, 250-pound tackle Ray Bray begged for a chance to score a touchdown, and Luckman had him line up at fullback and gave him the ball. (It's not so uncommon today for bulky lineman to be used for goal-line plunges.) When Bray was stopped for no gain, Luckman said mildly, "OK, get back where you belong, chum." In another game, Luckman let each of his linemen call a play on one drive. When the strategy paid off in a touchdown, they teased him mercilessly about how easy it was to be a quarterback.

The regular season over, the undefeated Bears and the once-defeated Redskins, 10–1 for the season, prepared for a championship rematch back in Washington, DC, on December 13, 1942, two years after the Redskins' ignominious defeat. The Bears had won 39 of their last 40 football games, including exhibitions and all-star games, and were being referred to as "the Dream Team." Arthur Daley of the *New York Times* wrote the Washington team's obituary the day before the game: "What the Monsters from the Midway will do to the capital Braves makes strong men shudder. . . . None but the Washington Braves and a few fanatical rooters can see the slightest hope for George Preston Marshall's team." He called Luckman "a flawless operator and a fine passer" and his backup Charlie O'Rourke "perhaps a better mechanical passer than Luckman but not yet his equal in poise or experience." After calling the Bears' group of running backs "terrifying," Daley noted: "The gamblers have stopped posting odds and have devised a system whereby a bettor can take Washington and 14 points or take Chicago and give 20 points." Then, as if he hadn't intimidated Washington fans sufficiently with his prose, Daley ended his article by recapping each of the 11 touchdowns the Bears had scored against the Redskins in the 1940 title game.

The advance sellout came to a record gate of $113,260.40. The payoff would work out to $966.87 for each member of the winning team, for some a bonus equal to a third of their salaries. The Redskins team accepted only money orders and certified checks as payment for tickets, and local banks complained about the long lines at teller windows. The club turned away more than $200,000 in tickets requests. The cover of the game's program featured the number 310, representing the number of NFL players, coaches, and executives serving in the armed forces.

"Hard-fought" barely describes what happened on the field. There was almost more fisticuffs than football; neither team managed even 200 yards of offense. "Never has there been a game of such intensity," Arthur Daley reported. "Enough punches were thrown to serve for a Madison Square Garden main event as the short-tempered athletes, particularly the Bears, went at it in earnest." The Bears outgained the Redskins and held Sammy Baugh to a paltry 65 yards on five-for-13 passing.

And yet the Bears lost. After gushing touchdowns all season, they came up dry. Only once did the Bears' vaunted "quick-openers" open a hole in the Redskins' defensive line, springing Ray Nolting for 17 yards. Aside from that, it was gridlock at the line of scrimmage. Chicago averaged barely more than a yard and a half per carry. Baugh quick-kicked three times in the first half to pin the Bears deep in their own territory, and although Chicago came close to scoring on a couple of occasions before turning the ball over, their only points in the 14–6 loss came in the second period, when tackle Lee Artoe picked up Dick Todd's fumble and ran 50 yards, untouched, for a touchdown. It was the bizarre antithesis of their 1940 offensive outburst.

Although there was talk in the press that the Bears' concentration had been disrupted by a pregame meeting in which several Bears complained about having to play two weeks later, over Christmas, in the Pro Bowl, pitting the champions against a team of NFL all-stars, Luckman took personal responsibility. He blamed himself for calling too many slow-developing long passes and abandoning the disciplined ball-control game plans that got them where they were. Slow-developing pass plays also gave the Redskins opportunities to avenge 1940 in the most crowd-pleasing way—by sacking Luckman. "I was combing those wild men from Washington out of my hair all afternoon," he said.

"We were great in our own minds," was Luckman's assessment 55 years later. "We felt superior to every other team."

"The Redskins were terrific today," Daley wrote. "The Bears had been handing it out for almost two years but they could not take it when the pressure was on. Sid Luckman, wonder operator of the T-formation, completed five of 12 passes for a total of just 2 yards. He was harried and slammed to earth, treated with such disrespect that one hardly could believe it."

At the end of the bench all George Halas could do, sitting in his naval uniform on weekend leave from Oklahoma, was jut his jaw and keep his mouth shut.

In the *Chicago Tribune* on Monday, Edward Prell's first sentence was, "A football dynasty fell with a thud today on the frozen turf of Griffith Stadium, where two years ago it came into power."

Worse, though, his story wasn't even the lead in the hometown sports section that day, ignominiously taking a back seat to the headline SCHWOEGLER WINS NATIONAL BOWLING TITLE.

20

Casualties

In February 1943, the United States Supreme Court declined to hear an appeal in the case of *Buchalter v. New York*, but it reversed field a month later and granted a review.

The case was argued before the court on May 7 and 10; and three weeks later, on June 1, 1943, seven months after the New York State Court of Appeals had upheld the convictions of Lepke, Capone, and Weiss, the Supreme Court spoke. Justice Owen Roberts delivered the unanimous opinion of the court.

> The petitioners were convicted of first degree murder in the County Court of Kings County, New York, after a trial lasting over nine weeks. The printed record consists of over twelve thousand pages. . . . In his concurring opinion, the Chief Judge said that he agreed with one of the dissenting opinions that errors and defects occurred in the trial which could not be "disregarded without hesitation lest, in our anxiety that the guilty should not escape punishment, we affirm a judgment tainted with errors and obtained through violation of fundamental rights." His conclusion was, however, that the errors did not affect the verdict. . . .

The petitioners rely not on any one circumstance, but insist that they were not afforded a fair and impartial jury free from influences extraneous to the proofs adduced at the trial, that they were deprived of an impartial and unbiased judge to preside at the trial, and that the prosecutor resorted to unfair methods to influence the jury. . . .

The petitioners assert that, in view of unfair and lurid newspaper publicity, it was impossible to obtain an impartial jury in the county of trial, and that the rulings of the court denying a change of venue, and on challenges to prospective jurors, resulted in the impaneling of a jury affected with bias. We have examined the record and are unable, as the court below was, to conclude that a convincing showing of actual bias on the part of the jury which tried the defendants is established. . . .

As already stated, the due process clause of the Fourteenth Amendment does not enable us to review errors of state law, however material under that law. We are unable to find that the rulings and instructions under attack constituted more than errors as to state law. We cannot say that they were such as to deprive the petitioners of a trial according to the accepted course of legal proceedings. . . .

As we have recently said, "it is not asking too much that the burden of showing essential unfairness be sustained by him who claims such injustice and seeks to have the result set aside, and that it be sustained not as a matter of speculation, but as a demonstrable reality."

The judgments are *Affirmed*.

That should have been it, but the ruling was only the beginning of what Burton Turkus, who had won Lepke's conviction, would later call "probably the longest and certainly the most bizarre and needless controversy ever waged between national and state authorities over one man. . . . The developments were so weird they left any number of observers with the distinct impression that persons in very high places were most meticulous about keeping this underworld king, with seventy murders on his tally sheet, from the electric chair he so justly deserved."

Lepke became a political football that the United States government and the newly elected governor of New York, Thomas Dewey, punted back and forth for months. Dewey and Turkus needed the federal government to pardon Lepke so that New York could claim him and put him, finally, to death. But the Roosevelt administration had every reason to drag its feet. Putting America's most wanted criminal to death would enhance Dewey's chances of winning the Republican presidential nomination in the summer of 1944 and the White House in the fall. Furthermore, Dewey suspected that President Roosevelt's close labor adviser Sidney Hillman had turned a blind eye to mob interference in the garment industry when he was the president of the Amalgamated Clothing Workers Union and had even cut a deal with Lepke to keep the peace in the 1930s. If Lepke, back in New York's custody, were to testify to that fact, he might save his own life and put a Republican back in the White House.

On July 8, 1943, the New York District Attorney's Office appealed directly to US attorney general Francis Biddle to release Lepke to the state. On July 10, the US Department of Justice refused, then a week later it announced that it would produce Lepke for resentencing for murder. On July 20, Lepke, Capone, and Weiss were resentenced to death by New York, their punishment to be carried out at Sing Sing during the week of September 13, but the feds nonetheless failed to deliver Lepke yet again. On September 2, Governor Dewey demanded that President Roosevelt pardon Lepke. A new execution date was set for October 18. When Roosevelt failed to release Lepke by October 14, a new date was set for November 29. On November 20, Dewey accused Roosevelt of protecting Lepke by refusing to grant him "the customary unconditional" federal pardon. A fourth new date for execution was set for January 3, 1944. On November 30,

Attorney General Biddle refused to formally request that Roosevelt commute Lepke's sentence. It was the second anniversary of Lepke's conviction, and Americans could be forgiven for believing that the mobster would never be strapped into Old Sparky. On New Year's Day, 1944, Governor Dewey postponed the executions a fifth time, to February 6.

Dewey challenged the Roosevelt administration in the press, asking whether it was unwilling to turn Lepke over to Dewey for execution because it was afraid the country would discover something very unpleasant about FDR if Dewey got his hands on Lepke. And if it did turn him over, Attorney General Biddle wanted Dewey's assurance that Lepke would be executed promptly—that is, before he had a chance to talk.

Dewey replied that his own demand for Lepke was unconditional. If Roosevelt wanted to hold on to him, it would be his sole responsibility if Lepke happened to escape. Given public opinion, Roosevelt really had no choice now and turned Lepke over to Dewey, at which point Dewey in effect taunted Roosevelt by granting a series of reprieves to postpone the electrocution of Lepke and his two cronies, Louis Capone and Mendy Weiss, who had been waiting for him at Sing Sing for the last year and a half.

When the 1943 NFL season began, Meyer Luckman's chances of not dying in prison were growing smaller. The lawyer to whom Sid Luckman had paid an exorbitant retainer still had not been able to make any progress. Only in rare cases could a commutation of or a pardon for a state prison sentence come directly from the US president or vice president, so Meyer Luckman's fate was most likely in the hands of New York's governor. But agreeing to any form of leniency for him would only undercut Governor Dewey's current winning streak

of mob convictions and look hypocritical in light of his hard line
with the feds regarding Lepke.

Sid Luckman continued to bear his burden in silence. During the summer of 1943, he kept busy tutoring several colleges, including his alma
mater, in the nuances of the T formation. When Columbia coach Lou
Little hired him to conduct a clinic on the T formation for the school's
football coaches, Luckman donated the paycheck to its scholarship
fund. He told Coach Little that at the University of Pittsburgh all he
had had to work with were 17-year-olds and 4-Fs—those deemed unfit
for military service—but he had been impressed by their determination. World War II didn't ruin football, but it certainly put the sport in
some perspective as the sublimated combat that it was. Luckman, who
so far enjoyed a military deferment as a father and sole breadwinner,
told Arthur Daley of the *Times* that he couldn't begin to predict what
would happen to the Bears in the fall, as he ticked off the team's wartime "casualties": "Since last year we've lost Stydahar, Kolman, Artoe,
O'Rourke, Gallarneau, Bray, Nowaskey, Pool, Petty, Maznicki, and
maybe Fortmann. However, we should have Turner, Clarke, McLean,
Nolting and Famiglietti returning. Osmanski and Siegal are full-fledged
dentists now and they may be available. And we've picked up Jim Benton and Dante Magnani from Cleveland, which was so short-handed it
had to suspend operations for the season." Luckman even talked, once
again, about going into the trucking business. So many players had gone
to war that the Pittsburgh Steelers and Philadelphia Eagles had to join
forces to field an NFL-quality team, now called the "Steagles," which
won half its games. In the same column, Daley seemed to acknowledge
how different the world was, relegating the Bears' superiority to the past
tense: "The Bears were the best football team in the world in their day
and no one knew it better than they."

In 1943, the quality of play across the NFL declined for every team, yet the Bears were once again the best team in the league: they scored the most points, gave up the second-fewest, and gained 600 yards more than the next best offensive team, the Green Bay Packers. In a season that produced the fewest passing yards since 1937, Sid Luckman's passing statistics took a considerable leap forward. Until 1943, Luckman had not come close to being the league's best passer statistically; from 1940 to 1942, he'd lagged well behind both Sammy Baugh and Green Bay's Cecil Isbell in both yardage and touchdown passes. Now, with George Halas in the navy, Halas's replacements Luke Johnsos and Hunk Anderson let Luckman, in his words, "go hog-wild on passes." In one game fewer than the number he had played the year before, he threw for more than twice the number of yards, a career-record 2,194; and almost three times the number of touchdowns, a league-record and career-best 28.

After tying the Packers at Green Bay to open the season, Chicago won six straight before heading to the Polo Grounds for a game against the 2–2–1 Giants on November 14, billed as "Sid Luckman Day." Although the Bears quarterback wouldn't turn 27 for another week, he had been making headlines in New York for more than a decade. The game would also serve as a hometown send-off for Luckman, who would be joining the war effort as a merchant marine after the season; for the next two years, he wouldn't be able to practice with the team but would arrange to play with them on Sundays as often as possible.

Before the game Luckman was presented with two $1,000 war bonds, one from his admirers in Brooklyn and Chicago, the other from his fellow football players. "For what earthly reasons," Luckman whispered to teammate George Wilson during the ceremony, "are these fans giving a thousand bucks to a high-priced pro who probably needs it much less than they do?"

"If football fans want to go sentimental," Wilson replied, "who are we to complain?"

Any sentimentality on the part of Giants fans was short-lived. Luckman not only did not reciprocate New York's hospitality but chose Sid Luckman Day to have the single best game of his long career. Perhaps his archrival was on his mind; two weeks earlier, Sammy Baugh had thrown a record six touchdown passes against the NFL's Brooklyn Dodgers. In five games, Baugh had already passed for 15 touchdowns while Luckman had thrown for 17 in seven games. In light of his own poor performance in the 1942 championship game, Luckman was especially motivated to prove himself against one of the league's better teams.

Sid was inspired by the presence of almost 57,000 hometown fans in the same stadium where Benny Friedman had once shown him how to grip a football. In the first quarter, he passed to Jim Benton for a four-yard touchdown. Connie Mack Berry caught a 31-yard touchdown toss. Hampton Pool scored on a 27-yard sideline route. In the second half, George McAfee and George Wilson crisscrossed, clearing out for Harry Clarke to haul in a 62-yard touchdown pass. The T formation had never looked more unstoppable, receivers flooding the field. Benton, again, caught a looping 15-yard Luckman pass in the corner of the end zone. Coach Hunk Anderson attempted to replace Luckman with backup quarterback Bob Snyder, and spare the Giants further humiliation, but Luckman's teammates rebuffed him, smelling a passing record they wanted to be part of. In the fourth quarter, Wilson caught a three-yarder, Luckman's sixth touchdown pass. Late in the game, on the Giants' 40-yard line, Pool ran a deep post pattern from the right side, and three Giants defenders closed in on him; Luckman had no other option but to let the ball fly. Miraculously—it was that kind of day—Pool leaped and outfought the defenders for the ball at the 10, then pivoted away for Luckman's seventh touchdown toss of the game.

The Bears crushed a solid Giants team by an embarrassing score of 56–7, and Luckman had treated everyone to something no one had ever done before. A smaller ball, a better team, and a talented quarterback converged in an unprecedented passing performance. Seven touchdown passes in a game wouldn't be equaled for another 11 years. Luckman passed for well over three times the league's average yards, while completing 66 percent of his passes during a season when quarterbacks averaged well under 50 percent. The team set five more single-game records that day: most yards gained by a team (702); most yards passing by a team (508); most yards passing by one man (453); most touchdowns by a team (eight); and most extra points (eight). "If they had added a broad jump or pole vault to the program," William Richardson quipped in the *New York Times*, "he probably would've broken those marks also." As the *Chicago Tribune*'s Ed Prell wrote the next morning, "Sid Luckman, the kid who used to chuck a cheap football while dodging automobiles in the streets of Brooklyn, today pitched a pigskin as it was never pitched before."

And he had done it against a team whose coach, Steve Owen, was an acknowledged master of defense. Although he was an earthbound coach—averse to the possibility of gaining many yards quickly with a forward pass—Owen had once coveted Luckman. "Make no mistake about it," Owen had said when Luckman was playing for Lou Little at Columbia. "Luckman is one of the best passers in the East. I can't see a weakness in him. I'd grab him for the Giants in a second."

After the game, Luckman made his way to the Giants' locker room to apologize to Owen for running up the score. He told Owen that his teammates wouldn't let Hunk take him out of the game until near the end.

"If I'm gonna be beaten," Owen told him, "that's the way I want it done. I don't want anyone to feel sorry and kick on first down.

Since it had to happen, I'm genuinely glad you were the one that did it. That's what I think of you."

A few minutes later, in the Bears' locker room, 35-year-old Bronko Nagurski, who had been lured out of retirement to help the war-depleted Bears, tried to keep the game ball. Luckman couldn't tell whether the big man was teasing as he pleaded with Nagurski: "Let me have this ball, and I'll buy twenty others for you. For God's sake, if I never keep a football again, I've got to have this one. Gotta show it to my offspring."

"OK, sure, kid," Nagurski replied with a smile, gently tucking the ball in Luckman's arms.

The Bears' victory was another emblem of their offensive dominance during the era of the smaller football. Between 1935 and 1945, NFL teams averaged just over 15 points a game, while the Bears averaged 22. During Luckman's nine peak seasons, 1940–48, the team scored an average of more than 28 points a game.

The Sid Luckman Day rout of the New York Giants provided Sid with more than records: it gave him one of his favorite memories. He had called his mother from Chicago a few days before the game and convinced her to attend with his brother and sister. During the game, there was so little cheering from local fans as the Bears ran up the score that Sid could hear his entourage hollering its support from the box seats. As he dropped back to pass on one third-down play, his pass protection broke down for once, and the Giants' huge defensive linemen were chasing him out of the pocket.

"*Sideleh! Sideleh!*" he heard someone screaming in the stands.

It was his mother, shrieking in Yiddish: "*Gebn zey di pilke, Sideleh!* Give them the ball, Sidney! You're going to get hurt! Let them have the ball!" At the end of his life, Sidney was still laughing about it.

21

A Surprising Comment

L uckman was careful in his 1949 autobiography to explain that the team's success in passing was the result of plenty of hard work, teamwork, and analysis. Today, the most casual fan takes for granted the complexity of the passing game and the defenses against it, but Luckman needed to spell it out for a readership whose understanding of football was still mired in a simpler era. After workouts at Wrigley, he wrote,

> I would sit down with the boys and discuss each obstacle—how the secondaries are employed, how this halfback or that operates against a receiver, which of our plays have worked best lately, and whether the enemy's fullback [middle linebacker], stationed just back of scrimmage, will pull over on flat passes. Take that last case—if the fullback does shift his position, then the thing to do is fake a pass to the right and then slam it down the middle to a guy like "Rabbit" McLean, who can grab it and break away in a hurry. Hour after hour, these tactical plays were taken up, though many of them would be altered during a game, since some defenses have the ornery habit of switching from their familiar styles when you least expect it.

After the Giants game, Luckman remained behind in Flatbush for a couple of days to visit his family. The house on Cortelyou Road had been refurnished. Ethel, of course, was overjoyed to have everyone together again. "We still ribbed one another good-naturedly," Sid recalled in his autobiography. "Otherwise we were a good sight more settled and surer of ourselves." His brother Leo now had 33 trucks, while Dave was a successful young salesman for Gimbel's department store and being groomed for bigger things. Blanche was married to Harry Fleischer, and had had a baby, Myrna. And Sid and Estelle dandled nine-month-old Bobby. "This night," Luckman recalled, "they generously forgot their personal problems and began to rave about the Giant–Bear game. It was replayed almost in its entirety in that living room on Cortelyou Street."

Dave, who still lived with Ethel, told Sid that the touch-football kids in the neighborhood kept pestering her for his address so they could write to him for advice. Dave took Sid over to the small lot where they now played their games. In his book, Sid recounts discovering that the T formation's more wide-open style of football had trickled down to the sandlots. The best player, an elusive kid named Boodey, came over and said, "Show us how, Sid. Come out and show us."

"Kid, you don't need me," Sid said, content to watch. "Why, you showed me a few stunts out there I'd like to copy myself."

"You're not so bad yourself, big-timer," the kid said, with typical Brooklyn moxie, as the others crowded around. "But I don't see how you missed that last-quarter pass against New York the other day."

"Which one?"

"Where Wilson was supposed to catch it in the end zone. You had the ball on their thirty-yard line. It was third down."

"Well, I tried my best," Luckman said, "but they had me covered there. You should've known that. Did you see the game?"

"I'll say. Saved up for three weeks from my newspaper route."

"Boodey," another boy interjected, "how many touchdowns did you expect Sid to throw? Ain't seven enough?"

"I still hate to see a guy miss a cincher like that. Wilson was waitin' out there all alone."

It wasn't lost on Sid that with all the newspapers trumpeting his seven touchdowns, he had to come to his own Brooklyn neighborhood to find critics. Boodey wasn't the only one, it turned out. Once the kids saw it was open season on Sid Luckman, another boy cited a missed first down in the second quarter, and yet another complained that the coach had pulled Scooter McLean out of the game just when he was going great guns.

The next day, the family dined at the famed Toots Shor's on 51st Street in Manhattan, where Toots joined them and even ordered "a special home-style plate fixed up for Ma." Ever the fan, Toots looked Luckman up and down, saying, "By God, Sid, you were in action fifty minutes yesterday, and there's not a scratch on you." He turned to Leo. "Seems to me Sid's takin' less knocks now than he did at Columbia. I used to invite him down to my place with Oscar Bonom and Art Radvilas, and the three of them usually had faces that looked like overdone pot roast."

"Look at his right leg," said Ethel, the mother who had been opposed to this football thing all along.

"Don't be bashful, Sid," Toots said with a belly laugh. "Lift your trouser leg and show us the scars. You're among friends."

In Sid's book at this point, eight years and more than 100 pages of memoir have passed since the last mention of Meyer Luckman. Now he reappeared, but only as the subject of one of Sid's many lies to explain his father's absence from the family. Luckman writes that his mother "had been alone since Dad Luckman passed away early in 1943." But in 1943, Meyer Luckman was alive in Sing Sing, though not in good health. Describing that visit back on Cortelyou Road, Sid continued his invented story: "She poured a glass of sweet wine for me in the kitchen, and as I was sipping it, she made a most surprising comment: 'You know, Sid, Pa would have loved to see this game. How proud he would have been.'"

The Bears seemed to have used up their offensive brilliance in New York. The team stumbled badly in Washington the following week, on Luckman's 27th birthday, losing 21–7 to the undefeated Redskins, even though an injured Sammy Baugh could make only occasional appearances and the Redskins gained only 44 yards in the air. Luckman threw his 24th touchdown pass of the season, but, pressured again by the Redskins' pass rush, he also threw three interceptions. This didn't bode well, especially since it looked as if the Bears might play the Redskins yet again in the championship game a month hence, provided Washington could beat out New York for the Eastern Division title and the Bears could beat the winless Cardinals at Comiskey Park in their final regular-season game.

Against the hopeless Cardinals, the Bears looked as if they might have been playing over their heads all along, even in a depleted league. Luckman, weakened by a bout of flu earlier in the week, had checked out of the hospital against doctors' orders and got the team in hot water by throwing a first-quarter interception that quickly resulted in a Cardinals touchdown. Down 24–14 at the beginning of the fourth quarter, and about to end up in a tie for first place with the Packers, Luckman supplied two fourth-quarter touchdowns—his third and fourth of the game. Reclamation project Bronko Nagurski did the rest. Earlier in the season, the 35-year-old fullback, who had last played in 1937, had barely got his uniform dirty in part-time blocking during previous games. Thanks to injuries to first-string running backs, he volunteered this day for fullback duty, a dubious proposition considering his old legs. Amazingly, he contributed 84 yards on 15 carries and helped carry the Bears to a 35–24 come-from-behind win and another championship date with the Washington Redskins, this time at home.

A full house of 34,320 fans showed up the day after Christmas for Chicago's fourth straight championship appearance and a resumption of the duel between the league's two marquee passers. Early on, the Bears sent Baugh to the sideline, and the perpetrator was none other than Luckman himself. In the first period, Baugh punted and Luckman, who returned punts only 11 times in his career, took the ball near the sideline and headed upfield, where Baugh confronted him after a 20-yard return. Perhaps it never would have happened had Halas still been on the sidelines and not in the navy. The two most valuable players in the NFL collided and went down, but only Luckman got up. Baugh had to be carried from the field and didn't return until the third quarter, at which point, according to Luckman, Baugh said to him during a time-out, "Ah admired that hip or knee you handed out, Sid. Guess Ah lost track of the fact you used to be a fair ball carrier." No doubt Baugh's actual language was less genteel.

Ironically, Luckman, who very rarely carried the ball during his career, and would end it with a negative 1.2 yards per attempt, was about to have by far his best day as a rusher in the pros, leading the team with 64 yards on eight carries, 30 yards more than the next best rusher, Nagurski. With Baugh on the bench for half the game, Luckman completed 15 of 26 passes for 286 yards and five touchdowns, two more than anyone had ever thrown in a title game, although, to be fair, two of them were short swing passes that Dante Magnani turned into long touchdowns. Luckman threw no interceptions, and he intercepted two Redskins passes himself. With Nagurski plowing his way for some valuable yards while yelling, "Let the farmer through!"—it would be his last football game—the Bears avenged their recent losses to Washington with a 41–21 victory that wasn't even as close as the score would indicate.

Luckman considered it the best game he had ever played, more masterly than the 73–0 game or even the 56–7 extravaganza six weeks before. Despite Luckman's early wildness, statistically it was one of the better all-around individual football performances ever. "Now the championship is back where it should have stayed all the time," Bears captain Bob Snyder said in the locker room afterward. "What right have those Redskins to our championship, even for one season?"

Three months later, in March 1944, Redskins owner George Preston Marshall finally decided that if he couldn't lick the founders of the modern T formation, he would join them, hiring Clark Shaughnessy as an adviser to teach the T to the team's new head coach. No one was happier about the change than Sammy Baugh. "I switched from a single-wing tailback to a T-formation quarterback in 1944, and that was the most difficult thing I'd ever had to do in my football career," Baugh would remember. "The hardest parts were the simple things, like just taking the ball from the center, turning and faking to one man, and then giving it to another. You had to have such precision working out of the T. Hell, I remember talking to Sid Luckman one time, and he told me when he switched over to the T at the Bears he darn near cried it was so damn frustrating." On the other hand, Baugh said, "Actually the T was good for me. I'd played about ten or eleven years of single-wing ball, counting college, and I figured I only could go maybe another year or two as a tailback. Hell, I was getting beat up and hurt all the time. Never had a broken bone but I was hurt a lot. But with the T formation, that enabled me to play another seven or eight years."

By the following fall, Ensign Sidney Luckman had completed a 12-week course at the U.S. Maritime Service Training Station at Sheepshead Bay in Brooklyn, not far from his family and within relatively easy commuting distance to Sing Sing, which was about to receive, after a protracted wait, its most famous prisoner to date.

22

Last Dance

On January 21, 1944, Louis "Lepke" Buchalter was handcuffed to corrections officer John McAvoy and loaded into a black bulletproof sedan at the Federal House of Detention in lower Manhattan. He was accustomed to captivity after two years in hiding and another four in federal prison. Up the West Side Elevated Highway they rode, up into the Bronx, where Lepke had been driven in the fall of 1937 to inform Max Rubin that he had already lived to a ripe old age, only to have Rubin survive a bullet to the back of the head—so that, instead of Lepke putting Max Rubin away, Max Rubin had survived to put Lepke away. They drove up through Yonkers, where his men had told Walter Winchell to go to make sure he wasn't being followed on the night Lepke turned himself in.

Up through Hastings-on-Hudson, Dobbs Ferry, Irvington, Tarrytown, and Sleepy Hollow they drove, little piles of snow everywhere. Finally, they arrived at Sing Sing, the rambling fortress overlooking the Hudson, looking more like a factory than a prison. It wasn't Lepke's first visit; in 1918 he had served a year and a half there for robbery. The sedan pulled up at the curb in front of the death house, and when its big barred doors swung open for them, Lepke was walked up the steps between McAvoy and another detective. Three more detectives trotted behind while yet another stayed with the sedan. They all wore dark overcoats and fedoras, except for Lepke, who was hatless.

The mug shot of prisoner 102894 shows a mild-looking, clean-shaven man with short brown hair parted on the left side, wearing a white shirt, tie, and chalk-striped suit jacket. The photo's accompanying admission record, filled out in black typescript, is chillingly terse about Louis Buchalter, whose aliases are listed as "Lepke," "Buckhouse," "Cohen," "Kauver," and "Louis Cohen." His crime is listed as "Verd Murder 1st," his term as "EXECUTION," and his criminal act as: "Joseph Rosen—prop. candy store—day—gun—because he threatened to disclose Buchalter's racketeering activities to district attorney of NY county." Once Lepke was processed, he was taken to a cell in the death house on a different corridor from Weiss and Capone, whom he was allowed neither to see nor to speak to.

Elsewhere in Sing Sing that day, in the prison hospital, Meyer Luckman was suffering from the late stages of heart failure. Like everyone else, he had heard the news of Lepke's arrival. His time has come too, Luckman must have thought. But Lepke and his lawyers were hardly ready to give up. They played his few remaining cards for all they were worth in the next few weeks. In this, he had an ally in New York's ambitious governor, Thomas Dewey. Having broken the back of Murder, Inc., Dewey and his successor as Manhattan district attorney, Frank Hogan, hoped to break Lepke and make a deal that would expel Lepke from the death house and propel Dewey into the White House. With Lepke at last in New York State's custody, no longer sheltered by the federal government, his lawyers leaped into desperate action. First, they asked for a new trial because Judge Franklin Taylor had been "prejudicial." Denied this, the lawyers for Lepke, Weiss, and Capone asked for a special commission to investigate the facts but were turned down again. The execution was rescheduled yet again, for March 2. The executioner, Joseph Francel, was told to report to work on that night, a Thursday, the night when Sing Sing traditionally executed prisoners, at 11 o'clock.

Lepke played his penultimate card, telling DA Hogan on Wednesday, March 1, that he wanted to talk. "If I would talk," he had once said, "a lot of big people would get hurt. When I say big, I mean big. The names would surprise you." The sensational threat to talk had kept him on front pages, and kept several prominent men up at night. Hogan hurried to Sing Sing, hopeful that the prospect of imminent death really had loosened Lepke's tongue, and spent an hour and a half in his cell. When he left, he said nothing to anyone. The *New York Mirror* reported, "It is said Lepke offered material to Governor Dewey that would make him an unbeatable presidential candidate." In fact, Lepke had delivered nothing of value, none of the incriminating revelations that had been rumored: a murder by a nationally prominent labor leader, a conspiracy charge against a high-ranking New York City official, the relative of a high-ranking officeholder who was a front for two crime lords. "Lepke knew what he was doing every minute," Hogan said later. "He knew just how far to go—and we knew pretty fast that we weren't going to get anywhere with him."

Expecting Lepke to talk was a bad bet. If he had talked, he would have been no better than Kid Twist Reles, than Tick-Tock Tannenbaum, than Sholem Bernstein, Mikey Syckoff, and dozens of others. Not talking was the difference between him and everyone else. Not talking was what made Lepke Lepke. Besides, if he had told Hogan anything that compromised his syndicate associates, his wife, Betty, and their adored adopted son, Harold, would never have been safe. Hoodwinked, Hogan returned to the city, and Lepke and the others prepared to die.

On the night of March 2, all three were shaved, bathed, dressed in traditional execution attire—black pants, white socks, slippers—and

served their last meal. Lepke ordered roast chicken, shoestring pota-
toes, lettuce and tomato salad, rolls, and coffee. As if to express their
undying loyalty to him, Weiss and Capone ordered the same. Rabbi
Jacob Katz, Sing Sing's Jewish chaplain, visited Lepke and Weiss.
When they were taken to the pre-execution cell known as the Dance
Hall, 25 feet from the execution chamber, Lepke, Capone, and Weiss
still couldn't see one another, but they could talk. "Something can
happen yet!" Lepke told them. "I can feel it."

A little more than an hour before the scheduled executions,
something did happen. Lepke's last move had been to seek a writ of
habeas corpus on the grounds that his transfer from the feds to the
state was illegal. The federal district court and circuit court of appeals
turned him down, and he appealed to the US Supreme Court, which
agreed to hear his final appeal but not until Saturday. As a courtesy,
Governor Dewey granted him and the others a two-day stay of execution, now set for Saturday night, March 4. If it took place, it would be
the first Saturday night execution in 27 years. Meanwhile, two other
men waiting to die that night, for killing a detective in Brooklyn 15
months earlier, 26-year-old Joseph Palmer and 28-year-old Vincent
Sallami, were executed on schedule.

Lepke, a man who never enjoyed the spotlight, was a bigger story
than the war, even in the august *New York Times*. LEPKE GETS 2-DAY STAY
TO PERMIT A NEW APPEAL; HAS A TALK WITH HOGAN, read the lead
front-page headline on March 3, given equal weight with U.S. UNITS
REPEL FOE ABOVE ANZIO, ERASE GAINS UNDER VAST AIR COVER; ALLIES CUT
OFF ARMS FOR TURKEY. In the Dance Hall, the men entertained a steady
stream of visitors. To his wife, Betty, Lepke dictated a statement that
she took down on a legal pad and read to reporters on the afternoon
of March 4 at Ossining's Depot Square Hotel, where the press had
been gathering, waiting for Lepke's end.

"I wrote this down, word for word," Betty told the reporters. "He said, 'I am anxious to have it clearly understood that I did not offer to talk and give information in exchange for any promise of commutation of my death sentence. I did not ask for that! The one and only thing I have asked for is to have a commission appointed to examine the facts. If that examination does not show that I am not guilty, I am willing to go to the chair, regardless of what information I have given or can give.'"

On the afternoon of March 4, reporters listened to the announcement on the radio that the US Supreme Court had denied the men's appeal. After the ghoulish déjà vu of another last meal, they were readied for death. Three dozen reporters and witnesses filed into the death chamber and waited. Joseph Francel took his place, out of view of everyone. At 10:55 p.m., the warden checked for a last time with Governor Dewey's mansion in Albany, only to be told there was no news.

Louis Capone went first, because the authorities didn't want a man with a heart condition to die prematurely of a coronary at the news that Lepke had been put to death. At a couple of minutes after 11, Capone emerged from the hallway connecting his cell to the execution chamber and, saying nothing, sat down in the chair, which had electrocuted its first four prisoners in July 1891 and would execute its last, its 614th, a higher number than any other prison's, in 1963. A few minutes later Capone's body was wheeled out to the autopsy room, and Mendy Weiss entered the chamber, chewing gum, and was strapped to the chair. He, alone among the three, spoke. "I am here on a framed-up case, and Governor Dewey knows it," he announced, before the head electrode was lowered into place. "I want to thank Judge Lehman. He knows me because I am a Jew. Give my love to my family and everything."

Weiss's body was wheeled out to make room for Lepke. Burton Turkus described Buchalter's gait as "brisk, almost defiant" and could not resist a last reference to his eyes. "The collie-dog softness was no longer in Lepke's eyes as he strode into the harsh chamber that reminded one newsman of a chapel." Lepke sat in the chair and surveyed the room as he was strapped in and the electrode was attached to his bare leg through the slit made in his pants. He was imperturbable and all business, as always, and, moments later, became the first organized crime boss to be legally executed in the United States and the last to date.

The syndicate, Turkus wrote later, "had lost its first major figure to the Law. Ironically, for all his power and his killings, it was the murder of a little man that caught up with Lepke, and ended him."

In death, Lepke got front-page treatment in the Sunday *New York Times*, taking precedence over the first US bombing of Berlin. LEPKE IS PUT TO DEATH, DENIES GUILT TO LAST; MAKES NO REVELATION, read the headline. "The people of the State of New York," read Alexander Feinberg's lead, "closed a long-due account last night."

Lepke was given an Orthodox Jewish burial the next afternoon in Mount Hebron Cemetery in Flushing, Queens, and laid to rest next to the mother who had left him years before to move to Colorado. Only his wife; his adopted son, Harold; and two of his brothers watched his plain wooden casket lowered into the grave. Harold, who would live to be 76, was thereafter known to many as Harold Wasserman, taking the surname of his birth father, Jacob Wasserman, who had died in 1928.

Several days later, Louis Capone, described in the *New York Daily News* as "the fat fingerman for the late Louis (Lepke) Buchalter," was buried in Brooklyn's Holy Cross Cemetery. Only a few "underworld-lings" attended, according to the police, and the newspaper compared the skeleton crowd with attendance at the lavish funeral of gangster

Frankie Yale 16 years earlier. "There were no police mingling with the mourners," the article reported, "seeking to discover a slayer, as had been done with Yale. The state, not gangland guns, had done Capone in."

"Well, they certainly tried everything," New York's Mayor La Guardia quipped to the *Times*, alluding to the six reprieves Lepke had been granted.

Turkus put the long ordeal into somber perspective, alluding to the man who would redefine human evil: "With the international gangster still to be brought to justice, a process which will cost the lives of thousands of innocent persons, the passing of Lepke is of comparatively little significance." He could not yet know that the Nazis would murder six million Jews and that, all told, the war Hitler started would cost at least 10 times as many lives.

In his 1951 book, Turkus thrust Lepke's death further into historical, almost cosmic perspective, writing, "In dealing with national organized crime, it must always be remembered that no matter how many ganglords and torpedoes are eliminated today, a new crop flowers tomorrow.... Already the Lepkes, the Al Capones, the Buggsy [*sic*] Siegels are shadows. But when they fell, the holes were quickly filled and mob business went on as usual. For, though the faces change, the blueprint remains indelible."

The faces of the good guys changed too, of course, but not so abruptly. In 1945, Brooklyn district attorney William O'Dwyer became New York's mayor. Soon after being reelected in 1949, he was politically destroyed by the kind of racket he had once crushed: a new Brooklyn district attorney, Miles F. McDonald, exposed a scandal involving hundreds of New York police officers who were on the payroll of one Harry Gross of Flatbush, who operated a $20 million-a-year illegal gambling empire that employed more than 400 bookies. The scandal forced O'Dwyer's resignation in 1950, and questions about his association with organized crime dogged him until his death in 1964.

In 1944, New York governor Thomas Dewey won the Republican nomination for president, getting his chance to defeat Franklin Roosevelt, but lost the election by a wide electoral vote. In 1948, Dewey ran again, against Harry Truman, but was victimized by his own complacency about a predicted landslide, and lost again. Dewey would eventually die of a heart attack on a golfing trip to Florida in 1971.

For two months in the summer of 1952, Brooklyn assistant district attorney Burton Turkus was host of a weekly ABC television program, *Mr. Arsenic*, that provided inside information on real-life, headline-making crimes. "Mr. Arsenic" was the name Turkus had been given by contract murderer Buggsy Goldstein, one of the first two mobsters to die in the electric chair. "That Turkus," Buggsy had quipped to a reporter during his murder trial, "they oughta call him Mr. Arsenic. He's poison."

Meyer Luckman had missed all of Lepke's 11th-hour machinations and maneuverings. Just two days after Lepke arrived at Sing Sing, Meyer Luckman died of heart failure in the prison hospital at the age of 67. We'll never know whether any of his children was there at the end. Although he was a minnow in the sea of crime and corruption that had engulfed New York City for so long, his crime had earned him a modicum of renown, and his death made newspapers across the country. The *New York Times* certainly hadn't forgotten him, running a short obituary on page 21 of the January 25, 1944, edition, next to a story about a Brooklyn housewife who was awarded $400 in a lawsuit against two butchers who had overcharged her a total of $1.11, in violation of rules set by the US Office of Price Administration.

The 250-word story was headlined MEYER LUCKMAN DIES IN SING SING HOSPITAL. The subheading read, "One of Slayers in Notorious Drukman Crime Is Heart Victim." The sinister synchronicity of the event didn't elude the reporter: "Meyer Luckman was an associate of Louis (Lepke) Buchalter who, oddly enough, was admitted to the death house in Sing Sing prison only a few days ago." The Drukman murder case, readers were reminded, "precipitated a political crisis. . . . The motive for the killing was Drukman's alleged diversion of a few garage checks to get money for racing wagers, but other checks and other vouchers that turned up in the case started the political and public furore."

In its own front-page story, the *Brooklyn Daily Eagle* reprised some of the gruesome details of the crime, in which "Drukman was beaten to death with a loaded billiard cue after being trussed in a self-strangling killer's noose. . . . The names of Meyer and Harry Luckman had been linked with that of Louis Lepke Buchalter, now in the Sing Sing death house, after belated surrender of him by federal authorities. The Drukman murder, trial juries were told, was patterned after the methods used by killers of the Lepke mob."

The *Eagle*, however, contained a piece of information not available elsewhere. It noted that Meyer Luckman, who would not have been eligible for parole for another five and a half years, died "just when a petition asking for his release was being prepared."

Perhaps Sid Luckman's expensive effort to free his father had been about to bear fruit.

The obituary didn't mention that Meyer Luckman had a surviving wife or four surviving children, one of whom was now, for football fans, a household name.

In another 54 years, obituary writers returned the favor, and not a single one of Sid Luckman's death notices and prominent obituaries mentioned his father.

A week after Meyer Luckman's death on January 23, the man whose father had never seen him play in college or the pros was voted the National Football League's most valuable player of 1943.

23

Bingo Keep It

In winning the MVP award, Sid Luckman edged out Green Bay Packer end Don Hutson, who had won it the previous two years. Green Bay coach Curly Lambeau remarked in the newspapers that "playing against Luckman is like playing against a team with a coach on the field."

His enlistment in the US Merchant Marine interfered only intermittently with the 1944 season. Ensign Sidney Luckman of the merchant marine drew a short furlough from a sympathetic officer and made the trip to Green Bay for the opener, where several Packer fans, enraged that Luckman had been granted the privilege of facing their team, heckled him badly. He remembered the experience as "the most disturbing thing I ever faced in my career." Although Luckman threw three touchdown passes to help the Bears come back from an early 28–0 deficit, he was jittery and the Packers won 42–28. A week later, he was aboard the SS *Christy Payne* on a coastal mission from Portland, Maine, to New York as an assistant purser and pharmacist's mate. Four days after docking, he was back in uniform at Wrigley Field, tossing one touchdown pass in a 28–21 victory over the Cleveland Rams. On the next four Sundays, he was in a Bears uniform to throw two touchdown passes and score another on a one-yard quarterback sneak to shut out Green Bay in a rematch, 21–0, then throw three touchdowns against the Boston Yanks, two more against Detroit, and another against Philadelphia.

All in all, he managed to appear in seven of the team's 10 games, completing half of his passes, and Chicago's 6–3–1 finish was good for second place. But the 1944 season—and Luckman's 11 touchdown passes—deserved a big fat asterisk. Nineteen of the 28 Bears from the 1943 roster were gone. Two of Chicago's wins, by a combined score of 83–14, were over the wartime consolidation of the Chicago Cardinals and the Pittsburgh Steelers into a winless collection of remnants called the Card-Pitts, mocked as the Car-Pits, on which the rest of the league also wiped their feet. Luckman had already noticed the decline in the quality of play during 1943, but the 1944 team had to be cobbled together from spare parts. "We held tryouts and signed up anybody who could run around the field twice," co-coach Luke Johnsos recalled. "We had players forty, fifty years old. We had a very poor ball club." Good college players were all in the military and so were many of the best pros. "The balance of power generally shifted to service teams," Luckman wrote, "made up of the cream of civilian stars, including a host of pros."

In February 1945, Luckman made the first of three roughly one-month foreign voyages on the ship *Marine Raven* as assistant purser, assigned to the ship's accounts, payroll, and customs paperwork. In his autobiography, Luckman remembers seven overseas trips, transporting wounded servicemen and delivering ammunition and rations, but the US Coast Guard records show only three foreign trips, including a final one in July 1945, when Luckman had been promoted to chief purser.

Luckman recalled, presumably with far more accuracy, the night that he was awakened by three rings of the *Marine Raven's* bells, which he construed as the signal for an attack by German U-boats. He dressed in seconds and raced to the sailors' quarters, shouting, "Wake up, fellas! This is it! Attack!" It took his lieutenant to finally subdue him and explain that three bells were merely the signal for a change of watch. A few days later, on leave in liberated Paris, he was rudely awakened again, this time to the anonymity of celebrated American athletes. No one knew who he was. The real hero was any American soldier who treated a young Frenchwoman to a glass of beer.

By the fall of 1945, the 28-year-old quarterback was again with the team full-time, playing in all 10 games, and beating out Sammy Baugh to lead the league in passing yardage. But if the 1944 team was poor, the 1945 edition was pathetic. Despite Luckman's performance, the Bears won just three of 10 games, experiencing their first losing season since 1929. The war was over, and reminders of life on real battlefields were everywhere. Some players picked up where they left off. Ken Kavanaugh, who had flown 25 missions over Germany and never lost a man—"We were just flat-assed lucky," he told sports historian Robert W. Peterson—scored three touchdowns in his first game back. George McAfee, who returned from the navy late in the 1945 season, after almost four years away and despite his insistence that he wasn't ready, scored four touchdowns in his second and third games back and averaged almost nine yards a carry.

Others were too hardened by war, or battered by it, for professional football. Mario Tonelli, a fullback from suburban Chicago and Notre Dame, had last played as a rookie for the Chicago Cardinals in 1940. Before the Bears' last game of the 1946 season against the Cards at Comiskey Park, Luckman was introduced to Tonelli, a player he barely remembered and wouldn't have recognized anyway. The 200-pound Tonelli had enlisted early, then survived the Battle of Bataan in the Philippines in 1942, the Bataan Death March, and four Japanese prison camps. He had seen most of his comrades die

of starvation, exhaustion, and beatings. He was one of the lucky
ones, and in more ways than one; he was relieved of his Notre Dame
class ring in prison, but a Japanese lieutenant who had attended the
University of Southern California and seen Tonelli play against the
USC Trojans in 1937 returned it to him with instructions to bury
it under his barracks in a tin can. By the time Tonelli and his ring
made it home in the fall of 1945, he weighed 109 pounds and had
to undergo two operations on his parasite-ravaged intestines. After
he put on 60 pounds, the Cards signed Tonelli for the last few games
of 1945, but he never left the bench. When he told Luckman that
football seemed like a breeze compared with what he had endured,
and that he would be back on the field before long, Luckman got a
lump in his throat and said, "I sure hope so," though he could see
Tonelli was one hero who wouldn't play again.*

Pro football was now more firmly entrenched in a postwar society whose very survival had been in jeopardy during the worst of the
war years. Television, which had experimentally broadcast the first pro
football game in 1939, was poised to deliver the game to the brains
of the country's sports fans, although it wouldn't be until 1951 that
an NFL championship game was televised coast to coast.

By 1946 pro football had won the hearts of enough Americans that Halas, back at the wheel after 39 months in the navy, was
busy warding off talent raids from the new All-America Football
Conference, which was expanding the game geographically north to
Buffalo, south to Miami, and, thanks to commercial air travel, west
to Los Angeles and San Francisco. Fullback Norm Standlee, who
had last starred for the Bears in 1941, signed with the San Francisco
49ers. The Miami Seahawks plucked end Hampton Pool. The Los

---

* He did not. Tonelli went into Illinois politics and outlived just about everyone on
the field that day, dying in 2003 at the age of 86.

Angeles Dons signed Bears All-Pro halfback Harry Clarke, end Bob Nowaskey, and Luckman's backup, Charlie O'Rourke, who had played for Boston College. Some of the offers were almost irresistible; Bill Osmanski, who had been making $12,000 before he went to war, was reportedly offered $40,000 to jump leagues, but the dentist chose instead to accept a small salary bump from Halas, to $15,000. The new league's instability was a factor, and for a certain type of individual, Halas inspired a degree of respect and loyalty that was almost filial.

That was never more the case than with Luckman, who also found himself in play. The day after the Bears opened the 1946 season with a 30–7 victory at Green Bay, John Keeshin, the president of the Chicago entry in the AAFC, the Rockets, offered him a three- to five-year coaching contract for an alluring $25,000 a year and claimed Luckman had agreed to it. Keeshin told the press that Luckman wanted to make coaching football his lifework, but in good conscience needed to discuss the offer with Halas. For a man like Halas, who had pinched pennies for a quarter of a century to keep the Bears in business, the size of these postwar offers was scandalous. Halas countered with $20,000, up from $12,000, and Luckman decided to remain with the Bears.

Some sportswriters wondered whether Luckman might be holding out for an even bigger offer from the Rockets, but Luckman was smarter than that. "Trite as it may sound to some," Luckman wrote in 1949, "I simply couldn't see myself forsaking a club that had given me all the benefits a player could wish for, and joining a team in a newly-organized league that may or may not succeed." Success was not likely in a city that already fielded two teams (the Rockets had to compete with both the Bears and the Cardinals), and it didn't come as a shock when the mostly woeful new team folded after four years. The upstart league it belonged to folded too, but bequeathed to the

NFL the AAFC's three strongest franchises: the San Francisco 49ers, the Cleveland Browns, and the Baltimore Colts.

There was another reason to stick with the Bears. NFL commissioner Bert Bell had adopted a free-substitution rule during the war to help compensate for the lower quality of talent; depleted teams wouldn't have to exhaust their men by requiring them to play both offense and defense for at least an entire quarter before being replaced. Players could be replaced freely, to conserve their energy for what they did best and limit injuries. In 1946, the league rescinded free substitution, limiting substitution to three men at a time, but at least it meant that vulnerable quarterbacks could be better protected than before by fresh blockers.*

Even limited free substitution was essential to refining the game's focus on expertise and tactical coaching. The sport that once looked like a cottage industry, with each man striving to turn in a complete game, was now beginning to resemble an assembly line in the best sense, a game in which various specialists all added their expert touches to the finished product.

However strong Luckman's loyalty was, Halas had to begin thinking of an eventual replacement for his most valuable player, who was going to turn an ancient 30 before the end of the season. While Halas had been serving in New Guinea during the war as welfare and recreation officer for the Seventh Fleet, one of his stand-ins, Luke Johnsos, had been eyeing a young man from Waukegan, Illinois, named Otto Graham, who played tailback at Northwestern in the single-wing formation. Like Luckman, Graham could pass and run and had the makings of

---

* The league restored free substitution in 1950, and has kept it to this day. To accommodate the change, the active-roster limit of 30 players in force in 1940 was raised in 1964 to 40.

a leader. He was a religious kid who didn't drink or smoke, and the Bears were determined to draft him first in 1944; however, the team lost a coin flip to Detroit, and Graham ultimately signed with Paul Brown of the AAFC's Cleveland Browns, where he would lead the team to 10 championship games in his 10 seasons (the last six as part of the NFL), winning seven of them.

Luckman took control in 1946 and led the Bears to a resumption of something they were accustomed to: winning. McAfee, Osmanski, Kavanaugh, Gallarneau, Turner, and Wilson were all back at work and out to prove that not even a world war could interrupt the arc of their greatness. They breezed through the schedule, losing only to the reconstituted Cardinals and the New York Giants, and led the league in points scored and point differential. Along the way, the Bears celebrated their own Sid Luckman Day at Wrigley Field, on Sunday, November 17. In the Bears' late-game 24–20 victory over the Redskins, Sammy Baugh tossed two touchdown passes to Luckman's one. At the end of the regular season, it was the New York Giants, not the Redskins, who earned the right to face the Bears in the NFL championship game, played before almost 60,000 fans at the Polo Grounds. The last time the two teams had met for the championship, at Wrigley Field in 1941, two weeks after the attack on Pearl Harbor, only 13,000 fans had bothered to show up.

The match would be remembered more for the scandal surrounding the suspected throwing of the game, by Giants quarterback Frank Filchock and halfback Merle Hapes, than for anything that happened on the field that day.* The Giants had already beaten the Bears once that year, at the Polo Grounds, 14–0. Luckman, who had had one of his worst days ever, throwing five interceptions, wanted badly to avenge the loss before his hometown friends and family,

---

* The Filchock–Hapes scandal is discussed in chapter 15.

and the Bears, despite the earlier loss, were favored by 10. Luckman opened the scoring by threading a perfect pass to Ken Kavanaugh in stride under the goalposts. Dante Magnani, Luckman's roommate on the road, returned one of Filchock's six interceptions later in the first quarter to make it 14–0, and the Bears seemed to be off and running. But New York's defense tightened up, Filchock threw for two touchdown passes, and the fourth quarter began with a 14–14 tie.

With a couple of minutes gone in the fourth, Luckman scored the most unlikely touchdown of his career. He had long been relieved of any obligation to run the football, and knowing that it was the last thing opponents looked for, Halas and Luckman had devised a play they named "Bingo Keep It." It called for him to fake a handoff to a back going left, then take off around right end. It was a fairly simple bootleg play whose surprise factor was Luckman's being allowed to lumber with the ball at all. With the ball on New York's 19-yard line, Luckman walked to the sideline during a time-out and said to Halas, "Now?" "Now," Halas replied. Luckman couldn't remember the last time he had had to run with the ball except when being chased from the pocket.

Luckman bent over Turner and barked his signals. On the snap, in unison, like a small chorus line, the Bears' two running backs dipped and pivoted their upper bodies to the right, then pivoted back and went left. Luckman faked a handoff to McAfee. Most of the left side of the Giants line fell for it, following the backs, and Luckman hid the ball against his hip and rolled right, cut inside the Giants' outside linebacker, and picked his way downfield, weaving and stumbling finally into the end zone for the touchdown. It wasn't elegant, but it did the trick. On the Giants' following possession, after Filchock threw an unpressured pass right into Bulldog Turner's hands, it looked as though Filchock could easily have been in some bookmaker's pocket.

The ensuing late field goal clinched the Bears' 24–14 victory. It was not an impressive win for Chicago—neither team managed 250 yards of offense, and Luckman completed only nine of 22 pass attempts and called it "one of the most vicious games I've ever played in in my life"—but it was good for the Bears' fourth NFL championship in seven years.

24

A Congestion of Quarterbacks

The Bears came close to the championships during the next four years, and winning would have made them the greatest dynasty in NFL history. From 1947 through 1950, Luckman's twilight years, the Bears actually had the best won-lost record in the NFL (36–12), edging out the Chicago Cardinals (31–16–1) and the Philadelphia Eagles (34–12–2), the two teams that met in the championship games in 1947 and '48. But Chicago never made it to the big game in those four seasons, despite the team's impressive consistency, with records of 8–4, 10–2, 9–3, and 9–3.

Sid Luckman was at his postwar peak in 1947, passing for a career-high 2,712 yards and career second-best 24 touchdowns but also throwing a career-high 31 interceptions with a right wrist that had undergone two operations over the summer for growths on the tendons. Better-disguised pass defenses also made his job harder, as the league had by now wised up to the T formation, and other teams practiced their own versions of it. But Luckman was not through making history; on a sunny October afternoon at Griffith Stadium in Washington, DC, the Bears and Redskins set an NFL record for combined passing yardage, throwing for 731 yards and seven touch-downs between them. Luckman did the most damage, throwing three touchdown passes for the third straight game. Despite Washington's 411 yards in passing, the Bears' 56–20 victory was a nightmare for the Redskins—a terrible reminder of Washington's nadir as a franchise. All in all, eight Bears scored, including Bulldog Turner on a record-setting 96-yard interception return for a touchdown, at the end of which an exhausted Sammy Baugh, who had pursued him the length of the field, was dragged by an equally exhausted Turner into the end zone.

That aside, the T formation agreed with Baugh in 1947. He had a career year; he had more completions, more touchdowns, more passing yards, and a higher pass completion percentage than his rival Luckman, with half as many interceptions. The evolution of the passing game in general was a major factor in the league's increasing popularity. Average game attendance had reached 30,000, doubling the average in 1936 and almost quadrupling the 8,211 people who on average attended a game in 1932. Under the influence of rules guru Hugh "Shorty" Ray, whom Halas had presciently recruited to stabilize and streamline pro football, as he had done with the high school and college game, points per game had tripled between 1932 and 1947, total yardage and passing yardage had doubled, and the average number of plays needed to score a touchdown had decreased from 35.7 to 21.6.

Of course, passing alone didn't guarantee a team's success, as Baugh's 1947 team discovered. The Redskins managed to win only four games and achieved only a single (barely) winning season between 1947 and 1950.

On the other hand, the Bears, winners of eight straight, needed to win only one of their last two games of 1947, both at home—one against the Rams, now based in Los Angeles, and the other versus the crosstown Cardinals—in order to win their division. On December 7, the Bears outgained the Rams by a wide margin, but Luckman's one touchdown pass to Ken Kavanaugh wasn't enough to offset his four interceptions, and Los Angeles came from behind to win, 17–14. The next week, the Cardinals ventured to the North Side with a strong, young team and built a 27–7 half-time lead, helped considerably by four interceptions thrown by Luckman. Halas had seen enough at the beginning of the fourth quarter and pulled Luckman, subbing in 17th-round draft pick rookie Nick Sacrinty, who proceeded to have the best day of his very short-lived NFL career, throwing two long touchdown passes, but the Cardinals held on for a 30–21 victory and the team's first division championship since 1925.

"It was a new experience for me, leaving a game with twelve minutes, and the game hanging fire," Luckman wrote. "I had seen many a player pulled out for a 'pinch hitter,' and I knew now exactly how it felt." The 31-year-old, who considered the game his worst performance ever, brooded in the locker room until only he and his 245-pound roommate, tackle Fred Davis, were left.

"As your friend," Davis told him, "I should beat that game out of you. But it'll be much easier on the system to take in the town tonight." After he dragged Luckman to several nightspots, the two ended up at Chez Paree on the near North Side to hear comedian Joe E. Lewis's act. Luckman's old pal Irv Kupcinet sat down and called over Lewis and singer Tony Martin, who had both seen the loss to the Cardinals and now offered to help Luckman brood.

"Don't look so doggone sad, gents," Davis told the entertainers, "or you'll kill our boy."

In the summer of 1948, Luckman, Sammy Baugh, Rams quarterback Bob Waterfield, and several other players traveled to Los Angeles to shoot a forgettable, and forgotten, B movie for Columbia called *Triple Threat*, in which, for "a fancy weekly stipend," as Luckman put it, they pretended to play football in the LA Coliseum. Intimations of his football mortality were hard to avoid, however, even in the land of make-believe. When Waterfield, who was married to actress Jane Russell, took Luckman home for a party, Al Jolson complained to Sid about the Bears' loss to the Cardinals the previous December. "I had dough on the Bears last year, and you bums disappointed me in that Cardinal fracas. I really ought to be more sympathetic. Nobody knows better than Al how it feels for a champ to fall. It took me eight years to climb back. Hope you can turn the trick sooner."

"I'd already begun to contemplate the pressure of another pro season," Luckman wrote about that time, "and the new worries it might bring on." One of those worries was getting his weight back to an optimal 192 after a summer of lolling and hobnobbing in the California sun. He worked off 20 excess pounds at Postl's Health Club, a 27th-floor gym at 188 West Randolph Street, a notorious building in Chicago's Loop. Unbeknownst to Luckman, 188 West Randolph was, according to Gus Russo's *Supermob*, a "point of convergence for Syndicate members, their lawyers, and paid-for-officials," and would remain one for decades. Postl's steam room was illegally bugged by the FBI.

No one had been a Chicago Bear longer than Luckman, and only four NFL players had been in the league longer. When he showed up at camp for his 10th season, he was confronted with his own demise in the form of a man he had tutored in the nuances of the T formation five years earlier. Heisman Trophy winner Johnny Lujack had been a Notre Dame sophomore then; after serving on a sub-chasing destroyer during the war and returning to Notre Dame, he became the Bears' first-round draft pick in 1946. When he finally joined the Bears in 1948, he was Luckman's heir apparent. Like Luckman, Lujack had turned down a fatter contract from the Chicago Rockets to play for Halas. He signed for four years, at salaries of $17,000, $18,500, $20,000, and $20,000, and went to work. Like Luckman in 1939, Lujack was eager, easygoing, diligent, and humble. He pestered Luckman constantly with questions about the game and how to tweak his own skills. When Lujack worried that his bootlegging left something to be desired, Luckman counseled him to draw the ball into his hips a little quicker, just as he started his pivot. Ten years earlier, Luckman had turned to veteran quarterback Bernie Masterson for similar advice.

As if Lujack's presence wasn't sufficient to light a fire under Luckman, Halas had drafted another first-round quarterback, Bobby Layne, of the University of Texas. "The three L's" were photographed in identical poses, kneeling and looking off into the distance, no doubt trying to figure out what Halas had in mind with his embarrassment of quarterback riches. "There's room on the field for all these men, in steady switches," Halas said. "I'm against any feuds for positions. We're all equal here—no first- or second-stringers."

Sid's family didn't help; when six-year-old Bobby Luckman came to camp with Estelle, he announced to some of his father's teammates that his favorite Chicago Bear was Johnny Lujack.

The Bears as a team were undergoing a remodeling, and not just at the quarterback position, where Halas had invested heavily, paying Luckman $23,000 and Layne $22,000 plus a $10,000 signing bonus that kept him out of the hands of the other league's Baltimore Colts. Halas had new players and lots of new tricks up his sleeve, including using Luckman more on defense. Against the Packers in the teams' traditional opener in Green Bay, Halas started Lujack at quarterback and Luckman at defensive halfback. Ironically, in the 45–7 victory— the most lopsided in the two teams' already long history as rivals— Lujack intercepted three Packer passes while Luckman and Layne each threw a touchdown pass to Ed Sprinkle.

Using all three L's at quarterback, the Bears breezed to a 10–1 record with one game to go, beating everyone handily except Green Bay, whom they beat by a single point in a rematch, and losing only to Philadelphia. Luckman still carried most of the quarterback load during the season, throwing 13 touchdown passes, cutting his interceptions down to 14, and for the second straight year completing more than 54 percent of his passes. Lujack contributed six touchdown passes (and eight interceptions) and, with the hard-partying Layne mopping up, the team amassed a 31.3 points-per-game average, while the defense was the best in the league. But the Cardinals, with an identical 10–1 record, were every bit as good, and, with the West Division championship at stake, the two teams met once again at Wrigley Field in the final game of the season.

On a warm December day, before 51,285 spectators, the largest Bears crowd ever at Wrigley Field, Lujack started strong against the Cardinals, throwing two touchdown passes, and the Bears, who would gain 460 yards for the game, were ahead 21–10 in the fourth quarter, when they ran out of steam. The Cardinals scored twice, the second time after a tired Lujack, who had played the whole game on defense as well, threw an interception on third down in his own territory. With the Cards leading 24–21, Luckman spelled Lujack and drove the Bears to the Cardinals' 14-yard line but two plays later was intercepted in the end zone—to finish the Bears' season. For the second year in a row, their crosstown rivals would go to the title game.

During the 1948 season, Bobby Layne had started just one game and completed a mere 31 percent of his passes. With a quarterback to spare, and then having drafted University of Kentucky quarterback George Blanda as insurance, Halas traded Layne after the season to the lowly Boston Yanks, who were about to become the even lowlier New

York Bulldogs for the 1949 season. In trading Layne, for $50,000 and two draft choices, Halas's fabled intuition failed him. With all the traffic at the quarterback position, Layne had not had a chance to prove himself, which the Bulldogs gratefully provided. Starting every game for them, Layne completed 52 percent of his passes, for 1,797 yards and nine touchdowns, although the team managed only a single win.

If Halas wasn't kicking himself yet, it was because Lujack would go on in 1950 to have a career year, leading the league in attempts, completions, yardage, and touchdowns. When the troubled New York Bulldogs folded after the 1949 season, the Detroit Lions claimed Layne in the team's dispersal draft. He would lead the Lions to four first-place finishes and three NFL championships in his six seasons in Detroit, while, during the same period, the Bears would lose their one title game, in 1956, and endure three losing seasons. While Layne prospered, a separated shoulder in 1950 would compromise Johnny Lujack's passing arm, and he also grew disenchanted with the intemperate Halas and his financial sleight of hand. Moreover, the trading of Layne forced Halas to overuse the injured Lujack, which further alienated him from Papa Bear. By 1951 Lujack had quit football.

While for Luckman the 1948 season was blessedly free of injuries, "There were days," he recalled, "when I felt my active grid time running short, and all this commotion drawing to a close." After the season he went to the Mayo Clinic for a delicate operation to remove a goiter from his neck; he had to remain awake during the procedure, talking to a nurse, in order to alert the doctors if they were too close to the laryngeal nerves.

Sid tried his hand at radio, hosting a sports show in Chicago, but was told that his "high-pitched Brooklynese" was too hard to listen to. In any case, he was now in the automobile business. In early 1948, Donjo Medlevine, a mob associate and part owner of the Chez

Paree nightclub in Chicago, had helped set Luckman up in a Chrysler-Plymouth new car dealership on Chicago's West Side. "If you can cling to a business for over a year, Sid," said Estelle, who could see the approaching end of his football career more clearly than her husband, "you'll accomplish something as big as winning the Carr trophy [for most valuable player]." Estelle and their expanded brood—Bobby and his two younger sisters, Ellen and Gail—moved to Chicago and Sid hired Bears trainer Andy Lotshaw as Sid Luckman Motors' manager, buyer, and goodwill man. Luckman applied himself to learning the automobile business with the same zeal he had brought to mastering the Bears' playbook. When Halas paid him a visit at the showroom in 1949 to entice him to play another year, Luckman balked, then realized he wasn't ready to let go of football.

"If I had been intending to quit at this stage," he said that year, "I was only kidding myself again, just as I had in 1939, in '42, '45, and '47. Each time I found it tougher to retire. The bug that had bitten me back in Flatbush couldn't be shaken loose."

Luckman backed up Lujack in 1949, but not well. He started only two games and threw for only 200 yards and a single touchdown. While Halas licked his self-inflicted wounds, watching Bobby Layne play brilliantly for a losing team in New York, the genius whose inspiration had carried Halas and Luckman to football immortality, Clark Shaughnessy, was busy cooking up pro football's next big innovation. Shaughnessy, now in his fifties, thought the game could be opened up even more, with a passing formation called the three-receiver set, which paved the way for further, ever more scientific future refinements of the passing game by Sid Gillman's San Diego Chargers (of the American Football League) and Bill Walsh's San Francisco 49ers. Shaughnessy unveiled the three-receiver set in 1949 as the new head coach of the Los Angeles Rams, a team with two excellent passers—Bob Waterfield and rookie Norm Van Brocklin—and the accomplished receivers Tom Fears, Elroy "Crazy Legs" Hirsch, and Verda "Vitamin T" Smith. The three-receiver set would make the Rams the most explosive offensive team for the next several years, while the Bears, with neither Shaughnessy nor the right personnel, slipped further and further behind.

In 1949, Shaughnessy's Rams and their wide-open passing game beat the Bears twice. Still, the Bears would have won the division had they not lost a third game, at New York—and, in the eyes of many, unnecessarily. After their first loss to the Rams in the fourth week, the Bears visited the Polo Grounds, the scene of so much of Luckman's best—and some of his worst—play during the past decade. It was where Halas had first thrust Luckman into game action as quarterback. Once again, Halas tapped the fading Luckman to start, even though Lujack had quarterbacked the team so far to a 3–1 record. It was a sentimental coaching decision and a dubious one. On this day, only 30,000 fans were in the stands, 25,000 fewer than on Sid Luckman Day six years earlier. By halftime, the Giants were up 21–0. Halas finally sent in Lujack, who mounted a brilliant second-half comeback that pulled the Bears even, at 28–28, in the fourth quarter; but a late Giants touchdown won the game, 35–28, and, in the end, cost the Bears the division title.

The lights on Luckman's brilliant career were flickering out, and if anyone needed proof it could be found in the next day's coverage of the game in the *Chicago Tribune*: Luckman was not mentioned once. After being the face of the team for almost a decade, he was enduring the fate of all aging athletes.

Still, with the added title of quarterback coach, he returned for the 1950 season, during which he would turn 34, but he would not start a single game. The man who had thrown 135 touchdown passes in his first 10 seasons would manage only one in each of his last two. The end finally came at Wrigley Field on a bitter December Sunday in 1950, against the Detroit Lions, led by Bobby Layne. Luckman asked Halas to put him in the game in the second quarter. On fourth down in Lions territory, Luckman dropped back to pass but slipped in the mud, and Detroit took over.

As Luckman trudged to the sideline in his familiar number 42 navy-blue jersey, he heard boos. After all, there were thousands of people in the stands who had never seen him play in his prime. To the younger fans, he was just another guy not doing his job. He took a seat on the cold bench, pulled his heavy cloak around him, and watched the Lions' young Bobby Layne take the snap from Detroit's center.

After a moment, Halas came over and put his hand on Luckman's shoulder. "Don't worry, son," Halas told him. "You've done more than your share to make them happy."

Luckman wouldn't play again. He sat on the bench the next week in Los Angeles, watching Johnny Lujack as the Bears lost the Western Conference playoff game to the Rams, 24–14. A week later, in the NFL championship game in Cleveland, the Browns' Otto Graham and the Rams' Bob Waterfield, both operating out of the T formation, each threw for 300 yards in the Browns' thrilling come-from-behind 30–28 victory. It was the apotheosis of the formation that Clark Shaughnessy and George Halas had engineered and that Luckman had executed, exactly a decade before, and which, in the face of ridicule from football's best minds, had changed the game forever.

25

Gifts

It would surprise no one who had seen Sid Luckman's muddy, beaming face on the cover of *Life* magazine in 1938 that he would be successful after his playing days were over. Well-known New York sports broadcaster Marty Glickman, who had been Sid's high school football rival, said when they were both old men, "He was a star that first day, and he stayed a star his whole life."

In the end, Sid Luckman's greatest asset in life was not his right arm, or his astute leadership on the field, but his personality and character. He had shouldered a special burden at an early age, knowing what his father had done and what pro football needed him to do. As Halas said at Luckman's retirement ceremony at the Sherman Hotel in Chicago on February 13, 1951, "In Sid, we created a new type of football player, the T quarterback. Newspapers switched their attention from the star runners to the quarterbacks. In Sid's twelve years with the Bears, football was completely revolutionized."

Like baseball's Hank Greenberg just before him, and Sandy Koufax 15 years later, Sid was a rare Jewish athlete whose success had broad appeal in mid-20th-century America. His Judaism was incidental to his talent but could never be divorced from it. He was the frequent target of anti-Semitic name-calling and worse, in Brooklyn, the NFL, the merchant marine, and business. At a historic height of Jewish vulnerability, he was a symbol of physical courage, quiet indignation, and social acceptance. The acknowledgments page of Luckman's 1949 autobiography shows how quickly he had become a darling of power brokers and bold-faced names: Jake Arvey, industrialist Henry Crown, Joe DiMaggio, Sid Korshak, Irv Kupcinet, Toots Shor. He may have never forgotten who he was and where he came from, but he had traveled a long way from Flatbush.

After his playing days, Luckman became a good friend of DiMaggio, who was two years his senior. They shared singular athletic achievements with dynastic teams during the same decade, and they also shared an ambivalence toward celebrity's hot glare. During his "lost" years after his divorce from Marilyn Monroe, DiMaggio was always on the move, turning up among friends he could trust. When Sid's daughter Ellen was a girl, she came home from school one day in the 1950s to discover that her babysitter was going to be Joe DiMaggio, who was taking temporary refuge with the Luckman family and sitting right there in the living room. During the same year, Peter Luckman's parents, Leo and Leona, took him and his sister to call on the elusive DiMaggio at New York's Madison Hotel, where he was staying in the suite of his old friend George Solotaire, a powerful ticket broker to the stars of the stage, screen, and underworld. DiMaggio came to the door in a bathrobe. In countless cities, DiMaggio had well-connected friends who looked after him. Sid and Estelle did so in Miami Beach, where they lived part of the year in a Mimosa Hotel apartment. It was as if DiMaggio had his own "underground railroad" of hosts who opened their homes to him and protected him from the press. When DiMaggio needed a job in the late 1950s, Luckman introduced him to Valmore Monette, whose company, V. H. Monette, was the main supplier of merchandise for post exchanges on US military bases all over the world. DiMaggio was essentially a greeter for the next three years, traveling around the globe with his boss to play golf with the brass at various military bases.

Luckman also became close to DiMaggio's good friend Frank Sinatra. A photograph captured the middle-aged Luckman sitting with Sinatra in California, both in bathing suits, beaming at the camera, flanked by their close associates, Sinatra's right-hand man Jilly Rizzo and Luckman's close friend and Chicago neighbor, construction-company owner Jack McHugh. When Estelle was dying of lung cancer at New York's Memorial Sloan Kettering in 1981, Bob Luckman was sitting with his intubated mother, when Sinatra, in town for one of his cancer-research fund-raising concerts, popped in unexpectedly and spent half an hour chatting with Bob while a dozen ICU nurses craned their necks to get a look at Sinatra through the open door. Later, Luckman prevailed on Sinatra to appear at the opening of Miami's deluxe Turnberry Isle resort, where Luckman purchased a condo after Estelle's death.

Luckman's children, nieces, and nephews basked in the reflected warmth of his celebrity. DiMaggio put in an appearance at the bar mitzvah of Sid's nephew Peter in 1957. Peter was a standout high school basketball player on Long Island, where he grew accustomed to seeing some of his father's illustrious friends in the stands. Among them were New York Giants coach Allie Sherman; financier and phi-lanthropist Cecil Wolfson; and Red Auerbach, who worked for a company Sid now partly owned, Cellu-Craft, as a sales representative during the off-season to supplement his income as the coach of the dynastic Boston Celtics. While Peter was a student at Syracuse University in the 1960s, he went to see Sammy Davis Jr. perform at the Three Rivers Inn near the university; when he knocked shyly on the singer's dressing-room door between shows to introduce himself as Sid Luckman's nephew, Sammy invited him in for an hour of conversation.

When Sid's older daughter, Ellen, got married, Gale Sayers, the newly minted Chicago Bears superstar, was a guest.

Sid's likability was inextricable from his humility. Having been ignored by an inebriated Babe Ruth when he wanted the Sultan of Swat's autograph as a kid—he finally obtained it when they met years later during a US war bond rally—he never turned down an autograph seeker. In the 1970s, when he was approached by a boy who recognized him in the stands at a Chicago Cubs game at the same Wrigley Field where he had once played, he signed his name, only to then find a long line of other youngsters queuing up to get the famous man's autograph too. After shaking everyone's hand, asking everyone's name, and scrawling his own, he turned to his son, Bob, and whispered, "Except for that first one, not one of those kids knows who I am."

New York Times sportswriter Dave Anderson called Sid "the most humble and the most polite of all of America's best athletes. After a telephone interview several years ago, he said: 'I'm grateful for your call.' Grateful? You don't hear that word much anymore from anybody about anything." When *Sports Illustrated* writer Paul Zimmerman interviewed Sid in the 1990s at his Florida home for an article about the quarterbacks who changed the NFL—"It was like interviewing Orville Wright for a piece about flying"—Luckman not only insisted the journalist stay with him, but pressed a shopping bag of gifts on him when he left, saying, "These are for your wife and children. It's a family tradition that whoever comes to our house must take a gift along with him."

Luckman made a religion out of generosity. He always sent people away with gifts—ties, perfume, candlesticks, crystal bowls, golf shirts—whether he had just met them or had known them for years. His friend Jay Pritzker, one of the wealthiest men in America, once left Luckman's apartment with his wife in hysterical laughter; the topic of men's shoes had come up, and now Pritzker was carrying two shopping bags full of shoes that Sid had given him. Luckman had a walk-in closet full of gifts, and his Christmas gift list, with approximately 4,500 recipients, was famous and finally became a kind of joke. "Easy to get on and hard to get off," people said. "At one point," Bob Luckman remembers, "a hundred people had died already, and he was still sending them gifts." Every fall, Sid's assistant and a group of other women sat at tables in his office in Chicago and wrapped and addressed every single gift. He bought many of the gifts in bulk from a friend who had a corporate gift company—he even traveled to China with Jay Pritzker for the purpose of getting more gift ideas—and he couldn't resist making a purchase if he saw something he loved. If he saw a jacket he liked at TJ Maxx, he'd order 50 of them. Once he sent his daughter Ellen and her husband to buy 100 framed prints whose artlessness was so memorable that they still talked about it 30 years later. His generosity often exceeded his taste, never more so than with an anatomically distorted sculpture of a quarterback in passing position that he insisted on giving to some of his closest friends. Kathie Lee Gifford made the mistake of regifting hers to a guest on morning television, only to be told by the guest that Sid had already given her one. Sid's own home was filled with paintings "in the style of" great artists.

Sid Luckman's generosity would not have been possible without his wealth, for which he had a childhood summer camp friend, Sam Levy, partly to thank. In the 1940s, Levy learned that Sid was working during the off-seasons as a salesman for a Midwestern packaging company that competed with his own New York firm, Cellu-Craft, which made flexible packaging for companies including Kraft Foods, Quaker Oats, and Sara Lee. Levy prevailed on Luckman to open a Cellu-Craft office in Chicago and sell for him, a job at which Luckman proved so successful—who wouldn't want to buy cellophane packaging from one of the greatest quarterbacks ever?—that Levy made

Luckman an equal partner after he retired from football. Luckman proved as unbeatable at selling as he had been at running the Bears' offense. It became axiomatic in the packaging business that no one could sell against Sid Luckman; if he set his sights on a new account, you couldn't beat him to it, and if you wanted an account he already had, you couldn't get it away from him. His son, Bob, who joined the company in the late 1960s and remained with it until his own retirement, recalls that Cellu-Craft was once about to lose its huge Quaker Oats account to a lower bidder. "Sid went to the purchasing guy, and the next thing you knew, he got the business back, because Quaker wanted a better presence in a big grocery chain, and Sid happened to be friendly with one of the chain's executives." He had a killer instinct; in 1959, he underbid a rival packaging-printing firm and won the huge Kraft Foods' caramel-candy-wrapper contract, even though the rival company was co-owned by Bears assistant coach Luke Johnsos and the team's single largest season-ticket holder.

In a book from the 1960s, *The Pro Quarterback*, Murray Olderman captured Luckman nearing 50, "black-haired and tan, dressed in a dark suit," a long black limousine waiting for him in front of the Randolph Tower in the Loop, when he was vice president of Cellu-Craft. In the back of the limo, he had one of the first mobile phones, which he used to call Estelle in Highland Park to tell her of his plans to stay in the city for dinner with friends. He and Estelle, once just two kids at Erasmus Hall, were empty nesters. Bob had recently married Gale Lassman, his neighbor, and daughters Ellen and Gail were at Syracuse and the University of Miami, respectively. He instructed the driver to take him to the venerable Drake Hotel. "There's a big round table reserved for him in the International Room overlooking Michigan Boulevard," Olderman wrote. "His companions are the chairman of the board of a vending company, the founder and president of a national bakery chain and an oil magnate who made

$20 million in the last three years. The talk is of Palm Springs and Honolulu and New York." Long after Cellu-Craft was merged into a larger company, even after the technical aspect of the business became too complex for him, Luckman stayed on, opening new accounts and handling old ones.

During much of the 1950s and 1960s, Luckman was also officially an unsalaried Bears quarterback coach, but his business career left little time for coaching, and his value to the team was questionable and often the object of media criticism. His heart wasn't always in it. He's remembered by some less for his coaching than for using his coaching position to reward business customers by inviting them and their families to observe Bears team practices. The young man who once knew the playbook for every position wasn't concerned any longer with X's and O's.

By the 1970s, Luckman's talk was also of nursing homes. He invested heavily in Aviv Assets, a company that would eventually own 249 skilled-nursing facilities in the United States that the company rented to individual operators. Aviv's founder, a self-described "deal junkie" named Zev Karkomi, was a Russian-born immigrant (like Luckman's own father) who had served in the Israel Defense Forces in the 1950s and had immigrated to Chicago in 1960 with no English-language skills. He evolved from a door-to-door insurance salesman to become owner of one of the country's largest privately held owners of nursing-home properties and a major philanthropist for Israeli causes.

Sid's generosity had to be reined in when it came to his own family. "My mom used to have to calm him down," his daughter Gail says, "because he'd buy us anything we wanted." As long as he lived, Sid sent his sister, Blanche, a monthly check, whether she needed it or not. "Whenever he saw me," Blanche's daughter, Ronnie, says, "he'd hand me a hundred bucks. He was the most generous person I ever met." Hundred-dollar bills flew out of him. "He used to walk around handing them out," a close friend of his daughter remembered. "When I was eleven, I remember him handing me one. We were once all in Florida together watching jai alai and he gave everybody a hundred bucks to bet on the action." Luckman treated his teenage daughters' friends "like royalty," for instance sending a group in a limousine down to Chicago's Loop to eat dinner at Fritzl's, the Toots Shor's of the Second City.

When Sid's niece Ronnie mentioned to him that she and her husband wanted to live in a certain sought-after New York apartment building, he was on the phone immediately to the management company to arrange it. When Ronnie became infatuated with Rudolf Nureyev after his defection to the West, Sid bought her front-row tickets for one performance after another. They were sitting together at one when Nureyev stumbled and fell; Luckman, perhaps remembering his own clumsy first efforts with the T formation's footwork, turned to Ronnie and announced, in too audible a stage whisper, "He fell!" and laughed. "He was a wonderful uncle because anytime I needed something in life, I had someone to call," she says. "He was always funny, involved, always joking, laughing. Everyone loved him." One of Gail's friends, who ate many a dinner at the Luckman home, recalls everyone laughing so hard at Sid's teasing and joking that no one could get any food down. It wasn't a Luckman dinner if Sid didn't pass gas and immediately blame it on someone else.

No one else ever paid for a restaurant meal if Sid Luckman was seated at the table. He was offended if you didn't take advantage of his connections; he once complained to his son-in-law Dick Weiss, a businessman, "There's no one in the world I couldn't get in touch with to help you, and you never ask."

Although Luckman lent his name, presence, time, and money to dozens of worthy organizations, his compulsive generosity was not for public consumption; few people other than the recipients of it knew of his personal acts during his lifetime. He would help anyone in need that he could, whether former teammates down on their luck or simply someone whose path he crossed who hadn't had his advantages. No shoeshine man ever got away from Sid without a pep talk. He was legendary among his family and close friends for stopping his car in Chicago, leaping out, and handing 20 bucks to panhandlers, even during snowstorms and oblivious to the traffic that he might be holding up behind him. His son likes to remember a lunch he and his father ate in a small-town diner outside Kansas City, after which Sid left the waitress, an older woman, $100.

"What are you doing, Dad?" Bob protested. "The check was less than fifteen dollars!"

"Bobby," he replied, "do you think this woman wants to be on her feet all day, at her age? This will help make her week."

"He taught me what it meant to be in life," his son says. "He taught me how to love life, how to handle people, how to be with people."

At times, Luckman's giving had a curiously adamant edge to it. Once, in Tiffany's, he approached another shopper, an elderly woman with a small dog. Luckman insisted on knowing what tricks the dog could do, and when its owner demurred, he offered to pay her 10 bucks for each trick the animal could perform. Although it clearly wasn't about the money, the woman couldn't refuse.

A close friend paints a picture of Sid on four phones at once, finding a job for this one, getting that one's son into college, promising Super Bowl tickets to someone else. "All he did," Bob Luckman says, "is help people."

"Sid wanted to fix the world," Rabbi Jonathan Magidovitch would tell mourners at his memorial service, in 1998. "We call it *tikkun olam*. He lived it as a personal crusade to get rid of war, disease and poverty. . . . Sid made people happy with his money. It was as if he felt it were not his. It was a gift to him which he just passed along."

Sid's wife, Estelle, who was noted for her relative indifference to materialism, had to go to extreme lengths to stem his lavish generosity. When she needed a car and Sid sent her out to buy whatever she wanted, she returned with a Chevrolet. "Why would you buy a Chevy?" he protested. "You can have any car you want." When his gifts of fine jewelry over the years reached critical mass, she couldn't stand it any longer. Sid came back to the house in Highland Park one day and found her waiting for him, wearing every piece of jewelry he had ever bought her—every ostentatious ring, every antique brooch, every necklace, every bracelet.

"What's going on?" he asked.

"Sid," she said, "if you buy me one more thing I'm taking all this uptown to Leeds Jewelers and selling it."

In his 1962 book *Kup's Chicago*, Irv Kupcinet reports that Luckman had inscribed a game ball to Charlie Baron, writing, "To the dearest friend I have in the world—this is the ball used by the Bears in winning the 1946 championship." Visitors to Baron's Lake Shore Drive apartment in Chicago weren't allowed to leave until they had admired his prized possession, which sat on the mantelpiece. Later, while at the home of another friend of Luckman's, John McGuire, Baron spotted an NFL football with the identical inscription, word for word. And it turned out that a dozen of Sid's "dearest" friends, including Joe DiMaggio, had the same.

It was an unusual mix, this deeply felt, private compassion for others on one side, and the glad-handing "star" on the other. Luckman enjoyed the perks of his status. He loved his Florida tan. He loved the conveniences of wealth. He owned the second mobile phone in Chicago. He loved women. He loved fine clothes. Later in life, he had an enormous walk-in closet in Florida with a mechanized, revolving rack like the kind at a dry cleaner's establishment. At the push of a button, the machine would hum and spring to life, while Sid waited for the perfect suit for the occasion to turn the corner and rumble into view. It was all the more of an extravagance because he was color-blind —which is why every Hart Schaffner & Marx suit on the rack already had a shirt and tie hanging inside it, courtesy of a clothes coordinator who came in once a week. As Luckman's niece Ronnie says, "If I'd been through what he went through with his parents, I'd want to look good too."

With few exceptions, Sid didn't drive, an activity at which he was widely regarded as incompetent. In Chicago, he walked everywhere he could. As a favor to a friend, he once hired a man who proved to be generally useless, but rather than let him go, Sid bought a Cadillac so the man could become his driver and become useful. He remained his driver for 15 years before Sid finally found him a job as a tollbooth collector. In the back seat, Sid could touch up with his Norelco electric shaver on his way to dinner, to meetings, or to one of the many speeches he continued to give throughout his life. As Irv Kupcinet said late in Luckman's life, "You can't name an organization in Chicago that hasn't honored Sid Luckman or used him to raise funds." In 1989, Democratic senator Alan Dixon of Illinois read into the *Congressional Record* a long tribute to Luckman on his 73rd birthday, and for his 74th, US Congressman Frank Annunzio of Illinois presented Sid with an American flag that had flown over the Capitol.

While Sammy Baugh retired to his ranch in Rotan, Texas, and held forth with a trucker's hat on his head, a plug of chewing tobacco in his cheek, and a hunting dog at his feet, Luckman always looked prosperous and required of his own family members a high standard of grooming and comportment in public. His children knew just how to behave in restaurants when the inevitable fan approached to ask for an autograph or merely to express his or her gratitude for all the great memories. For Estelle, however, his fastidious standards could verge on tyrannical. In later years, when they often spent time apart during the winter—she in Florida, Sid going back and forth to tend to his business in Chicago—Estelle dreaded his arrival as much as she would a military inspection, fearful he would scowl at her new hairstyle or eye shadow.

It had been a long time since Sid was life-size to his children. Bob remembers, as a boy, overhearing some Chicagoans talking about Sid Luckman and the Bears as he was sailing his toy sailboat in a pond in front of the Shoreham Hotel in Chicago, where the family first lived after leaving Brooklyn for good in the late 1940s. He thought, "Wow, Dad must really be somebody." A decade later, in Highland Park, Gail, the youngest, was at the Ravinia Elementary School across the street from the family's house, playing tetherball. She was uncommonly good at the game. When one of her victims, a boy, rationalized his loss by telling friends, "What do you expect? She's Sid Luckman's kid," Gail went home and confronted her mother.

"Mom," she said, "I know Sid Luckman is Dad's name, but who's 'Sid Luckman'?"

"Oh, he's a pretty famous football player," came the reply.

As Bob Luckman matured, though, his father was a force to be reckoned with: "I was always Sid Luckman's kid, never Bob." Sid was a difficult man to get a compliment out of, and he couldn't always turn off his quietly competitive spirit. When Bob was in his early teens, he was playing lineball, a two-person Midwestern variation of New York's stickball, in the grammar school playground across the street from his house. Players took turns: one pitching a tennis ball against a brick wall on which a strike zone had been painted, while the other player batted, with strict rules determining which batted balls were singles, doubles, and triples. A shot over the chain-link fence that surrounded the blacktop was, naturally, a home run. On this particular day, Bob was overmatched, trying to hit against a starting pitcher on the Highland Park baseball team, when Sid happened to walk over, saw his son's difficulty, and asked him for the bat. Sid, who had once been the starting shortstop for Columbia University's baseball team in addition to its star football player, promptly smacked a couple of the pitcher's tosses over the fence and handed the bat back to Bob, saying, "I don't want to press my luck." Point made.

"It's hard on a kid, but Mom kept me normal, if there is such a thing," Bob says now. "She accepted people for who they were, not what they were." For Gale, Bob's wife of over 50 years, Estelle was likewise a boon: "Estelle was my best friend. She was incredible. She was the most caring, wonderful human being, and I felt like I was her daughter. A very special human being. I could talk to her about anything. I was closer to her than my own mom." About Sid, Gale says, "He was the best father-in-law. He couldn't do enough for me."

And, yet, with the exception of Estelle, Columbia's Lou Little, George Halas, a few lawyers, some inmates at Sing Sing, and, for a few years back in the 1930s, most of Brooklyn, no one really knew the most unbelievable fact about him. When told recently about the details of Meyer Luckman's crime, a close family friend thought for a moment and then said, "Well, that explains Sid's whole personality. He spent his life trying to undo what his father had done."

26

Secrets

Meyer Luckman had been airbrushed from the family history and from memory as well. Because Meyer had murdered his own brother-in-law, both sides of Sid Luckman's clan had been disgraced. No one spoke of the past, and no one spoke of how the past was not spoken of.

"Sid never talked to us about his family, his mom, or his dad," Bob says today. "It's kind of unusual. What's amazing is I spent a lot of time with Ethel, and she never mentioned a word about her brother or her husband. Nothing!"

Ethel, who never once spoke to, or of, Meyer after his conviction, certainly never said a word to her grandchildren about her past. She rarely sat and talked with her grandchildren at all. Ethel was stately and quiet, "sullen" in the words of a family friend who knew her, almost a ghost. She left behind a handful of generic memories—she sat in a corner, she knitted, she had a beautiful laugh—but no one knows where she and Meyer met. Ethel would spend her last years living with Sid's sister, Blanche, and her husband on Long Island, but even their daughter, Ronnie, who grew up with Ethel living in her house, would have few memories of her.

If it hadn't been for a time in the early 1960s when Estelle Luck-man was trying to help her daughter Ellen through a rough period, no one in the younger generation would have known about Meyer for decades, if at all. Ellen was having a trying time at school, and to provide some perspective, Estelle told her what Sid had had to go through at the same age—disgraced by Meyer's arrest and conviction, he had been shunned by classmates, who called him a murderer's son. It was a shocking form of consolation for Ellen, who was too astonished to ask for details, and knew better than to confront her father about it, but she did confide in her first cousin Ronnie, Blanche's daughter, to whom she was very close. Ronnie was visiting Highland Park when she learned about Meyer, but the information was scant. Was their grandfather guilty? Who knew? Family secrets of a certain magnitude are highly toxic, and the less that is known about them, the better. However, Ronnie was curious and went to the New York Public Library when she got home, scanned some of the newspaper coverage on microfiche, and saw that it was a big deal, but she still couldn't draw any conclusion except that "according to the papers, everyone thought he was guilty." She wasn't even clear who the murder victim was.

Ellen did mention it to her cousin Peter, Leo's son, who eventu-ally tracked down the *New York Times* coverage of the trail and educated himself. However, Ellen neglected to mention to her siblings, Bob and Gail, that their grandfather was a convicted murderer, so it was another 25 years before Bob heard the first thing about it. Until then, all he had known was that his father's father had had some money but lost it in the Depression.

Sid Luckman had no greater ally in keeping his secret than the press itself. Even without the general taboo against trespass-ing on the personal lives of athletes and other public figures— the press obediently kept FDR's invalidism, JFK's unbridled womanizing, and countless professional athletes' offensive conduct out of view—no sportswriter in the 1930s and 1940s would have been eager to invoke Meyer's crime in his or her coverage of Luckman's football career. As a teenager, Sid already showed signs of high character, as when Allison Danzig of the *Times* cited his selflessness as a sophomore quarterback at Columbia in 1936. Sid was exactly the kind of young man one wanted to protect from any adverse publicity. Two years later, *Life* magazine officially severed Meyer Luckman's saga from his son's. Even Johnny Lujack, Luckman's protégé, teammate, and friend, now in his 90s, never heard Sid mention either of his parents and was shocked to hear about Meyer. Another nonagenarian, hall of fame NFL football coach Marv Levy, another of Luckman's many friends, had a one-word response when told about Sid's father: "Wow."

Luckman broached the subject later in life to a few intimates but not in much detail. In the 1970s, Sid befriended a young Chicago restaurateur named Steve Lombardo and changed Lombardo's life. Calling on his wealthy friends in the late 1980s, Sid lined up financing for Lombardo and his partner Hugo Ralli's now famous Gibsons Bar and Steakhouse on the Near North Side. Gibsons, today among the top-grossing restaurants per square foot in the country, became Sid's Chicago hangout and soon his buddy Irv Kupcinet's as well. Its frequent appearances in Kup's column—in addition to its bountiful servings and excellent service—secured its reputation as a destination for celebrities, including the sports and entertainment stars whose framed and autographed photos cover every inch of the walls of the stairwell that leads up to the Club 42 private dining room, named after Sid Luckman's uniform number. Sid insisted that Gibsons offer gargantuan desserts, modeled after those at Wolfie's in Miami; he even shanghaied Lombardo onto a plane to Miami to show him what he meant. Until his death, Sid was a father figure with whom Lombardo spoke almost daily, but only once did Sid mention his own father's fate, and then in such vague terms that Lombardo remains under the impression that Meyer Luckman murdered someone in self-defense while being muscled in some kind of "union beef."

Sid never felt completely safe from the buried past. In the late 1940s, the twilight of his playing career, when Sam Drukman's murder was still a recent memory, he had no compunction about entrusting his autobiography to ghostwriter Norman Reissman. However, in his 70s, after a lifetime of letting the sleeping crime lie, he had second thoughts about tempting fate; he rejected his son's suggestion to write a book, out of fear that some enterprising reporter would dig up old headlines. It made no sense, after all that time had passed, to be revealed as the son of a murderer, especially since he himself was the intimate of men who were intimates of organized crime figures.

The world in which Sid Luckman landed in Chicago—a vast gray area where figures like Irv Kupcinet, Charlie Baron, and Sidney Korshak operated—was in many respects the white-collar extension of his father's. Luckman's friend Frank Sinatra would never deny his relationship with mobsters and fixers like Lucky Luciano, Frank Costello, Meyer Lansky, and Bugsy Siegel. And to have Sidney Korshak's ear, as Luckman did, was to own the ultimate insurance policy against harm. The two Sids were not just friends but close friends; it was Luckman who hosted parties for Korshak when the latter visited from Los Angeles. As Korshak's niece says, "My uncle Sid, Sid Luckman, and my father [lawyer and Illinois state senator Marshall Korshak] were one big *moosh*. They loved each other."

Luckman once called on Sid Korshak, by then one of Hollywood's most powerful figures, to make a relative's labor problems disappear by having a strike at his business called off. It was a Korshak specialty. Bob Luckman remembers that while he was driving his father to a lunch with Korshak, Sid said that he would kick Bob under the table as a signal for him to excuse himself so the two men could conduct business. Korshak's stock-in-trade was making big problems disappear. His personal physician once sat poolside with him in California when a phone was brought to Korshak, who listened to a caller complain about having trouble getting a liquor license for an establishment in Las Vegas. "Have fifty thousand dollars in cash brought to me by tomorrow," the physician heard Korshak respond, "and I'll take care of it." As Gus Russo writes in *Supermob* about the young Korshak, "The all-solving telephone call would become a leitmotif of Korshak's 'practice.'" Sid Luckman never ran afoul of the law, but as one of America's rare Jewish sports legends, as the immensely appealing human being he was, he enjoyed the benefits of powerful friends whose financial and business dealings were often less than transparent.

It seems hardly possible that Sid Luckman's well-connected friends did not know that his father was a convicted murderer and had been an associate of Louis "Lepke" Buchalter. Much more likely they knew but considered Sid a brother to be protected from any unwanted scrutiny—in exchange for Sid's discretion in all matters concerning them. (In the same way, DiMaggio could be counted on never to breathe a word to investigators of his friendships with Chicago mob kingpin Sam Giancana, Longy Zwillman, and others).

Sid Luckman would not have lived in that world were it not for his early prominence as an athlete. He was cut out of a different cloth from the men of that era who set out to make a fortune at almost any cost. He needed to be loved, not feared. As Sid's children grew, they got a better view of his essential modesty, even vulnerability. "Dad needed the accolades," Gail says. "He did." "He was a little insecure in that way," chimes in Bob. "So confident," Gail adds. "But then insecure." In his 1949 autobiography, Sid had called himself "a nervous runt" as a boy and "thin-skinned." Yet it was his anxiety and very eagerness to please authority—at 19, he saw the power that state authority could wield—that contributed to his coachability and conscientiousness. Whereas someone else might have bristled at Halas's abrasive personality, Luckman holed up in his room and memorized hundreds of plays.

The casualness of Sid Luckman's relationship to money—the impression he made that it was simply passing through his hands on the way to more deserving recipients—never impressed his intimates more than when he forgave a business friend's six-figure debt to him or when he paid $100,000 to settle another's nuisance suit rather than become embroiled in a legal battle certain to make a few headlines. His son protested in the latter instance, worried that his father was being taken advantage of, but to no avail. "He always turned the other cheek," Bob says, "always gave people the benefit of the doubt." Virtuous acts become second nature to Sid, every bighearted gesture perhaps expunging a little more of his family's shame.

Meyer Luckman too had possessed virtues: a loving, if coarse, concern for his children, and a determination to provide for them and also for his poorer in-laws and other relatives, several of whom he hired. In the murder trial, the victim's own brother testified that Meyer had bought a house for the Drukman parents, had paid their medical bills. Sid was raised in a home that took seriously its obligations to family—the only people you could trust when you were an immigrant in a land of strangers. Sid's generosity was both an apologia for, and a tribute to, his father.

Good fortune followed Sid. When he said, "There but for the grace of God go I," it was hardly a generic sentiment. To make a living, his father worked in a world where his violent nature would be first an asset, then a catastrophe, and finally his undoing. The "accident" of athletic talent and then unexpected stardom spared Sid from the rough-and-tumble world of Brooklyn business. "There's no question he felt guilty that his brother had to take over the business," says Ellen Luckman. When Leo died mere months before Sid in 1998,

Sid wrote Leo's son, Peter, a warm letter of condolence, saying, "In my youth, he was my inspiration, my mentor, and having him for my brother played a major role in whatever success I obtained. . . . Your Dad had a very tough life and bore all the heartaches through some real difficult times. What a great man—they do not make many like him. I have gone to temple every Saturday for Kaddish and will for the next months."

Sid's younger brother, David, perhaps the most charismatic of them all, an up-and-coming executive for Gimbel's department store in New York, developed a tumor in his early 30s that was misdiagnosed by a doctor friend, and then it was too late to save him. Sid could have been either of them, and he knew it. He could have been Davey O'Brien, two spots behind him in the 1939 draft and five inches shorter, who quarterbacked a miserable Philadelphia team for two years and died at 60. He could have been any one of a hundred college quarterbacks who didn't make the pros at all, or Young Bussey, who did, rode the bench for 10 games with the Bears in 1941, and died in battle in the Philippines in 1945. Luckman's good fortune made him superstitious, since gifts so inexplicably bestowed might be taken away quickly; he always straightened pairs of shoes, stepped onto airplanes with his right foot, removed hats from tables, and threw salt over his shoulder to ward off evil outcomes. Once, he sent his daughter to catch a black cat that had crossed his driveway in Highland Park.

Fate put him in the path of coaches Paul Sullivan at Erasmus Hall, Lou Little at Columbia, and, finally, George Halas. Of all the many friends Sid Luckman made in his lifetime, no one was more important than the man who had watched him play in the mud at Baker Field in 1938 and realized he had discovered a crucial ingredient for his mission to ensure the National Football League's survival.

27

Who Do You Think You Are, Sid Luckman?

In 1939, Luckman filled a hole in George Halas's plans for the team's future, and Halas filled a hole in Luckman's life; having lost his own father's presence in his life, Sid was about to lose the guidance of his father substitute, Lou Little. Had Halas not pursued him so ardently, Luckman would likely have disappeared back into the family fold and applied his considerable business instincts to the trucking business. For decades after Luckman's retirement, the two men met for a weekly Tuesday lunch. In public, they formed a mutual admiration society. Luckman forever lobbied to have the T formation referred to as the Halas Formation, and he honored Halas whenever possible. As the former *Chicago Tribune* sports editor Cooper Rollow told Halas's biographer, Jeff Davis, at countless banquets "Luckman practically made a career by saying, 'And now let's all stand and voice our admiration for the greatest coach of all, Papa Bear!'"

In private, though, there was nothing ceremonial about their affection for each other. Luckman became more than Halas's trusted friend. They had collaborated on a history-making sports dynasty, but they touched something deeper in each other. Luckman was drawn to an older and wiser man whose irascibility and chicanery veiled rock-solid values of family, hard work, and compassion that mirrored his own, and which his own father had betrayed. Unlike many of Halas's detractors, especially among players, Luckman saw past his camouflage and that secrecy bordering on paranoia. "He meant to me as much as anybody on this earth has ever meant to me," he said of Halas at the end of his own life. "He took me under his wing and nurtured me until he felt I was what he wanted me to be as a player, a teammate, a man. We were inseparable. He was a second father to me."

And Luckman was a son to Halas, never more so than after Halas's only son, George Jr., known as Muggsy, died suddenly of a heart attack in 1979, when Halas was 84. Luckman, along with Irv Kupcinet, was summoned early one morning to Halas's apartment to deliver the tragic news. After that, Luckman said bluntly, "He made me his son."

Halas was able to express to Luckman the tenderness that lurked in the shadows of his nature. In 1983, five months before Halas died at the age of 88, he sat down and typed a letter to Luckman—a letter so meaningful that Luckman kept the original framed in his apartment and a copy of it folded in his wallet for the rest of his life. When Luckman spent time in his later years at the Mayo Clinic—where he endowed a scholarship for medical students—he always hung a copy on the wall of his hospital room for everyone to admire.

My dear Sid,

"I love you with all my heart."

When I said this to you last night as I kissed you, I realized 44 wonderful years of knowing you were summed up by seven words.

My boy, my pride in you has no bounds. Remember our word "now!" Every time I said it to you, you brought me another championship.

You added a luster to my life that can never tarnish. My devoted friend, you have a spot in my heart that NO ONE else can claim.

God bless you and keep you, my son. "I love you with all my heart."

Sincerely yours,
George

In the few years between Halas's son's death and Halas's own, Luckman and his billionaire friends Abe Pritzker, then in his 80s, and Abe's son Jay tried to buy the team from Halas. Forty years after his teammates wanted Halas to get rid of the rookie quarterback, Luckman was in a position to own the team. At lunch, Luckman and Pritzker said to Halas, "Coach, we'd like to buy the team. You name the price and you run the team as long as you want to. You'll be chairman of the board, we won't do anything."

Halas replied, "If ever in my life I wanted to sell the team, I'd sell it to you," but he wanted to keep it in the family. Luckman understood.

Following his triple-bypass heart surgery in the early 1980s, Luckman rebelled against his new lifestyle and diet restrictions and ended up back in the hospital. Halas read him the riot act at lunch, bawling him out as he never had had occasion to do when Luckman played for him. When Halas had finished his obscenity-laced denunciation of Luckman's stubbornness, he fell silent for a moment, then reached across the table and took his old quarterback's hand in his and said softly, "Sid, what would I do without you?" Luckman paid the lesson forward a few years later in a letter to a similarly obstinate Jay Pritzker after Pritzker's heart attack. "In closing," he wrote, after urging Pritzker to "stick to the rules," "I paraphrase Coach—'Jay, what would we all do without you?'"

Not long after that, in 1983, the 88-year-old Halas was being treated for pancreatic cancer, and Luckman was with him in the hospital every night for months. When Halas lay dying at his home in the

Edgewater Beach Apartments, it was Luckman he wanted to see. The 66-year-old Luckman was there almost every night, just the two of them in Halas's bedroom, the man who had seemingly willed into existence a game that has become the richest sport in America having his cold feet massaged by the man who had helped him do it at a critical juncture in the game's history. Between 1968, when Halas retired from coaching, and 1983, the once mighty Bears had had only two winning seasons, and it must have been a great comfort for Halas to see Sid Luckman, the friendly ghost of championships past, next to his bed.

"To be a Bear is something very few people understand," Luckman said in a rare interview when he was a frail 80 and his voice had grown wispy. "If you're a member of the Bears you have a heritage and understanding very few people understand. I loved being a Bear. The camaraderie, the friendship, the roar of the crowd, the emotion. . . . You can't imagine the extreme emotion of winning. Nothing in the world can ever replace the years I played for the Bears."

Luckman couldn't bring himself to be present on Halloween when Halas's death was imminent, but he made the initial call to tell the press that he was gone.

The T formation had given the Bears teams of the 1940s a competitive edge that they could not sustain as the odds against them mounted and the rest of the league caught up. After his retirement, Luckman was succeeded by a welter of quarterbacks, none of whom had his leadership skills or the same favorable historical conditions. But if the Bears no longer dominated, the league prospered. By the 1960s, Halas's once ragtag league had overtaken baseball as the national pastime. The passing era that Luckman helped usher in transformed football. Thanks in part to new rules protecting receivers and quarterbacks, in 1982 pass attempts exceeded rushing attempts for the first time in NFL history.

During the next two decades, San Francisco coach Bill Walsh's West Coast Offense, Cincinnati coach Sam Wyche's no-huddle offense, and Buffalo coach Marv Levy's K-Gun Offense further insured the passing game's dominance. In 2018, when the NFL set records for touchdown passes and pass completion percentage, the ratio of the league's passing-to-rushing attempts had never been greater.

Beginning in the 1950s, television brought the NFL's thrilling new offenses into millions of American homes, and with it the league's increasingly cathartic violence. The surreptitiously dirty play of the early years that Halas loved, and that often went unnoticed and unreported in the print media, was replaced by images of overtly brutal hits—like Chuck Bednarik's flattening of Frank Gifford in 1960, or Dick Butkus's crunching tackles later in the decade—that became emblems of the NFL's crowd-pleasing aggression.

No small part of the NFL's appeal was enhanced by a company founded in 1962 by a World War II veteran and men's clothing salesman named Ed Sabol, who paid the NFL $5,000 for the rights to film that year's championship game. Eventually, NFL Films' novel ground-level camera angles and telescopic lenses captured the nuance of every colorful collision in slow motion. When NFL Films packaged these clips with Sam Spence's heart-pounding score and John Facenda's godlike narration, the effect was an exquisite double message: NFL Films transformed the game's viciousness into ballet while exalting it through martial music and relentless metaphors of war. The now iconic footage of Wilson's Duke footballs revolving slowly in the air on their way to a receiver's hands was a poetic distraction from the game's reality: concussions were the new broken noses, and a culture of taunting and showmanship was about to replace the older generation's gratitude for being allowed to play at all. A game once overshadowed by college football was on its way to becoming a big business synonymous with a conservative fantasy of America itself.

Luckman had no illusions about the good old days, even in 1970: "There's no comparison. Today's players are far superior to those of my day. They're bigger, stronger, faster, better coached all the way from high school, and they start football younger. . . . Of the thirty-man squads I played on, I would say from twelve to fifteen might have made the 1970 Bears, but lack of size and speed would bar the others. Such Bear stars as George McAfee, Bill Osmanski, Bulldog Turner, and Joe Stydahar would have made any of today's NFL teams."

He might not have said the same about himself. Without his extraordinary teammates and the secret weapon of the T formation, Luckman might have been a merely average quarterback. He wasn't very mobile. He didn't have a great arm. Sammy Baugh lasted longer and threw 50 more touchdown passes in his career; Baugh also had more completions, more passing yards, and a higher completion percentage. But Luckman had a slightly higher quarterback rating and four championships to Baugh's two. And his greatest skill lay in making everyone better when he was on the field.

"He understood the whole game, the burdens of the other players," says Marv Levy, the hall of fame coach who took the Buffalo Bills to four consecutive Super Bowls in the early 1990s and became a friend of Luckman's. "He was that era's Peyton Manning and Tom Brady—innovative, bright, team-oriented."

Ironically, the Bears were the very last of the old teams to have a quarterback break Luckman's team record of 137 career touchdowns. Strong-armed Jay Cutler finally did it in 2015, but in the eight seasons it took Cutler to surpass Luckman, the Bears had a mediocre 58–70 record and went to the playoffs only once; by contrast, in Luckman's first seven years as the Bears' quarterback, his teams compiled a record of 86–20–3, went to the title game five times, and won four championships.

✳   ✳   ✳

On a chilly, sunny day in December 1994, 78-year-old Luckman returned to Brooklyn for the dedication of his old Erasmus Hall football field, renovated and renamed Sid Luckman Field. Sixty years before, he had run wild here. Now he didn't look well. He was just out of the hospital and had come against doctors' orders. He rode around the new artificial-turf field in a convertible and waved to the crowd, wearing tinted aviator glasses and a carnation in his lapel. When he addressed the crowd, he said the expected things—that it was one of the greatest days of his life, that it seemed just like yesterday.

Erasmus Hall High had changed. The teenagers who passed through the school's metal detectors were still largely the children of immigrants—but at the end of the 20th century they were Haitian, Caribbean, Indian, and Pakistani, not the Jews, Irish, and Italians of the 1930s. In one of the school's display cases honoring celebrated graduates, there was a clipping of a Jimmy Cannon column about Sid Luckman, but the Erasmus Hall Dutchmen's quarterback of the moment, 17-year-old Adrian Bailey, had never heard of Luckman. Of course he was glad to meet his predecessor: "I think it's great they're doing this," the young quarterback said, "to have all these people come out for it—the students, the coaches, all those old people."

Today, serious students of football don't have to be reminded who Sid Luckman is, and among older Jews of all kinds, the mention of his name often prompts smiles of recognition and ethnic pride and conjures up a distant time and possibly a stuttering newsreel. Several months before his death, in 1998, *Seinfeld* paid tribute to Luckman by naming one episode's minor character after him. Bob Luckman is constantly asked, when he introduces himself, if he's related to Sid Luckman and is then showered with exuberant reactions when he says yes. The world turns out to be full of people who grew up with fathers who idolized Luckman.

Sixty years after Bears fans started complaining, "Where's Sid Luckman when we need him?" his name suddenly was in the news again, thanks to the team's latest candidate for quarterback messiah, second-year-man Mitch Trubisky. Watching Trubisky during the Chicago Bears' home opener in 2018, ESPN's play-by-play announcer Joe Tessitore remarked that the city could use someone to rally around, like "a Sid Luckman." Mentions of Luckman proliferated in the following weeks when Trubisky threw six touchdown passes against Tampa Bay, the most by a Bears quarterback since Lujack's six in 1949 and Luckman's seven in 1943. Trubisky threw three more in his next game to tie Luckman's record of nine touchdowns in successive games. Toward the end of the season, Trubisky tied Luckman's record of three games in a season with a passer rating of 120 or better, helped carry the team into the playoffs for the first time in eight years, and surpassed Luckman's 1943 playoff passing record of 286 yards with 303 of his own against the Philadelphia Eagles. But Luckman was cited for a record from that war-depleted 1943 season that may never be matched:, 13.9 percent of his pass attempts—and 25 percent of his completions—were touchdowns. Twenty years after his death, Luckman's exploits still cast a long shadow.

When Sid was in his 70s, he heard his name invoked in a most unexpected place. In Israel, in 1987, American football was gaining a foothold, and the new International Jewish Sports Hall of Fame in Netanya included among the 300-plus inductees Luckman and his childhood idol Benny Friedman. A Luckman party of 14 led by Sid happened to be in Israel that year for the bar mitzvah of one of Sid's grandsons, and Sid arranged to also appear at the induction into the hall of fame. One afternoon, the Mercedes motor coach Sid had hired to ferry the group around dropped them off at their hotel.

In front of the hotel, a handful of boys were playing touch football. Suddenly, within earshot of members of the clan, one of the boys yelled at another, "Who do you think you are, Sid Luckman?"

Possibly only one child in the world that day, perhaps even that year, mentioned the name Sid Luckman while playing touch football, and he happened to say it when Sid Luckman was standing nearby. The story is part of Luckman lore; it comes up around a lunch table with all three of Luckman's children and their spouses present, as precious a memory as Joe DiMaggio showing up in the living room, or Frank Sinatra walking unannounced into Estelle's hospital room.

Meyer Luckman's murder of his brother-in-law, Sam Drukman, is not part of the family lore nor even an object of much curiosity. Sid never stopped avoiding the subject. In his autobiography, in which Meyer Luckman is barely mentioned after Sid goes to college, he wrote that his father had died in early 1943—he didn't die until 1944—in order to explain Meyer's absence from a family scene. In 1996, when he was 80, Sid Luckman was still ducking the truth. When explaining to an interviewer why he had considered dropping out of Columbia in his freshman year, he limited his comments to this: "My family wasn't doing well financially. My mother was having her problems."

He had spared the world, his loved ones, and himself the truth, which one can easily argue was the right thing to do. What upside was there—apart from satisfying some abstract commitment to total candor—in disclosing a distant crime whose perpetrators had been convicted and out of the picture for so many years? He chose to spare his loved ones the burden he was used to carrying almost alone. Sid

Luckman's solution was to choose life, and his was by any measure one long success story that he would summarize for posterity on his gravestone, in Skokie, Illinois: "I had it all. I did it all. I loved it all." Whereas another man in his situation might have shied away from life, flinching at every bit of good fortune that came his way, Sid Luckman put the poisonous past aside; if it was going to leak into the present, somebody else was going to have to be responsible.

What Sid did for a man named Mohammed Sekhani shortly before he died was, like many of his acts, just extraordinary enough that it's tempting to reach for an explanation as extraordinary as his being the son of a murderer. Only after Sid Luckman died, from a heart attack in Aventura, Florida, on July 5, 1998, did anyone learn of the gesture. Bob Luckman got a phone call from Sekhani, a Pakistani who had come to the United States at the age of 20. For years, he had been Luckman's regular server at Gibsons Bar and Steakhouse, where Sid always ordered the 19-ounce New York sirloin (always with ketchup) and entertained at the restaurant's power table, number 54. Regular guests included Irv Kupcinet and his wife, Essie; Chicago Bears coaches and players; and assorted businesspeople. When other diners said hello to Luckman, he would often tell Mohammed to buy them dessert and put it on his account. Sometimes he'd call Mohammed from his home in Florida and ask him who was eating at Gibsons that evening, then tell him he wanted to pick up the tab, even if, as was occasionally the case, he didn't know the people. When Mohammed once decided on his own not to honor one of Sid's directives, Luckman jokingly threatened to have him fired.

When Sid got Mohammed tickets to Super Bowl XXIX in Miami in 1995—fittingly, the one where San Francisco quarterback Steve Young set the still-standing Super Bowl record for touchdown passes with six—he wondered if Sid could help him get a table at Joe's Stone Crab, an impossible task on Super Bowl weekend. Sid

said, "Just go and tell them your name is Mohammed Luckman."
Mohammed gave the maître d' his temporarily adopted name and was
seated immediately. Before Bears home games Luckman would often
host huge brunches at Gibsons, after which the guests boarded buses
he had chartered to take everyone to Soldier Field and back. When
Mohammed once asked him for 10 tickets to a game, Luckman left
him 20. Mohammed frequently helped Luckman entertain at home,
where he was given the keys to Luckman's cash drawer and told to take
whatever he needed to buy food and supplies for the party.

At Gibsons, Luckman always arrived punctually, before his
guests, and Mohammed would take the opportunity to chat alone
with a man whose generosity, affection, and impeccable attire came
to seem almost otherworldly. When Sid touched Mohammed—a
handshake, a hand on his shoulder, a hug—it was, he recalled, going
on 30 years as a waiter at Gibsons, "like being touched by an angel."

In 1995, toward the end of summer, when Mohammed was 37 and
Sid Luckman was 79, Luckman took one look at Mohammed before dinner and said, "What's wrong, Mo? What is it? You're not looking so good."

Mohammed's six-month-old son, his first child, had a tumor on
his head and was in the hospital, where it needed to be removed. It was
complicated; the doctors were concerned that the tumor was attached
through the skull to brain tissue and removing it might cause brain
damage or worse. Mohammed was emotionally drained.

Within days, Luckman had taken the case under his wing, made
all the necessary arrangements, talked to the neurosurgeon, and ascer-
tained he was the best man for the job. Over Labor Day weekend, little
Nabeel Sekhani underwent a delicate, successful six-hour operation.

Sid Luckman never mentioned it to anybody. Three years later,
when his family was sitting shiva for him in Bob and Gale Luckman's
Highland Park home in the summer of 1998, Mohammed told Bob
he wanted to drive up with his wife and introduce Bob to their kids.

He brought some of Sid's favorite desserts—Gibsons' immense carrot cake, Texas pecan pie, Jerry Cherry pie.

Mohammed took Bob aside; introduced him to his perfectly healthy son, Nabeel; and explained what Sid had done. Although accustomed to his father's compassion, Bob had tears in his eyes when he learned how his father had taken care of the man he knew only as the waiter who had taken care of him.

But it was the way Sid Luckman played the game; he was very good, but he made everyone else around him better.

Postgame Commentary and Acknowledgments

One of the by-products of writing this book was learning the extent to which I had been only a few degrees of separation away from Sid Luckman all along. My childhood playmate Jay Cassidy distinctly remembers concluding as a boy that his future was not in football, when Luckman's daughter Gail demonstrated that she could throw a football farther than he. The older sister of another close friend, Chuck Dawe, was invited to Ellen Luckman's "sweet 16" birthday celebration in 1960, when the girls all piled into a limousine Luckman had rented for the ride downtown to attend the premier of *Ben Hur*, followed by a Kingston Trio performance at Mister Kelly's on Rush Street. When my second cousin Nina Gilson, who grew up in Chicago, invited me for dinner at her Manhattan apartment midway through the writing of this book, and asked me what I was working on, I asked her if she knew who Sid Luckman was.

"Know him?" she said. "He was one of my father's partners. He used to have dinner at my house."

Nina's father, Joe Orloff, I had to be reminded, made his living as one of the preeminent gin rummy players in America in the 1960s. Challengers used to fly in to try their luck against him at the Covenant Club, Chicago's original club for Ashkenazi Jews on North Dearborn Street in the Loop. Sid Luckman, no slouch at gin rummy himself and a Covenant Club regular, was among the men who regularly bankrolled Orloff. And it turned out that the father of another Highland Park friend used to play gin at Luckman's house on Saturdays.

I also learned, beyond these intimate associations, that the tentacles of organized crime had touched my world more than I knew. The son of one of Al Capone's lawyers lived two blocks from my childhood house. My sister-in-law's uncle, Al Schultz, was married to Ida Greenberg, the daughter of Alex Louis "Louie" Greenberg, another refugee from the pogroms in Russia, who became a racketeer, a bootlegger, and Al Capone's accountant. A friend of my brother was the grandson of a mob bagman. Jay Cassidy, who lived across the street and right next to Sid Luckman's house in the 1950s, was the grandson of a first cousin of Sidney Korshak. Little did I know.

However, the original impulse to write *Tough Luck* had nothing to do with any of these connections. The book was born of a nostalgic urge in 2017 to write a short story about one of the countless touch football games I played at Ravinia Elementary School across the street from the Luckman house. In my story, I summoned the nerve to ask Luckman, retired and raking leaves, if he would fill in for one of our regular quarterbacks, a boy who was busy that afternoon studying for his bar mitzvah. After initially declining, Luckman surprised us by walking over later in sneakers, carrying a precious official NFL football.

In my story, he threw soft touchdown passes, including one to an overweight kid who had never caught one before. On defense, he let me catch a few passes, although my most devious moves were useless against him. We were all in love with him. After the game, we begged him to show us how far he could throw the ball and gathered at the far end of the field to catch his 70-yard heave. Then he let us keep the ball, saying we would grow into it, and walked back home, massaging his right shoulder.

That short story began its rapid evolution into this book as soon as I discovered Meyer Luckman's crime, although to this day I still daydream about being tutored by Sid in the arts of passing and punting. When I told Bob Luckman about my fantasy of recruiting his father to play with me, he said, "And Sid would have done it in a minute."

The story of Sid Luckman and his father is a portal through which I've addressed larger events that have been exhaustively studied by others in direct light. It's a truism—and few are truer—that every nonfiction book is a collaboration between the author whose name is on the cover and many other writers whose labor and talent make it possible to tell a true story in greater detail and with greater perspective. For their accounts of organized crime, I am indebted to Albert Fried's *The Rise and Fall of the Jewish Gangster in America*, Gus Russo's *Supermob*, Burton Turkus and Sid Feder's *Murder, Inc.*, Dan Moldea's *Interference*, and Rich Cohen's *Tough Jews*; for the history of the Bears and professional football's early years, I am indebted to Jeff Davis's *Papa Bear*, George Halas's *Halas by Halas*, and Robert W. Peterson's *Pigskin*. For readers in search of more information and texture in these areas, I highly recommend these books. Needless to say, Luckman's own *Luckman at Quarterback* provided priceless scenes, dialogue, anecdotes, and insights into Luckman's early life and character. I'm indebted to Dan Daly for being my original link to the Luckman family's forgotten drama.

For providing the statistical history of the NFL, Sports Reference LLC's Pro Football Reference (pro-football-reference.com) was invaluable, as was YouTube.com for supplying so much film of old football games, including many of Luckman's. For the details of Meyer Luckman's crime, trial, and associations, I am beholden to the many unsung newspaper reporters of the 1930s who diligently recorded the first, and only, accounts of those events. Without journalists, history would be a black hole.

Still, errors turn up in pixels and print. One author misses the date of Lepke Buchalter's arrest by an entire year; Luckman himself misremembers the number of touchdowns he threw in a game; and Halas mentions two players he added to his roster in 1941 who didn't become Bears until 1943. I double- and even triple-checked facts at every opportunity. When there was a discrepancy about something that happened in a game, I sided with pro-football-reference.com and game film over human memory. However, pro-football-reference.com isn't always the last statistical word; for instance, the website's box score for the Bears' 41–21 victory over Washington for the 1943 NFL championship credits Luckman with a fourth-quarter touchdown pass to Harry Clarke of 10 yards. The film of the play clearly shows it to be a 16-yard touchdown pass. When game film wasn't available, and book authors and daily newspaper accounts were in conflict, I sided with the beat sports reporter who had just witnessed the game. I apologize in advance for all unforced errors of fact, my own and others'.

Under the best of circumstances—access to a cooperative living subject and his or her letters and thoughts, in addition to friends and family members—writing a biography is still a surface-scratching, or perhaps surface-gouging activity. As Julian Barnes wrote in his novel *Flaubert's Parrot*, "The trawling net fills, then the biographer hauls it in, sorts, throws back, stores, fillets and sells. Yet consider what he doesn't catch: there is always far more of that." Writing about Sid Luckman at all posed special challenges because no one in the immediate or extended family kept or left behind any notes, journals, diaries, or family biographies. The cooperation of Luckman's living relatives was essential. For generously sharing their time, memories, and materials with me, I want to thank above all Sid Luckman's children—Bob,

Ellen, and Gail; and their spouses, Gale Lassman, Dick Weiss, and Al Gardner—as well as his niece Ronnie Suslow and his nephew Peter Luckman and Peter's wife, Geri. Bob Luckman was essential to the progress of this book, and I want to thank him especially for making peace with this project, for his candor, and for making introductions for me on several occasions.

Thanks to all the people who shared their knowledge, memories, and expertise, among them: Carol Felsenthal, Peter Gottlieb, Margie Korshak, Samuel Lawton III, Marv Levy, Todd Logan, Steve Lombardo, Johnny Lujack, Gerry Orlowsky, Ellen Alswang Rosen, Mohammed Sekhani, and US District Court Judge Jack B. Weinstein.

This book is rooted in my childhood, when several wonderful English and history teachers inspired me and set me on my journey as a writer. I have been remiss not to have acknowledged them earlier, since the years have proved to me how lucky I was to have had their wisdom, humor, attention, and encouragement. So, to Eunice Borman, Jerry Grunska, Helen Palmer, and Marguerite Prahl, formerly of Highland Park High School, a very heartfelt thank-you, wherever you are. To my far-flung posse—including Rob Battles, David Bloom, Sidney Blumenthal, Jay Cassidy, John Chamberlin, Charles Dawe, James Friedman, Gregory Jordan, Philip Koch, Khari May, Stephen Molton, Harry Prichett, David Smith, Alan Orlowsky, Ed Orlowsky, and Paul Solman—thank you, thank you. And thank you.

On an entirely different front, a big shout-out to my local Paris Baguette for serving as a home away from home that perfectly mimics the ambient sound of a busy office. The management and staff there will never know to what extent they, and their croissants, enabled the writing of this book.

My literary "family" consists of my agent, Victoria Skurnick, who understood my passion for this project and contributed several important suggestions, often over lunches filled with laughter and gossip; and my Grove Atlantic editor, George Gibson, who is also my valued friend and former actual teammate. He perceived the soul of this book early on and attended to the manuscript with a level of editorial skill and a pitch-perfect ear that are both, sadly, becoming rare in a time when the Internet does such a disservice to the very idea of good writing, to say nothing of truth. Whereas anyone can "publish" almost anything on the Internet without concern for truth, accuracy, or good grammar, it takes a village to get old-fashioned books into shape. Much gratitude goes to Grove Atlantic's outstanding village of professionals: powerhouse editorial assistant Emily Burns, eagle-eyed proofreader Susan Gamer, art director Gretchen Mergenthaler and cover designer Becca Fox, publicist Justina Batchelor, production director Sal Destro, production assistant Olivia Noel-Davis, publicity director Deb Seager, associate publisher Judy Hottensen, and publisher Morgan Entrekin.

Early in the process of writing this book, my daughter Isabel listened to my brief description of the story and immediately suggested, with her usual aptness, a title that condenses into two words the essences of Sid Luckman's life. Both Isabel and my daughter Lucy cheered me on from the sidelines. I can't thank my partner Ivy Austin enough; no stranger herself to the highs and lows of creation, she ran all kinds of emotional interference for me, in addition to modeling her talent for the art of living. I couldn't ask for a more perfect teammate. To my dear late parents, Carey and Sol, thanks as always for helping to make this writer's life possible—if you look down, you'll see I'm still at it—and to my sister Joyce Friedman, thank you for being such a loving, caring ally.

Finally, there's my older brother Rob, a lifelong Chicagoan who shared many impressions with me during the writing of this book but didn't live to see it finished. Our bond as the two most sports-crazed siblings in the family began in earnest when, in possession of a brand-new license, Rob drove the two of us down to Comiskey Park for the first game of the 1959 White Sox–Dodgers World Series. Our connection over the years intensified as we shared many basketball and tennis courts, mounting memories of Chicago's professional sports teams, and recollections of our own widely spaced, and gently exaggerated, moments of youthful athletic heroism. Rob, here's to you, our brotherhood, our friendship, and that one perfect baseline pick-and-roll we executed at the Standard Club in 2009.

Selected Notes

In cases where sources are not cited within the text of the book, I have provided them below.

Introduction: The Quarterback Next Door

The conversation between Dan Daly and the old-timer was recounted to me by Daly in an email.

1: Hog-Tied and Trussed

Details of Sam Drukman's murder and its aftermath come principally from articles in the *Brooklyn Daily Eagle* and the *New York Times*. Anecdotes about Sid's childhood relationships with his parents come from his 1949 autobiography, *Luckman at Quarterback*.

2: The Erasmus Terror

The story of Sid's broken hand is from the author's conversations with Luckman's children, nieces, and nephews, as are the stories concerning the death of the family's infant daughter and Meyer Luckman's violent temper. Stories about, and quotes from, Erasmus football coach Paul Sullivan come from *Luckman at Quarterback*, as do the conversation involving Sid, Leo Luckman, and Lou Little, and Estelle and Sid's high school conversation.

3: One Heartless Tangle

The sources for most of this chapter are the newspapers cited. That Ike Luckman's wife was also his niece was reported in the *Brooklyn Daily Eagle* of June 9, 1936. The "effect" of the crime on Leo and his wife was provided in an interview with Leo's son, Peter Luckman.

4: A Worrisome Gent

This chapter relies heavily on a combination of newspaper coverage, mostly in the *New York Times* and the *Brooklyn Daily Eagle*, and Sid's autobiography.

5: Specialized Persuasions

The portrait of Lepke has been assembled from a variety of sources (and photos), chiefly Burton Turkus and Sid Feder's *Murder, Inc.*, Albert Fried's *The Rise and Fall of the Jewish Gangster in America*, Rich Cohen's *Tough Jews*, FBI Records: The Vault (vault.fbi.gov), and photographs available on the Internet. The attendance of Meyer Luckman at the 1934 mob execution of William Snyder was a fact buried in a January 17, 1937, *New York Times* article about the Flour Truckmen's Association's "labor adjuster," Max Silverman.

6: A Good Future in Trucking

The quotes and anecdotes about Sammy Baugh draw from many sources, including *Luckman at Quarterback*, Richard Whittingham's *What a Game They Played*, NFL Films' *The Top 100: NFL's Greatest Players*, and Baugh's obituary in the *Washington Post*, December 18, 2008. Physical details of the 1937 NFL championship were gleaned from game film. The history of the football's dimensions comes from "The Evolution of the Football" in *Popular Mechanics*, February 1, 2018. The conversations between Lou Little and Luckman come from the latter's autobiography. Details of the Columbia–Syracuse and Columbia–Brown games come from *Luckman at Quarterback*, various newspaper accounts, and game film. *Luckman at Quarterback* provided the conversations between Sid Luckman, Lou Little, and Benny Friedman.

Details of E & A Transport Company's immunity from the flour haulers' strike come from the *Brooklyn Daily Eagle*. Leo Luckman's comment to Sid comes from the latter's autobiography, as does Halas's phone call to Sid. Halas's biographical information comes largely from Jeff Davis's *Papa Bear*. Halas's comment that Luckman "did so many tricks with the ball" appeared in Luckman's obituary in the *Chicago Tribune* of July 6, 1998.

7: Up the River

The history of Sing Sing is drawn from Ralph Blumenthal's *Miracle at Sing Sing: How One Man Transformed the Lives of America's Most Dangerous Prisoners* and Denis Brian's *Sing Sing: The Inside Story of a Notorious Prison*.

8: Captive City

The report that Irv Kupcinet had fought with the Northwestern coach's brother comes from a Jay Mariotti column in a *Chicago Sun-Times* special supplement on Kupcinet, "Kup's Chicago," published on November 12, 2003. The description of Charlie Baron as "handsome" is based on the only photograph of him that I could find, in *33 Division Pictorial History, Army of the United States, Camp Forrest, 1941–1942*; he served in the 33rd as an aide to Major General Samuel T. Lawton. Kupcinet's comment that "No charges were brought, but he was warned to be aware" is quoted in "Kup's last farewell to a 'Dearest Friend'" in the the *Chicago Sun-Times*, July 6, 1998.

9: A Fast Passing Game

Biographical information on Clark Shaughnessy is taken from James W. Johnson's *Wow Boys*, Jeff Davis's *Papa Bear*, and *Luckman at Quarterback*. Information on Hugh Ray Jr. comes largely from the biography by Ray's grandson James W. Stangeland, *Hugh L. Ray: The NFL's Mr. Einstein*. Shaughnessy's inspiration for the T formation in Nazi military strategy comes principally from William Barry Furlong's article, "The Blitzkrieg Comes to the Gridiron," in the February, 1986, issue of *Smithsonian* magazine. Ken Kavanaugh's anecdote about Buford "Baby" Ray can be found in Richard

Whittingham's *What a Game They Played*. Luckman recounts his conversation with Luke Johnsos in his autobiography, which is also the source of the note that Dashiell Hammett was his favorite author. Sprinkle's and Kavanaugh's comments about Luckman's passing are reported in Jeff Davis's *Papa Bear*, as is Halas's comment, "Sammy was the better passer." Luckman's conversation with Shaughnessy comes from Luckman's autobiography.

10: Runaround

I have drawn my description of Lepke's surrender to J. Edgar Hoover from existing accounts in Turkus and Feder's *Murder, Inc.*, Neal Gabler's *Winchell: Gossip, Power and the Culture of Celebrity*, and Rich Cohen's *Tough Jews*.

11: Rookie

Luckman's account of his first game at quarterback in the NFL is taken from a videotaped interview with him conducted by the Lincoln Academy of Illinois in 1996. The conversation between Luckman and Shaughnessy in the car comes from *Luckman at Quarterback*, as does the conversation between Luckman and Halas about Shaughnessy. Luckman's son, Bob, is the source for the story of Joe Stydahar rescuing Luckman from George Musso, as well as the story about Stydahar's upset stomach. The anecdote about Musso standing up for Luckman in the Detroit game is in *Luckman at Quarterback*. The McAfee quote comes from Richard Whittingham's *Bears: In Their Own Words*.

12: They All Laughed

Leo's son, Peter, is the source of the information that his mother, Leona, needed two bodyguards to protect her from the mob after Meyer went to prison. Anecdotes about Hunk Anderson can be found in *Luckman at Quarterback*. George McAfee's comment about wearing low-cut shoes appeared in his obituary in the *Washington Post*, March 8, 2009. Luckman's comment on "competent unknowns" is from his autobiography. Pop Warner's quip about Shaughnessy's "crazy formation" is quoted in James W. Johnson's *Wow Boys*.

13: Whiners, Crybabies, and Quitters

Frankie Albert's quote "This stuff really works!" is in James W. Johnson's *Wow Boys*. Bill Osmanski's account of the last-second incomplete pass can be heard on *The Sports Scrapbook*, a radio broadcast that accompanies film of the 73–0 victory that can be seen on YouTube.com. Halas records his response to the referee's call in the Bears' 7–3 loss in his *Halas by Halas*. Baugh's visit to Columbia is recounted in *Luckman at Quarterback*, as are the anecdote about Sid collecting Baugh's autograph on a football and Baugh's comment about bringing Northerners and Southerners together. The story of how Halas handed Luckman three plays in the locker room is reported in numerous places, including *Halas by Halas* and *Luckman at Quarterback*.

14: Barrage

Physical description of the Bears' 73–0 victory over the Redskins is based on film of the game available on YouTube.com. Harry Clarke recollects his lie about not having scored a touchdown yet as part of *The Sports Scrapbook* audio accompanying the game film.

15: Temptations

The source for the story about Ava Gardner's mash note to Luckman is his nephew Peter Luckman, who heard it directly from his mother, Leona. The accounts of NFL franchise owners' gambling habits are taken from Dan Moldea's *Interference: How Organized Crime Influences Professional Football*. Details of the scandal involving Filchock and Hapes are drawn from Moldea and the comprehensive December 16, 1946, *New York Times* article by Alexander Feinberg, "'Fixer' Jailed Here for Bribe Offers to Football Stars." The inclusion of Luckman's name in Dorfman's address book is reported in Moldea.

16: High-Priced Help

Bob Luckman is the source for the story of Baron's loan to his father, including his taking offense that Sid had not approached him earlier. The bugged conversation involving Baron in the North Michigan Avenue tailor shop comes from William F. Roemer Jr.'s *Man Against the Mob: The Inside Story of How the FBI Cracked the Chicago Mob by the Agent Who Led the Attack.*

17: Another Botched Job

Although I have drawn on several reports, the best detailed account of the Joe Rosen murder can be found in Turkus and Feder's *Murder, Inc.* The dialogue between Lepke and Max Rubin, presumably taken from courtroom testimony, appears in Turkus and Feder.

18: Almost to a T

The exchange between Luckman and the unnamed college coach about the intelligence required to run the T formation is reported in *Luckman at Quarterback.*

19: With a Thud

Luckman recounts his telegram to Halas and the latter's reply in his autobiography. His appearance at the Brooklyn Edison Club was reported in the *Brooklyn Daily Eagle.* The exchange between Sid and his wife, Estelle, comes from his autobiography. The "OK, get back where you belong, chum," anecdote was reported by Arthur Daley of the *New York Times* in a column on August 3, 1943. The Bears' complaints about having to play in the Pro Bowl were reported in the *New York Times* on December 14, 1942.

20: Casualties

The back-and-forth between New York State and the federal government over Louis "Lepke" Buchalter is drawn from the account in Turkus and Feder's *Murder, Inc.* The exchanges between Luckman and George Wilson before the Sid Luckman Day game and between Luckman and Bronko Nagurski after it both come from *Luckman at Quarterback.* The conversation between Luckman and Steve Owen is reported in a December 1946 *New York Times* column by Arthur Daley titled "The Stamp of Immortality."

The anecdote about Sid's mother screaming at him to give the New York Giants the ball was reported by Sid himself in his 1996 interview with the Lincoln Academy of Illinois.

21: A Surprising Comment

The accounts of the days following the Bears' 56–7 victory are drawn from *Luckman at Quarterback*, as were Baugh's comment to Luckman during the 1943 NFL championship and the information about Luckman's missions while he was serving in the merchant marine.

22: Last Dance

The description of Lepke's arrival at Sing Sing is drawn from various photographs and from Turkus and Feder, the source as well for Lepke and his lawyers' last-minute machinations and the firsthand details about the execution of Lepke, Weiss, and Capone. The origin of Burton Turkus's nickname, "Mr. Arsenic," was reported in Turkus and Feder's *Murder, Inc.*

23: Bingo Keep It

The Mario Tonelli anecdote comes from *Luckman at Quarterback*.

24: A Congestion of Quarterbacks

The stories about nightspot-hopping with Fred Davis and the Hollywood party were provided by Luckman in his autobiography, as was the anecdote about Halas's visit to Sid Luckman Motors. What Halas said to Luckman when he came out of his last game as a Bear was reported by *New York Times* writer Sam Goldaper in *Great Pro Quarterbacks*, edited by Lud Duroska.

25: Gifts

Marty Glickman was quoted in Mike Lupica's *New York Daily News* column of July 7, 1998. DiMaggio's work for V. H. Monette is reported in Richard

Ben Cramer's *Joe DiMaggio: The Hero's Life*. Luckman related the story about
Babe Ruth refusing to give him an autograph in his Lincoln Academy of
Illinois interview. The Jay Pritzker anecdote comes from Bob Luckman, who
was there. Luckman's son-in-law Dick Weiss provided memories of the gift-
wrapping parties. The assessment of Luckman as a salesman comes from
his son, Bob, who also shared his memories of Sid entertaining business
associates and their families at Bears team practices. Steve Lombardo of
Gibsons Bar and Steakhouse supplied the anecdote about the woman and
her small dog. Luckman's daughters, Ellen and Gail, provided the jewelry
story among many others in this and the following chapter. Irv Kupcinet's
quote about Sid being honored in Chicago comes from Kupcinet's interview
with the Lincoln Academy of Illinois.

26: Secrets

Both Johnny Lujack's and Marv Levy's reactions occurred in personal conversations with the author. Ellen and Gail Luckman provided examples of
their father's superstitions.

27: Who Do You Think You Are, Sid Luckman?

Luckman's "He meant to me as much as anybody" comes from his interview
with the Lincoln Academy of Illinois, as does the story of Pritzker offering
to buy the team. Luckman's posting of Halas's letter in his Mayo Clinic
room comes from his son, Bob. Dick Weiss provided Halas's admonition to
Luckman after the latter's bypass operation, as well as Luckman's subsequent
letter to Jay Pritzker. Luckman's 13.9 percent touchdown-per-pass-attempt
record was cited on Fansided's 12th Man Rising (12thmanrising.com), a
website devoted to the Seattle Seahawks. Luckman's return to Brooklyn for
the dedication of Sid Luckman Field was reported by Ira Berkow in the
New York Times.

Bibliography

Books

Anslinger, Harry J., and Will Oursler. *The Murderers: The Shocking Story of the Narcotics Gang.* New York: Farrar, Straus and Cudahy, 1961.

Arons, Ron. *The Jews of Sing Sing.* Fort Lee, NJ: Barricade Books Inc., 2008.

Blumenthal, Ralph. *Miracle at Sing Sing: How One Man Transformed the Lives of America's Most Dangerous Prisoners.* New York: St. Martin's Press, 2004.

Brian, Denis. *Sing Sing: The Inside Story of a Notorious Prison.* Amherst, NY: Prometheus Books, 2005.

Cannon, Jimmy. *Nobody Asked Me, But . . . : The World of Jimmy Cannon.* New York: Holt, Rinehart and Winston, 1978.

Cohen, Rich. *Tough Jews: Fathers, Sons and Gangster Dreams.* New York: Simon & Schuster, 1998.

Cramer, Richard Ben. *Joe DiMaggio: The Hero's Life.* New York: Simon & Schuster, 2000.

Daly, Dan. *The National Forgotten League: Entertaining Stories and Observations from Pro Football's First Fifty Years.* Lincoln and London: University of Nebraska Press, 2012.

Davis, Jeff. *Papa Bear: The Life and Legacy of George Halas.* New York: McGraw-Hill, 2005.

Demaris, Ovid. *Captive City: Chicago in Chains.* New York: Lyle Stuart, Inc., 1969.

Duroska, Lud, ed. *Great Pro Quarterbacks.* New York: Grosset & Dunlap, 1972.

Dyja, Thomas. *The Third Coast: When Chicago Built the American Dream*. New York: Penguin Press, 2013.

Elmaleh, Edmund. *The Canary Sang but Couldn't Fly*. New York: Union Square Press, 2009.

Fried, Albert. *The Rise and Fall of the Jewish Gangster in America*. New York / Chichester, West Sussex: Columbia University Press, 1993.

Gabler, Neal. *Winchell: Gossip, Power and the Culture of Celebrity*. New York: Alfred A. Knopf, 1994.

Halas, George, with Gwen Morgan and Arthur Veysey. *Halas by Halas*. New York: McGraw-Hill Book Company, 1979.

Jaworski, Ron, with Greg Cosell and David Plaut. *The Games That Changed the Game: The Evolution of the NFL in Seven Sundays*. New York: Ballantine Books / ESPN Books, 2010.

Johnson, James W. *The Wow Boys: A Coach, a Team, and a Turning Point in College Football*. Lincoln and London: University of Nebraska Press, 2006.

Kennedy, William. *Legs*. New York: Penguin, 1983.

Leonard, David, Kimberly B. George, and Wade Davis, eds. *Football, Culture and Power*. New York: Routledge, 2018.

Luckman, Sid, with Norman Reissman. *Luckman at Quarterback*. Chicago and New York: Ziff-Davis Publishing Co., 1949.

Moldea, Dan E. *Interference: How Organized Crime Influences Professional Football*. New York: William Morrow and Company, 1989.

Olderman, Murray. *The Pro Quarterback*. New York: Prentice-Hall, 1966.

Peterson, Robert W. *Pigskin: The Early Years of Pro Football*. New York and Oxford: Oxford University Press, 1997.

Roemer, William F., Jr. *Man Against the Mob: The Inside Story of How the FBI Cracked the Chicago Mob by the Agent Who Led the Attack*. New York: Ivy Books, 1989.

Russo, Gus. *Supermob: How Sidney Korshak and His Criminal Associates Became America's Hidden Power Brokers*. New York: Bloomsbury USA, 2006.

Smith, Robert. *Illustrated History of Pro Football*. New York: Putnam Publishing Group, 1972.

Stangeland, James W. *Hugh L. Ray: The NFL's Mr. Einstein.* North Charleston, SC: CreateSpace Independent Publishing Platform, 2014.

Thorn, John, ed. *The Armchair Quarterback.* New York: Charles Scribner's Sons, 1982.

Turkus, Burton, and Sid Feder. *Murder, Inc.: The Story of the Syndicate.* Boston: Da Capo Press, 1951.

Whittingham, Richard. *Bears: In Their Own Words.* Chicago: Contemporary Books Publishing Group, 1992.

Whittingham, Richard. *What a Game They Played: An Inside Look at the Golden Era of Pro Football.* Lincoln and London: University of Nebraska Press, 1984.

Zion, Sidney. *Loyalty and Betrayal: The Story of the American Mob.* San Francisco: Collins, 1994.

Websites

Besttickets.com

The Gridiron Uniform Database: gridiron-uniforms.com

Murderpedia: The Encyclopedia of Murders: murderpedia.org

Newspapers.com

NFL.com

NFL Films' "The Top 100: NFL's Greatest Players"

Pro Football Hall of Fame: profootballhof.com

Pro Football Reference: pro-football-reference.com

FBI Records: The Vault: vault.fbi.gov

YouTube.com

Index

A. E. Staley Manufacturing Company, 77–78

AAFC (All-America Football Conference), 227–228, 229

Abbandando, Frank "the Dasher," 133

Abraham, Jesse, 129–130

Achtung—Panzer! (Guderian), 105

All-America Football Conference, 165

All-Star league team (1940), 130

Alston, Walter, 109

Amalgamated Clothing Workers Union, 199

American Professional Football Association, 78

Anastasia, Albert, 114, 118–119, 179

Anderson, Dave, 245

Anderson, Heartley "Hunk," 134–138, 153, 202, 203

Anslinger, Harry, 115

anti-Semitism
in Chicago, 94
directed at Sid Luckman, 127, 243

Army football, 48

Aron, Ron, 60

Artoe, Lee, 148, 153, 195

Arvey, Jake, 92, 170

Associated Press, on Meyer Luckman's trial, 32

Auerbach, Red, 244

Aviv Assets, 248

Bailey, Adrian, 268

Baker Field (Columbia University), 44–45

Ballard, Dave, 134

Baltimore Colts, 165, 166

Barber, Walter Lanier "Red," 145, 153

Baron, Charlie "Babe," 92–94, 170–172, 251

Battles, Cliff, 63

Baugh, Sam Adrian "Sammy." *See also* Washington Redskins
gambling scandals and, 162
hired by Washington Redskins, 61–66, 70
1940 championship game, 146–149, 151–153, 155, 157
1940 season, 139, 142, 144
1942 season, 194–195
1943 season, 203, 209, 210
1945 season, 225
1947 season, 233
records held by, 127, 164, 267
retirement of, 252
on T formation adoption by Redskins, 211
in *Triple Threat* (film), 235

"Bear Down, Chicago Bears" (song), 2

Bee, Clair, 134

Belichick, Bill, 187n

Bell, Bert, 161, 162–164, 228

Berry, Connie Mack, 203

Biddle, Francis, 199–200

Bidwill, Charles W., 161

Black Sheep (Sing Sing football team), 86–87

Blumenthal, Ralph, 84

Bonom, Oscor, 208

Boodey (Brooklyn neighborhood football player), 207–208
Boston Celtics, 244
Brady, Tom, 110, 187n
Bray, Ray, 70, 193
Brickhouse, Jack, 3
Brocklin, Norm Van, 240
Brooklyn Daily Eagle
  on Meyer Luckman's criminal record, 29, 31–33, 36–37, 39, 40, 41, 81, 130
  on Meyer Luckman's death, 221
  on Sid Luckman's football career, 19, 43–44, 79–80, 108, 109–110, 134
Brooklyn Dodgers (football team), 67, 109, 161
Brooklyn Homicide Court, 30
Brown, Paul, 229
Brumbaugh, Carl, 96, 111–112
Buchalter, Barnett, 52
Buchalter, Betty (Wasserman), 50, 215–218
Buchalter, Harold (Wasserman), 50, 215, 218
Buchalter, Louis "Lepke"
  aliases of, 51
  appeals and US Supreme Court case of, 190–191, 197–198, 217
  biographical information, 51, 52
  characterization of, 50–53
  Dewey and Roosevelt on conviction of, 198–200
  early incarceration of, 113, 120, 130, 173
  execution of, 213–220
  film about, 93
  Flour Truckmen's Association and, 55–56, 130–131
  Meyer Luckman and, 56–60, 130–134
  Murder, Inc., overview, 81–82
  rackets and, 53–55
  Rosen murder and, 174–179
  surrender of, 113–120
Buchalter, Rose, 52
Bussey, Young, 189
Byk, Leo, 14

Camp, Walter, 100
Cannon, Jimmy, 71–72
Capone, Al, 57, 89, 93, 161, 171
Capone, Louis
  appeal of murder conviction, 190–191
  Buchalter's surrender and, 118
  Dewey and Roosevelt on conviction of Buchalter, 198–200
  execution of, 214, 216–220
  Rosen murder and, 174–175, 179
  US Supreme Court case, 197–198
Captive City (Demaris), 92, 170
"Card-Pitts," 224
Cell 202—Sing Sing (Lawes), 85
Cellu-Craft, 244, 246–248
Central Conference of Teamsters, 165
Chicago Bears. *See also* Halas, George; Luckman, Sid; T formation
  "Bear Down, Chicago Bears" (song), 2
  Bears-Redskins 1940 championship game, 145–149, 150–158
  interceptions and touchdowns of, 164
  legacy of, 265–266
  Luckman hired by, 70–82
  Luckman scouted by, 66–70
  Luckman's rookie season with, 121–128
  1940 season, 134–138, 139–145
  1941 season, 180–184
  1942 season, 103–106, 188–189
  1943 season, 206–211
  1944–1946 seasons, 223–231
  1947–1950 seasons, 232–241
  uniforms of, 3
  Wrigley Field, 2–3, 78n
Chicago Cardinals, 161, 180, 224, 237
Chicago (city). *See also individual names of mobsters*
  as "City of the Big Shoulders," 3
  organized crime in, 89–94
Chicago Rockets, 165, 227
Chicago Tribune
  on Bears-Redskins 1940 championship game, 156
  on Halas, 262
  on Luckman's acting career, 159
  on 1941 post-season, 182

on 1942 post-season, 193, 196
on 1943 season, 204
on 1949 season, 240
on T formation, 186–187
Clarke, Harry, 154, 203, 227
Cleveland Browns, 165, 229
Cobb, Ty, 76
Cohen, Philip "Little Farvel," 174–175, 179
Columbia University, Sid Luckman's football
    career at, 9, 22–25, 43–49, 201
Connor, George, 136
Cooper, John Miller, 157
Corbett, Charles, 14–15, 31, 39
Costello, Frank, 115, 176
Cota, Joe, 170
Crack-Up, The (Fitzgerald), 169

Daley, Arthur J., 48, 141–142, 155, 193,
    195, 201
Daly, Dan, 5–6, 8, 87
Daniel, Chase, 110n
Danzig, Allison, 45, 46
Davis, Fred, 234
Davis, Jeff, 262
Davis, Sammy, Jr., 244
Day in the Life of Sing Sing, A (short film), 85
Decatur Staleys, 65–66
Demaris, Ovid, 92, 170
Detroit Lions
    first integrated team of, 148n
    gambling scandals and, 161, 165
    Luckman's rookie season and, 122
    1949 season, 238
Detroit Tigers, 76–77
Dewey, Thomas
    Buchalter and, 113, 115, 119–120,
        173–179, 198–200, 214–220
    as Manhattan special prosecutor, 42,
        134
    Meyer Luckman and, 200–201
    as New York state governor, 191
    presidential campaign of, 220
    Schultz and, 58
DiMaggio, Joe, 243–244, 251, 259
Driscoll, Paddy, 77, 187
Drukman, Abraham, 35–36

Drukman, Samuel. See also Luckman, Meyer
    (Sid's father)
    gambling and alleged embezzlement by,
        13, 31, 34, 57
    Luckman family relationship of, 14, 15,
        260
    murder of, arrests, 28–33
    murder of, events, 11–17, 55, 57–60
    murder of, trial and sentencing, 33–42
Duke (Wilson), 65, 266
Dwyer, "Big Bill," 161
Dyja, Thomas, 91

E & A Trucking Company, 73, 129–134
Effrat, Louis, 142–143, 156
Erasmus Hall High School (Brooklyn)
    alumni of, 18n
    Luckman's football career at, 15–17,
        18–26, 268

Facenda, John, 266
Famiglietti, Gary, 154
FBI
    Buchalter and, 115–120
    on Chicago organized crime, 172
    gambling scandals in sports and, 165–166
    Hoover and, 84, 116–119
Fears, Tom, 240
Feder, Sid, 51, 55, 115, 176, 218, 219
Filchock, Frank, 154, 162–164, 165, 229–230
Fitzgerald, F. Scott, 169
Flagler Hotel, 27
Flaherty, Ray, 62, 145, 155
Fleischer, Harold, 27, 33, 207
Fleischer, Myrna, 207
Fleischman, Blanche Luckman. See Luckman,
    Blanche (Sid's sister)
Flour Truckmen's Association, 55–56,
    130–131
football, game of. See also National Football
    League; passing game; T formation;
    individual names of players
    footballs and regulation size, 17, 64–65,
        205
    leather helmets used in, 3, 49, 78, 86,
        122, 147, 156

"Football Meant Nothing Before Sid Luckman" (Cannon), 71–72
Ford, Gerald, 90
Ford, John, 85
Forster, E. M., 89
Fortmann, Danny, 135, 148
Francel, Joseph, 215, 217
Fried, Albert, 54, 191
Friedman, Benny, 16–17, 20, 74–75, 106, 146, 269
Frontline (PBS), on NFL and organized crime, 166

Gallarneau, Hugh, 181, 229
gambling scandals (sports), 161–167, 229–230
Gardner, Ava, 160–161
Geoghan, William F. X., 14, 15, 28, 30
Gibsons Bar and Steakhouse, 257–258, 271–273
Gifford, Kathie Lee, 246
Gillman, Sid, 239
Glebocki, Joseph B., 163
Glickman, Marty, 20, 242
Goldberg, Marshall "Biggie," 108, 110
Goldis, Wolfie, 57
Goldstein, Martin "Buggsy," 133, 174–175, 179, 220
Graham, Otto, 228–229, 241
Grange, Harold "Red," 4, 69, 79, 102, 122
Green Bay Packers
    Hutson and, 65
    Isbell and, 64
    Luckman's rookie season and, 121, 125
    1941 post-season, 180–182
    1943 season, 202
    1944 season, 223
Greenberg, Hyman "Hank," 4, 5, 242
Grip-Tite (Horween Leather Company), 65
Gross, Harry, 219
Gross, Louis, 33
Gross, Samuel, 120
Guderian, Heinz, 105, 144

Halas, George. *See also* T formation
    Anderson hired by, 134–138

Bears-Redskins 1940 championship game, 150–158
    "Bingo Keep It" play of, 230
    biographical information, 76–77
    death of, 263–265
    on Friedman, 16–17
    Luckman hired by, 20, 70–82
    Luckman's affection of, 107–112, 262–264
    Luckman's birth announcement to, 191
    Luckman scouted by, 66–70
    Luckman's move to Chicago and, 89
    Luckman's rookie season with Bears, 121, 122, 123, 125–126
    1940 season, 134–138, 139–145
    1941 season, 180–184
    1942 season, 195–196
    1947–1950 seasons, 234–241
    quarterback sought by, 61–66
    in US Navy, 189, 202, 226, 228
Halas, George "Muggsy," Jr., 263
Hall, Irving, 69, 72
Hapes, Merle, 162–164, 229–230
Harron, Bob, 67
Held, Aaron, 130
helmets, leather, 3, 49, 78, 86, 122, 147, 156
Hemendinger, Charles, 39, 40
Henderson, Elmer "Gloomy Gus," 136
Herber, Arnie, 125
Hersh, Seymour, 93
Highland Park (Illinois) High School, 4
Hillman, Sidney, 199
Hinkle, Clarke, 181
Hirsch, Elroy "Crazy Legs," 240
Hoffa, Jimmy, 165
Hogan, Frank S., 162, 214, 215
Holland, Jerome "Brud," 46
Hoover, J. Edgar, 84, 114–120
Hope (prisoner), 86
Hornung, Paul, 164–165
Horween Leather Company, 65
Huggins, Miller, 77
Hugh L. Ray (Stangeland), 104n
Hull, Fred J., 12–13, 25, 30, 32, 34, 59, 190

Hutchins, Robert Maynard, 101
Hutson, Don, 65, 90, 180

Illinois National Guard, 170, 171
Interference (Moldea), 162
International Jewish Sports Hall of Fame
     (Israel), 269
Isbell, Cecil, 64, 181

Jews of Sing Sing, The (Aron), 60
Johnsos, Luke, 107, 180, 202, 224,
     228–229
Jolson, Al, 235
Jones, Lawrence "Biff," 143, 158
Jones, Ralph, 76, 101, 102
Justice, Ed, 151

Kantor, Dora, 31, 33
Kantor, Harry, 30–31, 33–34, 40–41
Kantor, Louis, 40–41
Karkomi, Zev, 248
Karras, Alex, 164–165
Katz, Jacob, 216
Katzenberg, Yasha, 120
Kavanaugh, Ken, 94–95, 106, 152, 189,
     229, 230, 234
Keeshin, John L., 165, 227
Kelly, Jim, 110
Klappholz-Schornstein Baking Corporation,
     130–131
Klein, Edwin, 25
Kleinman (assistant district attorney), 14
Korshak, Sidney, 165, 170n, 258–259
Korshak, Signey, 93–94
Koufax, Sandy, 4, 5, 109, 242
Krause, Max, 151
Kupcinet, Essie, 271
Kupcinet, Irv
     career of, 3, 160
     Gibsons and, 257, 271
     Halas' death and, 263
     Kup's Chicago, 251
     Luckman's introduction to, 90–94
     Luckman's 1947 season, 234
     Meyer Luckman's legal defense and, 170n
     on Sid Luckman's personality, 251, 252

La Guardia, Fiorello, 58, 134, 219
Lambeau, Curly, 181
Lansky, Meyer, 52, 115, 171–172, 258
Largent, Steve, 65
Law, John, 86–87
Lawes, Cherie, 85
Lawes, Kathryn, 84
Lawton, Samuel, Sr., 170
Layne, Bobby, 111, 236–238
Leahy, Frank, 185–186
Lehman, Herbert, 30, 31, 59, 190–191
Lehman, Irving, 190–191
Lepke. *See* Buchalter, Louis "Lepke"
Levine, Abe "Pretty," 133
Levy, Marv, 257, 267
Levy, Sam, 246–247
Lewis, Joe E., 234
Life magazine, on Sid Luckman, 49, 66, 67,
     87, 257
Lindheimer, Ben, 165
Lipiansky, Lillie, 40
Little, Lou
     Columbia team of, 22–24
     on Luckman's professional football
          career, 68–70, 73–74
     Luckman's rookie season and, 122
     Luckman's T formation clinics at
          Columbia, 201
     Owen and, 204
     as Sid Luckman's mentor, 43–49, 111,
          146
     Sing Sing football clinic by, 87
Lloyd, Brandon, 187n
Lombardo, Steve, 257–258
Los Angeles Dons, 165
Los Angeles Rams, 148n
Lotshaw, Andy, 239
Luciano, Lucky, 52, 115, 258
Luckman, Abraham (Meyer's brother), 31,
     34, 40
Luckman, Anna (Meyer's sister-in-law), 33,
     39–40
Luckman, Blanche (Sid's sister)
     baby sister's death and, 26–27
     biographical information, 15
     daughter of (*See* Suslow, Ronnie)

Luckman, Blanche (*continued*)
    father's incarceration and, 87, 168
    husband's arrest, 33
    on mother's personality, 255
    Sid's generosity toward, 248
    on Sid's marriage, 80
Luckman, Bob (son)
    author's interviews of, 6–9
    Baron as godfather of, 94
    birth of, 191–192
    career of, 247
    childhood of, 207, 236
    on father's legacy, 253–264, 268–269, 273
    knowledge about grandfather, 6–9, 169,
        172, 255, 256
    mother's death and, 244
Luckman, David (Sid's brother), 15, 47, 80,
        168, 261
Luckman, Ellen (Sid's daughter), 239, 243,
        245, 246, 256, 260–261
Luckman, Estelle Morgolin (wife)
    characterization of, 251, 253–254
    Chicago move by, 75–76, 79
    children of, 207
    courtship with Sid, 25–26
    death of, 244
    on father-in-law, 256
    first child's birth, 192
    Gardner and, 160–161
    on husband's post-football career, 239
    later marriage of, 247, 253
    mother's death and, 192
    wedding of, 80
Luckman, Ethel (Sid's mother)
    baby's death and, 27
    characterization of, 255–256
    Drukman's relationship to, 14, 15, 260
    family visit (1943) and, 206–209
    husband's trial and incarceration, 37,
        38, 88
    Little and, 47
    on son's football career, 73–74, 122, 205
Luckman, Gail (Sid's daughter), 239, 248,
        259
Luckman, Gale (Sid's daughter-in-law), 254
Luckman, Geri (Sid's nephew's wife), 161

Luckman, Harry (Meyer's nephew)
    appeal withdrawn by, 59
    arrest of, 30, 32
    charges against, dropped, 25
    Drukman's death and, 12
    trial/sentencing of, 36
Luckman, Ike (Meyer's brother)
    jury-tampering trial and, 39, 41
    Kantor and, 34
    sons of, 132
    surrender and fine of, 132
    trucking business of, 13
    wife of, at brother's trial, 33
Luckman, Leona (Sid's sister-in-law), 38,
        131, 160–161, 243
Luckman, Leo (Sid's brother)
    childhood of, 15, 16–17
    children of, 243 (*See also* Luckman, Peter
        (Sid's nephew))
    death of, 260–261
    father's business assumed by, 38, 193
    Sid's college recruitment and, 22–24
    Sid's trucking company work and,
        129–134
    Tri-Borough Transportation Corpora-
        tion, 182–183
    trucking career of, 73, 80–81, 207
Luckman, Leo (Sid's cousin), 34, 39
Luckman, Meyer (Sid's father)
    appeal withdrawn by, 59
    Buchalter and, 56–60, 130–134
    characterization of, 26–27
    death of, 220–222
    family's lack of knowledge about crimi-
        nal history of, 6–9, 270–271
    first arrest of, 24–25, 34
    health issues of, 214
    incarceration of, 43–44, 49, 75, 87–88
        (*See also* Drukman, Samuel)
    jury-tampering trial and, 38–42
    legal defense obtained by Sid for,
        168–172, 200–201, 221
    Luckman at Quarterback on, 47–48,
        208–209
    Luckman family secrecy about, 47–48,
        255–261, 270

Murder, Inc. connection of, 130–134
obscurity of, 60
second arrest of, 28–33
son's football career supported by, 15–17
trial and sentencing of, 33–42
Luckman, Morris (Meyer's cousin), 13, 30, 32
Luckman, Peter (Sid's nephew), 38, 161, 243, 244, 256, 261
Luckman, Sid. *See also* Erasmus Hall High School (Brooklyn); *Luckman at Quarterback* (Luckman); passing game; T formation
   acting career of, 159–160, 234–235
   affection of Halas by, 107–112, 262–264
   as Bears' quarterback coach, 240, 248
   Bears-Redskins 1940 championship game, 145–149, 150–158
   on best game played, 211
   "Bingo Keep It" play of, 230
   birth of first child, 191–192 (*See also individual names of children*)
   car dealership of, 238–239
   Chicago Bears playbook introduction of, 94–98
   college football career of, 9
   at Columbia University, 9, 22–25, 43–49, 201
   compensation of, 79, 156–157, 227, 236
   death of, 222, 250–251, 260–261, 271–273
   family's secrecy about father of, 47–48, 255–261, 270
   father's legal defense and, 168–172, 192–193, 200–201, 221 (*See also* Luckman, Meyer (Sid's father))
   football injuries of, 46, 67–68
   friends of, in organized crime, 89–94, 258–261
   Gardner and, 160–161
   health issues of, 238, 264
   legacy of, 1–9, 253–264, 268–273
   on *Life* magazine cover, 49, 66, 67, 87, 257
marriage of (*See* Luckman, Estelle Morgolin)
   as most valuable player (1943), 222
   1940 season, 134–138, 139–145
   1942 season, 103–106, 188–189
   1943 season, 202–205, 206–211
   1944–1946 seasons, 223–231
   1947–1950 seasons, 232–241
   other sports played by, 46
   post-football career and characterization of, 242–254
   public speaking by, 192
   radio career of, 238
   records held by, 2, 164, 232, 267
   religion of, 4, 16, 242–243
   rookie season of, 121–128
   trucking company work by, 129–134
   US Maritime Service joined by, 212, 223–224
Luckman, Sidney (Sid's cousin), 15, 34, 132
Luckman at Quarterback (Luckman)
   on family visit (1943), 206–209
   Halas on T formation, 187
   Meyer Luckman omission from, 47–48, 258, 270
   self-characterization in, 259–260
   on Shaughnessy, 111
Luckman Brothers Trucking Company, 11, 13
Luisetti, Hank, 157
Lujack, Johnny, 111, 235–238, 239, 257
Lvovsky, Jake, 120

MacLeod, Bob, 125
Maffetore, Anthony "the Duke," 133
Magidovitch, Jonathan, 250–251
Magnani, Dante, 210, 230
Maione, Harry "Happy," 133
Malone, Charley, 151, 155
Maniaci, Joe, 122, 123–124, 135, 152
Manske, Edgar "Eggs," 70, 142
Mara, Tim, 161
Marino, Dan, 110
Marracco, Fran, 94
Marshall, George Preston, 64, 143–145, 147–148, 153, 162, 211
Martin, Bob, 166

Martin, Tony, 234
Masterson, Bernie, 64, 95, 121, 125
McAfee, George "One-Play"
    Bears-Redskins 1940 championship
        game, 148, 150, 153
    hired by Bears, 135–136
    legacy of, 267
    Luckman's rookie season and, 128
    nickname of, 4
    1940 season, 140, 142, 145
    1941 season, 180, 182
    1943 season, 203
    1945 season, 225
    1946 season, 229, 230
    in US Navy, 189
McAuliffe, John P., 11, 12
McAvoy, John, 213
McBridge, Arthur "Mickey," 165
McDonald, George, 64
McDonald, Miles F., 219
McGoldrick, Joseph, 15, 30, 31, 37
McGuire, John, 251
McHugh, Jack, 244
McLean, Scooter "Rabbit," 206, 208
Medlevine, Donjo, 238–239
Methodist Episcopal Zion Church (Brook-
        lyn), 15
Miller, Edgar "Rip," 22
Millner, Wayne, 63
Milwaukee Journal, on Bears-Redskins 1940
        championship game, 155
Miracle at Sing Sing (Blumenthal), 84
Moldea, Dan E., 162, 165, 166
Monette, Valmore, 243–244
Montgomery, Cliff, 22, 47
Moran, George "Bugs," 171
Morgolin, Estelle. See Luckman, Estelle
        Morgolin (wife)
Mr. Arsenic (television show), 220
Mulrooney, Edward, 87
Murder, Inc. See also Buchalter, Louis
        "Lepke"
    Anastasia's role in, 114
    Meyer Luckman's connection to, 130–134
    Murder, Inc. (Turkus, Feder), 51, 55, 115,
        176, 218, 219

Musso, George, 96, 137
    Bears-Redskins 1940 championship
        game, 148
    Luckman's rookie season and, 127
Mutual Broadcasting System, 145
My Sister Eileen (play), 159–160

Nagle, Browning, 110
Nagurski, Bronislau "Bronko," 4, 62, 65–66,
        79, 98, 205, 209, 210
National Collegiate Athletic Association
        (NCAA), 99–100
National Football League (NFL). See also
        individual names of teams
    college football's popularity vs., 43–44
    early drafts in, 70
    founding of, 16–17
    free-substitution rule, 228
    gambling scandals and, 161–167,
        229–230
    Luckman as most valuable player (1943),
        222
    in 1930s, 103
    players' salaries, 79, 156–159, 227, 236
    Storck and, 92
    television inception and popularity of, 266
National Forgotten League, The (Daly), 6, 8
National Industrial Recovery Act (1933), 54
Neale, Alfred "Greasy," 184
New England Patriots, 187n
New York Bulldogs, 238–239
New York Daily Mirror
    on Buchalter, 215
    Winchell and, 118
New York Giants
    first integrated team of, 148n
    gambling scandals and, 161, 166,
        229–230
    Luckman's rookie season and, 121–122
    1941 post-season, 182
    1943 season, 203
    1949 season, 240
    at Sing Sing, 86
New York Herald Tribune
    Luckman's job with, 129
    on Meyer Luckman's trial, 37

New York Times
  on Buchalter, 119, 216, 219
  on gambling scandals, 163, 164
  on Korshak, 93
  on Meyer Luckman, 11, 13, 31, 32, 35,
    41–42, 130, 132, 220–221
  on 1940 football season, 141–143, 155,
    156
  on 1942 football season, 193–194, 195
  on 1943 football season, 204
  on Sid Luckman, 19, 45, 46, 48–49,
    79, 245
  on World War II service of football
    players, 201
New York World-Telegram, on Luckman's high
  school football career, 19
New York Yankees, 76–77, 86
Nitti, Frank, 171
Nolting, Ray, 135, 145, 148, 153
Notre Dame Box, 101, 186
Nowaskey, Bob, 148, 227
Nureyev, Rudolf, 249

O'Brien, Davey, 70, 108, 126, 137, 261
O'Dwyer, William D., 132–133, 134, 162,
  173–174, 219
Olderman, Murray, 247
organized crime. *See also* Buchalter, Louis
  "Lepke"; Luckman, Meyer (Sid's
  father); *individual names of mobsters*
  Buchalter and, 50–60
  early executions of mobsters, 220
  gambling scandals in sports and,
    161–167, 229–230
  Murder, Inc. and, 81–82
  "specialized persuasions" of, 55
Orgen, Little Augie, 52–53
Orlovsky, Philip, 81
O'Rourke, Charlie, 194, 227
Osborne, Thomas Mott, 84
Osmanski, Bill
  Anderson and, 135
  Bears' 1940 regular season, 142, 145
  Bears-Redskins 1940 championship
    game, 148, 150–152, 156
  compensation of, 227

legacy of, 267
Luckman's rookie season and, 121, 125
1946 season, 229
rookie season of, 70, 94, 96
Owen, Steve, 130, 204–205

Palmer, Joseph, 216
Paris, Alvin J., 163
Parisi, Gioacchino "Dandy Jack," 81
passing game
  forward pass and Friedman, 17
  impact of, 266
  Luckman at Quarterback on, 206–209
  Luckman-Baugh rivalry and, 146–147
  Luckman's 1941 season, 183
  Luckman's 1943 season, 202–205
  in 1940 regular season, 139–140
PBS, on NFL and organized crime, 166
Pearl Harbor, bombing of, 181
Penn, Irving, 81
Philadelphia Eagles, 90, 126, 165, 184, 201
Pierson, Don, 156
Pittsburgh Steelers, 201, 224
Plasman, Dick, 122, 135, 156, 189
Pollard, Fritz, 147
Pool, Hampton, 152, 203, 226
Postl's Health Club, 235
Povich, Shirley, 62
Prell, Edward, 182, 187, 193, 196, 204
Pritzker, Abe, 264
Pritzker, Jay, 245–246, 264
"Pro Football, Major New Sport" (news-
  reel), 72
Prohibition, 32, 54
Pro Quarterback, The (Olderman), 247
Protective Fur Dressers Corporation, 113

race issues in football
  segregation of players, 147–148
  Sidat-Singh and, 67n
rackets. *See* organized crime
Radvilas, Art, 208
Ralli, Hugo, 257
Ray, Buford "Baby," 107
Ray, Hugh "Shorty," 102–104, 126, 233
Rayburn, Sam, 148–149

Reissman, Norman, 258
Reles, Abe "Kid Twist," 133, 173–174, 177–179, 215
Rice, Grantland, 67n
Richards, George "Dick," 161, 162
Richardson, William, 204
Rise and Fall of the Jewish Gangster in America, The (Fried), 54
Rizzo, Jilly, 244
Roberts, Owen, 197–198
Rockne, Knute, 101
Rogers, Erskine, 34–35, 38
Rollow, Cooper, 262
Rooney, Art, 70, 161
Roosevelt, Franklin D., 181, 191, 198–200, 220, 256
Rose Bowl (1941), 143, 158
Rosen, Joseph, 174–179, 190, 214
Rosenbloom, Carroll, 166
Ross, Barney, 4
Rubin, Max, 176–179
Russell, Jane, 235
Russo, Gus, 93, 235, 259
Ruth, Babe, 245
Ryan, Robert Emmer, 170

Sabol, Ed, 266
Sacrinty, Nick, 234
Saint Valentine's Day Massacre, 89, 171
Sallami, Vincent, 216
San Francisco Examiner, on Shaughnessy, 138
Sarcona, Frank, 28
Sayers, Gale "the Kansas Comet," 4, 107, 136, 245
Schayes, Dolph, 5
Schlichter, Art, 164–165
Schornstein, Abraham, 130–131
Schultz, Dutch, 58–59
Sedlak (policeman), 39
Seidel, Gerry, 48
Seinfeld (television show), 268
Sekhani, Mohammed, 271–273
Sekhani, Nabeel, 272
Shapiro, Jacob "Gurrah," 41, 50, 52–54, 56, 58, 82, 113–114, 179

Shaughnessy, Clark
    Bears-Redskins 1940 championship game, 143–144, 149
    Hall of Fame and, 106n
    as head coach at Stanford University, 137–138, 158
    as Los Angeles Rams head coach, 239–240
    Luckman at Quarterback (Luckman) on, 111
    Luckman's rookie season and, 124
    on T formation, 66, 97, 98, 99–107, 158
    T formation shared with other teams, 184, 186, 211
    three-receiver set of, 239–240
    as University of Maryland coach, 186
Sherman, Allie, 244
Sherman Antitrust Act, 113
Shonka, Dan, 110n
Sidat-Singh, Wilmeth, 67
Sid Luckman Day, 202–205
Siegal, John, 48, 135
Siegel, Bugsy, 52, 219, 258
Silverman, Max, 56–57
Sinatra, Frank, 244, 258
Sing Sing prison
    Buchalter's execution and, 179, 213–220
    "Dance Hall" of, 216
    Lawes and, 83–88
    Strauss and Goldstein executed in, 175
Sloan, James, 28
Smith, Verda "Vitamin T," 240
Smith, Wilfrid, 156
Snyder, Bob, 152, 203
Snyder, William, 56–57, 73, 120, 130
Solomon, Essee (Kupcinet), 90
Solomon, Joseph, 91
Solotaire, George, 243
Solovei, Joseph, 30
Spitz, Mark, 5
Sports Illustrated, on Sid Luckman, 245
Sprinkle, Ed "The Claw," 108, 236
Stacher, Joseph "Doc," 172
Stagg, Amos Alonzo, 99, 100–101, 147
Stahl, Eugene, 11

Standlee, Norm, 181, 182, 188, 226
Stanford University, 137–138, 143, 158
Stangeland, James W., 104n
Sternaman, Ed "Dutch," 77–78
Storck, Carl, 92
Strauss, Harry "Pittsburgh Phil," 133,
        174–175, 179
Strode, Woody, 148n
Strong, Ken, 22
Stydahar, "Jumbo" Joe, 127–128, 135, 148,
        267
Sullivan, Paul, 20–22, 24, 45
Supermob (Russo), 93, 235
Suslow, Ronnie, 26, 248–249, 252,
        255–256
Swisher, Bob, 125, 187, 189

Tammany Hall, 113, 161
Tannenbaum, Albert "Tick-Tock," 133,
        174–175, 178, 215
Taylor, Franklin, 214
Teamsters
    Central Conference of Teamsters, 165
    Central Pension Fund, 166–167
    Local 138, 55, 56–57, 73
Tessitore, Joe, 269
T formation. *See also* Shaughnessy, Clark
    Bears-Redskins 1940 championship
        game and, 150–158
    development of, 99–107
    Halas on, 64, 66, 70, 74–75, 76–77,
        95–98, 99–107, 184–188
    impact of, 266
    inception of, 2
    Luckman at Quarterback on, 207–208
    Luckman's clinics in, 184–188, 201
    Luckman's introduction to, 95–98, 106,
        211
    Redskins' adoption of, 211
    shared by Bears with other teams,
        184–188, 201
    Zuppke and, 76–78
"They All Laughed" (song), 138
Third Coast, The (Dyja), 91
Thorpe, Jim, 100

Todd, Dick, 142
Todd, Hiram, 35, 39, 42
Tolson, Clyde, 117
Tonelli, Mario, 225–226
Toots Shor's, 208
Topping, Dan, 68–69, 109, 122
Torrance, Jack, 154
Tose, Leonard, 165
Tri-Borough Transportation Corporation,
        182–183
Trubisky, Mitch, 269
Truman, Harry, 170n, 220
Turkus, Burton
    Buchalter and, 51, 177, 198–200, 218,
        219
    Mr. Arsenic (television show), 220
    Murder, Inc., 51, 55, 115, 176, 218, 219
    O'Dwyer and, 134
    on Reles, 133
Turner, Clyde "Bulldog"
    Bears-Redskins 1940 championship
        game, 148, 153
    hired by Bears, 136–137
    legacy of, 267
    on Luckman, 108
    1946 season, 229, 230
    1947 season, 233
20,000 Years in Sing Sing (Lawes), 85

Unitas, Johnny, 166
United Flour Trucking Company, 56,
        130–134
University of Maryland, 186
University of Nebraska, 143, 158
University of Notre Dame, 101, 185–186
US Martime Service, 212
US Military Academy, 48
US Narcotics Bureau, 115

V. H. Monette, 243–244
Valentine, Lewis, 31

Walsh, Bill, 239, 266
Ward, Arch, 159
Warner, Glenn Scobey "Pop," 100, 138

Washington, Kenny, 148n
Washington Post, on Bears and Redskins, 62
Washington Redskins
    Baugh and, 61–66, 70
    Bears-Redskins 1940 championship
        game, 2, 150–158
    gambling scandals and, 162
    1942 post-season, 103–106
    1943 season, 209–211
    1947 season, 232–233
    T formation adopted by, 211
Wasserman, Betty (Buchalter), 50, 215–218
Wasserman, Harold (Buchalter), 50, 215,
    218
Waterfield, Bob, 234–235, 240, 241
Weiss, Dick, 249
Weiss, Emanuel "Mendy"
    appeal of murder conviction, 190–191
    Dewey and Roosevelt on conviction of
        Buchalter, 198–200
    execution of, 214, 216–220
    Rosen murder and, 174–175, 179
    US Supreme Court case, 197–198
Whalen, Grover, 159–160
Wilbur, Ray Lyman, 137–138
Williams, Garland, 114
Williams, Henry, 100

Wilson, 65, 266
Wilson, George, 146–147, 148, 151, 156,
    165, 187, 202–203, 229
Winchell, June, 119
Winchell, Walter, 116–120
Winkeler, Gus, 171
Wolensky, Morris "Moey Dimples," 115,
    119
Wolfson, Cecil, 244
Workman, Charlie "The Bug," 59
World War II
    death toll of, 219
    football players'/coaches' service in, 189,
        201, 202, 223–226, 228
    Pearl Harbor bombing, 181
    postwar football, 226–231
Wrigley Field, 2–3, 78n
Wyche, Sam, 266

Yale, Frankie, 219
Yale University, 99
YouTube, 5

Ziffren, Paul, 170n
Zimmerman, Paul, 245
Zimmerman, Roy, 153
Zuppke, Bob, 76–78, 97, 103, 106